BEYOND OPTIMISM

JOANNA MACY writes of this book:

"This deep, wise, broad-gauged book is a major contribution to the sanity and healing of our world.

Combining astute social analysis with invigorating spiritual insight, it clears our heads and hearts for action. Ken Jones unmasks the dangerous delusions of ideology, while affirming our innate capacity to awaken from the collective nightmare created by fear and greed.

Stunningly relevant and rich in both political and contemporary experience, this superb book shatters dichotomies between 'inner' and 'outer' work—and shows us the wholeness to be found as we take action together to evolve a sustainable civilization."

JOANNA MACY is author of many books, among them *Despair and personal power in the nuclear age* (New Society Publishers) and *World as lover, world as self* (Rider Books, 1993).

How does it feel
To be an apple
In the barrel
Of this autumn's plucking?

BEYOND OPTIMISM:

A BUDDHIST POLITICAL ECOLOGY

KEN JONES

JON CARPENTER
Oxford

Also by Ken Jones:
The social face of Buddhism (Wisdom Books, 1989)

Jon Carpenter Publishing
The Spendlove Centre
Charlbury OX7 3PQ
Phone + fax 01608 811969

First published in 1993 by
Jon Carpenter Publishing
PO Box 129, Oxford OX1 4PH

The right of Ken H. Jones to be identified as author of this work has been asserted in accordance with the Copyright, Design and Patents Act 1988.

ISBN 1 897766 06 8

Designed and typeset by Sarah Tyzack, Oxford
Printed and bound by Biddles Ltd, Guildford, England

DEDICATED TO ALL FOLLOWERS OF THE WAY
IN ALL LANDS AND TIMES

'It is no longer possible to believe that any political or economic reform or scientific advance could solve the life and death problems of the industrial society. They lie too deep in the heart and soul of every one of us.'

E.F. SCHUMACHER

Acknowledgements

I AM grateful beyond measure to my Zen teachers Genpo *Sensei* and Ven Myokyo-ni for their support and guidance. Cynog Dafis, MP I wish to thank both for political opportunity and for the example of his warm hearted politics. Thanks are also due to Jon Carpenter, whose continued support through difficult times has made publication possible, and to Jonathon Porritt for timely support both in print and on the platform.

Verse by John Hegley is reproduced by kind permission of the author. The drawing of a forest-croft township on page 161 is reproduced by kind permission of the artist, Paul M. Thomas. Readers will observe that it was originally drawn for a Scottish context! I am also grateful to Messrs Faber and Faber and to Messrs Harcourt Brace Jovanovich for permission to reproduce the four lines from T.S. Eliot's poem 'East Coker' which appear in Chapter 8.

Apologies are due to any who may feel hurt by my wide ranging critique of what I perceive as ideology in certain green and spiritual movements. Manjushri, the great mythical Buddhist wielder of the sword-which-cuts-off-delusion, would have made a more elegant and compassionate job of it.

Contents

Foreword

by Jonathon Porritt

IT MAY seem a little over the top to compare the work of a largely unknown green activist living in Aberystwyth with the hugely successful book by Al Gore (the Vice-President of the United States of America) entitled *Earth in the balance*. Yet I believe it is a legitimate comparison: in terms of personal commitment, of incisive analysis, of historical understanding, of the readiness to envision pragmatic yet radical futures, of spiritual underpinning (from a Baptist and a Buddhist respectively), and of good old-fashioned wisdom in an age of quick fixes, clever dicks and brutal bottom lines.

At the time of writing this Foreword (May 1993) the Green Movement in the UK is in something of a mess. Three years of economic recession have driven 'the environment' right down that influential if illusory list of people's 'priorities'. The peace dividend accruing from the end of the Cold War is being cashed in to ameliorate budget deficits rather than meet those 'threats without enemies' that now imperil our long-term security. The Green Party has temporarily disappeared down a cul-de-sac entirely of its own making, and many of the mainstream environmental organisations are engaged in a process of 're-positioning' without necessarily having the appropriate maps to hand. The momentum created by the 1992 Earth Summit has slowed almost to the point of immobility. The so-called 'spiritual dimension' of the Movement seems stuck in limbo—albeit a reassuringly ecumenical and open-ended limbo.

Added to all that, the political and economic forces that have brought us to the edge of ecological collapse are in no way abashed at their achievement. The recession is seen as little more than a temporary downturn before the next spasm of growth. As Ken Jones points out, it is not 'post-industrialism' that we find ourselves engaged in, but rather an aggravated form of superindustrialism that pulverises communities and eco-systems alike. The collapse of communism has merely served to reinforce the all-conquering superiority of this freemarket capitalism.

Ken Jones brings the fruits of many years of committed political activism and equally committed spiritual reflection to bear on these problems. That remains an all too rare combination within a Movement that has so successfully accommodated itself to the 'scientific materialism' it opposes, that it has in many significant respects been subsumed by it. We've undoubtedly become more effective as a result, but at what long-term cost?

It never ceases to amaze me, for instance, how spirituality has been almost entirely privatised within the Green Movement. I would venture a guess that a very considerable majority of the millions of green supporters in this country either subscribe explicitly to an established religion or faith, or harbour nebulous but still powerful intimations of some spiritual force at work in them and the big wide world.

Yet for the most part such allegiances are rarely referred to and remain almost irrelevant to the green works that people undertake as individuals, let alone to the organisations of which they are members. Having dared to come out of the 'green closet', there are many who still return there to keep ever so privately in touch with the spiritual core of what they happen to believe in.

How appropriate therefore that the twin themes of this book should be 'the psycho-spiritual liberation' of socially-engaged Buddhists, progressive Christians, the Baha'is, and of all those for whom the pursuit of 'perennial wisdom' remains a crucial priority, and the 'eco-social liberation' of the kind espoused by libertarian socialists such as William Morris.

That powerful strand of socialism (buried so deep for so long by the Labour Party that many contemporary socialists are wholly unnerved by its current exhumation!) does more than keep our consciences awake. It provides some of the intellectual rigour without which the Green Movement can never seriously aspire to undertake the work of political transformation.

But this is no hack tract on how best to resuscitate moribund socialism. What makes Ken Jones' approach particularly useful is his passionate renunciation of ideology itself and of the paralysing certainties and self-deceptions that go with it. Many eco-socialists may find the call for 'unilateral ideological disarmament' a little difficult to stomach, but it diminishes the radicalism of his analysis and the creativity of his solutions by not one jot.

As many activists today will testify, it's not easy to be realistically optimistic in such a troubled and in-turned world. Pessimism is the favoured currency, even to the point of 'eco-catastrophism'. By the same token, it's not easy to find ways of working pragmatically within the world as we find it without losing in the process one's burning ambition to see that world change into something very different.

But neither the catastrophists nor the absolutists within the Green

Movement have yet found a way of empowering others through their own powerlessness, anger and despair. And any variation of green politics that ignores its responsibility to empower others (by helping them to accept both the necessity and the desirability of change at a time when change is often seen as deeply threatening) is ultimately a self-indulgence.

Whether we like it or not, there are two conflicting realities that green activists have to deal with today: the reality of a world now almost entirely dependent on jobs and wealth created by unsustainable economic growth; and the even deeper reality of a planet that is gradually crumbling under the impacts of that sysytem. It's hardly surprising that people tend to keep these realities apart in their minds and in their daily lives. Dealing with the one seems to deny the possibility of dealing with the other. And as a result, many people are apprehensive, insecure, frightened at the prospect of change even as they accept the need for change.

It's that act of denial we have to confront people with in a spirit of consolation not condemnation. It's that conflict we have to open up in people, exposing the absurdities of our 'false economy' whilst simultaneously exploring the opportunities for new systems of wealth creation and self-discovery.

And it's precisely in that spirit that Al Gore wrote his *Earth in the balance* and that Ken Jones now offers us this insightful and extraordinarily helpful account of green politics and spirituality at what is a crucial time for the whole Green Movement.

JONATHON PORRITT
May 1993

life passes like a flash of lightning

Whose blaze lasts barely long enough to see,

While earth and sky stand still forever.

How swiftly changing time flies across our face.

You who sit over your full cup and do not drink,

Tell me whom you are still waiting for!

Li Po

Introduction

WE LIVE in confusing, shifting times. Disillusionment, hope and uncertainty exist together. On the one hand, many now sense the need for radical new departures, social as well as personal. On the other, many of the beliefs of yesteryear are, if not discredited, at least wearing thin. For me, it was time to write a book which reflected my own search for how to be a radical and a visionary and, at the same time, practical, realistic and pragmatic.

My conclusion is that the crisis which afflicts our civilisation is so profound and potentially terminal that we must take the search for its origins (and its remedy) back beyond the usual kinds of economic, political and cultural analysis. Could it be that there is something self-destructive about the human condition itself which also requires our investigation—and in which a good part of the remedy may lie?

Therefore, throughout the book, human behaviour, whether personal or global, economic or political, is examined in terms of its subjective roots—the kind of people we are—and this is integrated with social analysis, and with an ongoing concern for the disabling effects of ideology and fundamentalism (ours as well as theirs) and the need for a unilateral ideological disarmament movement. This is perhaps the first study of its kind to make use of modern Buddhist social theory, as elaborated in an earlier book, *The social face of Buddhism*.[1] In particular, the critique of ideology, in a specifically Buddhist sense, runs like a thread throughout the book and provides its underlying unity.

The first part of the book shows how a prospective ecological breakdown is compounded by other potential crises which are economic and political, cultural and military, most crucially affecting the Third World as well as the Overdeveloped World and the recently 'liberated' Second World. The new vistas are seen to be opening up over once familiar landscapes, as so many taken-for-granted myths and assumptions crumble.

There follows an examination of the currently fashionable business-as-usual 'green growth', to be sustained by new 'clean' technologies, with the conclusion that this environmentalism could be as much a part of the problem as its answer.

The many varieties of deeper greenery—the green parties, red-greens, ecofeminists, green Christians, new agers, deep ecologists, and 'new economists'—are critically scrutinised in the light of the Buddhist parable of blind people each feeling a different part of an elephant and each arguing exclusive knowledge of the nature of the beast. The new phenomenon of 'econationalism' also appears here, reflecting my Welsh background and questioning metropolitan assumptions as viewed from the periphery. In order to recover a steady-state ecological harmony, it is argued that we may need to jettison the present hyper-individualism in favour of a return to community, tough and mutualistic, but now at a higher, civil society level protective of individual and minority rights.

The realistic proposals for laying the foundations for a green society as from now give as much attention to the psycho-spiritual 'inner work' as to the more familiar campaigning 'outer work'. There is a particular concern to make spirituality accessible to people in the secular, humanistic tradition, on the basis of our common experience of life. This exemplifies the book's overall strategy, which is an inclusive one valuing the potential contributions that can be made by many different traditions. The specific suggestions, for getting started with both the inner and the outer work, are drawn from my own experience and will, I hope, have wide appeal.

Part I: UNDERSTANDING OUR SITUATION

OUR FIRST task will be to attempt some diagnosis of the present human predicament. And since the ecological crisis could turn out to be the fatal end-product of human history, I shall begin there.

There is a tendency to treat the ecological crisis as an isolated 'issue', somehow separate from the forces which have created it. On the contrary, it could be that its greatest significance is that it requires us to undertake a penetrating social investigation of its origins. It is too important for the grinding of political axes or for the visionary system building which is the response of ideology to great crises. More challenging still is to take the search even further back, to the hidden and rejected parts of ourselves.

In the whole interactive and indivisible web—ecological, social and personal—there is need and suffering which must claim our attention. Social and economic forces cannot be viewed as significant only in the light of the ecological crisis. For example, the work of semi-official torturers and kidnappers in many parts of the world has its own claims upon us. The rainforests and their creatures disappear. People also disappear. Whole cultures and nations have disappeared.

In short, once we begin to explore the underlying impulsions of the fashionable (or boring) eco-crisis we may eventually come to see that all the different manifestations of 'the human problem' have common origins and equal validity.

1 The extraordinary history of the human race

WHEN viewed at the end of the twentieth century and from the unfamiliar vantage point of social ecology human history appears extraordinarily moving. There is a certain melancholy grandeur about it which warms the heart. It is as with a friend who seems wilfully bent upon her own destruction as her only way of coming to terms with life, but who somehow continues to manifest her humanity and integrity.

This chapter will draw attention to key episodes in our history which can help us to understand our present predicament and the awe inspiring revolution it requires of us. A preliminary overview of the whole sweep of history reveals three fundamental and persistent problems.

In the first place, the majority of the world's population (and until recently 'majority' meant almost everybody) has lived on the edge of starvation. Most of people's resources were spent on simply staying alive, with wretched living conditions and endemic ill-health. That there were indeed other sides to their lives which we may even hold to be compensatory should not blind us to this brute reality.

Secondly, almost everywhere the living standards of the common people have been further depressed by a ruling and privileged class which has appropriated their production, whether in food, labour or money, leaving them with little more than what was necessary for child rearing. Much of human history is about the acquisition, distribution and use of this appropriated surplus. For example, increasing malnutrition and famine in Europe at the beginning of the fourteenth century, due to a rising population pressing against agricultural productivity and the limits of cultivatable land, was made worse by the appropriation of half the peasants' output by the nobility and clergy in feudal dues and rents, tithes and taxes. The creation of affluent industrial societies in parts of the world has not changed these underlying realities.

Thirdly, the most significant activity to which ruling elites have applied this surplus has been military, both to retain their dominance at home and to seize wealth and power elsewhere. This has further contributed to the immiseration of the mass of the population, whether through crushing impositions, enforced military service, or the widespread devastation and plunder of armies.

Until recent times the Malthusian dynamics of population and poverty remained everywhere unchanged. Each increase in agricultural production (whether due to more intensive methods or to pushing forward the agricultural frontier) would set off a ratchet effect, whereby population would rise and eventually overshoot the sustainable limit, falling back through famine and the endemic ill-health and epidemic disease of people weakened by hunger. Favourable conditions would eventually develop for a new period of vigorous growth of wealth and the technologies of wealth creation, permitting a further rise in population. Contemporary records painfully recall present-day media reports of Third World famine, and up to the end of the nineteenth century the great majority of Europeans lived on a *maximum* of two thousand calories a day (little better than the present situation in India). Throughout all but recent human history overall economic and population growth has been slow and faltering. It took two million years for the global population to reach a billion, by 1825; but thanks to the industrial revolution the next billion was reached in a mere hundred years.

This kind of eco-social history, as exemplified in Clive Ponting's excellent *Green history of the world*,[2] is extremely valuable for bringing our present ecological and social crises into clearer perspective. With few exceptions, there has, at least in environmental and material terms, been no past golden age, some Eden from which we have since suffered an industrial 'fall'. The (relatively) good times, whether mesolithic, early medieval, or early industrial, were the times of an open frontier, when natural resources were abundant and exploitable relative to the prevailing population level. It took some 150 years of industrial development to bring into being an 'affluent society' able to provide adequately for the material needs of a majority of its citizens. Yet this mere fifty-year-old achievement of under a third of the world's people has, at least in part, only been made possible at the expense of the remainder of humanity and of the sustainability of the planetary ecosystem.

Potentially, however, what this latter-day industrial revolution has also done is to give promise of an ecologically sustainable wealth and technology which *could* support the whole of a considerable global population at an adequate standard of life. The prime task of any radical politics must be to achieve that potential.

The only historical event that can be compared with the social and ecological upheaval that presently confronts us is the neolithic revolution, better understood as the transition to agriculture and a settled population. Spread over some four thousand years, this was substantially completed by 2000 BC, the end of 'prehistory'. The conditions were created for a small warrior and priestly caste to take for themselves the tiny surpluses which the mass of the population in certain favoured areas was now able to produce. In these Syrian, Egyptian, Inca, Aztec and Mayan societies there evolved the first rudimentary state and religious apparatus, its management assisted by writing, mathematics, money and the calendar. Irrigation systems appeared as the first large scale environmental engineering schemes. Large scale warfare, and the first genocidal massacres, also now became practicable. The Assyrians alone are credited with the deportation of some four and a half million people.

Some of these early civilisations, like the Mayan, suffered dramatic collapse; most, like China and the Mediterranean civilisations, sank into long term decline. In all cases environmental degradation was a significant and often decisive factor. Salination, deforestation and soil exhaustion and erosion reduced the agricultural surplus at a time when the rulers were obliviously embarking on even more grandiose wars, pomps and projects. Their tighter squeeze on people and resources accelerated the crisis and provoked slave and peasant uprisings. The iron age empires like that of Rome, capable of annexing and exploiting whole ecosystems beyond their own, eventually suffered a similar fate.

In his remarkable study of the evolution of human consciousness,[3] Ken Wilber maintains that the beginnings of modern consciousness appeared with these first civilisations. It was characterised by a self-conscious and mutual recognition of personhood, a distancing of both body and nature, and conceptual thinking. But 'the new egoic structure also brought, necessarily, new terrors. The self-conscious ego was more vulnerable, more aware of its mortality; more guilty in its emergence; more open to anxiety. And the new terrors inherent in the ego, when coupled with the new powers of the ego, resulted in the possibility (not necessity) of even more brutal terrors exercised by the ego: new substitute sacrifices, oppressive exploitation, massive slavery, class alienation, violent inequality'. Wilber quotes a Babylonian of around 1750 BC, Tabu-utul-Enlil, as testimony of an unprecedented 'psychological anguish':

> Wherever I turned there was evil upon evil;
> Misery increased and justice departed.
> I cried to my god, but he did not show his countenance;
> I prayed to my goddess, she did not show her head.

This self-conscious ego did contain the potential for a higher evolution of consciousness. However, since the fitful dawn of civilisation periodic holocausts continue to bear witness to how little our historical evolution has enabled us to transcend our root existential fear and its terrifying consequences. The following account from the killing fields of Cambodia can be matched by almost daily reports in the media of ethnic, political or religious 'cleansing' in some part of the world or other:

> Tuol Sleng, a former school built in pretty French colonial style, is a grotesque shrine to the 20,000 people who died there after being tortured. Old classrooms stand as they were during the torturers' day, rusting iron-frame beds, with generators to provide electric shocks beside them, patches of dried blood on the floor, and large black-and-white photographs of the victims after torture on the wall. There are rooms full of mugshots of prisoners, only one smiling.[4]

A high point in the evolution of human consciousness was the emergence of the great world religions in the period from the sixth century BC to the sixth century AD. Stripped of their cultural and institutional encrustatations, they could be a major resource in responding to the multifold crisis of our times. What I have in mind here is not so much the theistic tradition of God the creator and lawgiver, but rather the monist, so-called mystical tradition, which offers a means of transcending the dualism of the alienated self and all that is other. Unfortunately the religions of the West became increasingly concerned with punitive morality, dogmatic orthodoxy and institutional authority, and it is only recently that the 'inner' truths are being reclaimed and socially engaged.

Further confusion is created by the phenomenon of religious fundamentalisms, super-ideologies which offer the most extreme kind of response to contemporary disorientation and nihilism. All depend upon a highly elaborated body of powerfully sanctioned revealed truth, literal and unambiguous (as with every sentence in the Bible). They tend to be even more intolerant, exclusive and closed to meaningful dialogue than their secular equivalents.

Resuming our historical enquiry, the medieval civilisation which preceded our own in the West is of particular interest in opening our minds to the very different assumptions and values by which Europeans once lived. Raymond Delatouche has even argued that medieval Christendom offers a useful development model of a highly sophisticated society, regulated by principles of justice and equity designed to sustain the stability and viability of both the environment and the social order.[5] However, it is not necessary to romanticise medievalism, implying that everything has been going downhill since the fourteenth century (or, in the opinion of Lévi-Strauss, since neolithic times). For example, medieval ecological sustainability was in fact due mainly to rudimentary agricultural methods and to the huge extension of cultivated Europe up to the end of the thirteenth century.

The notion of 'the environment' would not have been understood by medieval people, who felt themselves to be an integral part of a living, spiritually-informed universe. The doubtful morality of mining, as a raping of Mother Earth, was still a matter of debate as late as the sixteenth century. Technology was less about mechanisms than about an enormous range of traditional skills employed in intimate partnership with the powers and products of nature, as for example in the construction of wooden sailing ships and the sailing of them.

During the sixteenth and seventeenth centuries Copernicus, Bacon, Galileo and Newton developed the scientific method of investigation and a very different world view began to emerge. Nature was understood as a perfect machine, operating according to precise mathematical laws. All natural phenomena could be categorised and hierarchically related; objectivity, number, prediction and control were the only things that really mattered. This tradition has shaped every branch of modern science, and endures as a widely dominant mentality.

Unfortunately it was assumed that this particular Cartesian understanding of reality was itself the very mirror of reality, instead of being no more than one serviceable representation within the limitations of the culture in which it originated. This is a narrow definition of *scientism* as an ideology misappropriated from the scientific method of enquiry. A wider definition, used in this book, is that which assumes that the scientific method is the only valid means of understanding reality and shaping our future. It assumes that ordinary consciousness provides an optimal, value-free representation of reality (positivism) and that phenomena can be substantially known and explained through reductionist analysis into mechanistically related parts. Other forms of knowing are denied or downgraded. The *thinking* self is set over and against feelings, the body, and the whole universe, as the one certain observation platform. We can understand the world without understanding ourselves except as objects of this same mode of enquiry. This dualism implies an assured and arrogant anthropocentrism which justifies human ordering and control of all that is *other*.

Cartesian scientism was generalised to support the ancient tradition in social theory which conceives of society as an abstraction inhabited by isolated atom-like individuals, possessed of certain characteristics governing the way they interact with one another (e.g. through contractual relationships) and with institutional abstractions like 'the state' and 'the market'. This is dramatically exemplified in the thinking of Thomas Hobbes, the first great modern political theorist, who has influenced a whole tendency in radical green writing like that of William Ophuls. This mind-frame was carried forward into the 'dismal science' of Adam Smith and the classical economists and into much contemporary liberal political and ethical theory.

Scientism on the one hand and religious fundamentalism on the other are two major *evasions* which disempower our effective response to ecological and social crisis. The distinction between science and scientism is of major importance. Science is an enormously valuable methodology and body of knowledge without which civilised survival would be impossible. Ultimately, however, it is no more than a tool in the service of whatever level of personal and social consciousness we have attained.

For scientism there is an *environmental* crisis 'out there' from which science alone can procure our salvation. 'Even if the Earth's resources prove to be ultimately finite, those of the solar system and the great galaxy beyond are, for all practical purposes, infinite'.[6] But for the higher levels of consciousness, to which we have the potential to open through psycho-spiritual cultivation and growth, there is an *ecological* crisis of which we are a part, and for the remedying of which science is indispensable to us. Scientism is science controlled and exalted by a shallow 'cleverness', as E.F. Schumacher called it, which believes that there is a scientific fix to every threat to the personal and collective ego:

> The disease [affecting our civilisation] having been caused by allowing cleverness to displace wisdom, no amount of clever research is likely to produce a cure. But where is wisdom? Where can it be found? Here we come to the crux of the matter: it can be read about in numerous publications, but it can be found only inside oneself. To be able to find it one has to liberate oneself from such masters as greed and envy.[7]

Although I believe our history is very much a record of fear-driven folly, it is at the same time much more than that. Scientific and technological vision and enterprise have relieved much suffering and hold great promise if we can exercise them more wisely in the future. Thanks to the heroism and compassion of revolutionaries and reformers, rebels and philanthropists, the citizens of many countries now sleep peacefully at night, enjoy the dignity of representative democracy (however circumscribed), are well informed, and have many possibilities for developing their potential.

And in every age there have been eloquent (and silent) witnesses to the grandeur and the folly—unsaintly saints and steadfast searchers; poets, artists and music-makers; wise fools and others lost to history; and all the less deceived who were sufficiently at home in themselves as to be neither deluded about who and what they were nor to be socially corrupted and intimidated. Without being able to carry forward this heritage we would make a sorry job of trying to shape a better future.

In the next two chapters I shall examine the ecological crisis to which the historical 'ascent of *man*' has led.

2 The hot question of population

AS COMPARED with all the subtle and various forms of pollution and the arguments about the exhaustion of planetary resources, the surge in human numbers on planet Earth might appear the most straightforward of ecological questions. In fact, we immediately encounter mentalities which will become all too familiar in the course of this book.

Population growth and control are subjects which arouse strong emotions. Positions are taken up which are as much explicable in terms of unyielding ideological stances as of the data and arguments under discussion. Those who thus take a problem 'personally' become as much part of that problem as a resource for its solution. Refusal to acknowledge the complexities and uncertainties in the relationship between population, the environment, the economy and the social culture is widespread. The controversies feed on themselves, as in the long-running dispute between catastrophist Paul Ehrlich[8] and cornucopian Julian Simon ('Natural resources are not finite').[9]

Some people undoubtedly display an Armageddon streak. Like the Fat Boy in *Pickwick papers*, they like to make our flesh creep, and sometimes give the impression of not being all that fond of human beings anyway. (In the *Gaia atlas* we are dismissed as a malignant cancer on the face of the Earth). And for radicals who feel an understandable detestation for the established social order and long for it to be transformed, the eco-crisis is a godsend. It would be difficult to imagine a more absolute mandate for change, especially when contrasted with the now unserviceable Marxist promise of the inevitable-collapse-of-capitalism-due-to-its-own-inherent-contradictions. No less outspoken on the subject of population control is a variegated opposition of religionists and socialists.

In the last thirty years world population has risen from two billion to five billion in a continually climbing curve. The United Nations Population Fund estimates that it will nearly double by the middle of the next century.

In the Overdeveloped World the fall in the death rate in the nineteenth century was followed by a falling birth rate and a near stabilisation of population levels. Changing social conditions led parents to see large families as more of a liability than an asset. However, this 'demographic transition' has not occurred in the Third World. The better control of disease has indeed led to a fall in the death rate. But poverty continues to encourage large families, which provide security in old age and infirmity. Patriarchal values, machismo, religious taboos, and the socially depressed and poorly educated condition of women are other factors which have tended to keep the birth rate high. Moreover, several governments, like those of Japan and Indonesia, actually encourage large families in order to provide more workers, to outbreed and 'bury' subordinate peoples, or to ensure continued racial predominance in the face of immigration.

Overall, however, women in the Third World are giving birth to fewer children than in the past. In 1960 they had an average of 6.1 children, as compared with 3.7 today. And yet not only are total numbers still rising; in the late 1980s the *rate* of increase started to climb again, reversing the post-1970 trend. This is mainly because the Third World age structure is weighted heavily in favour of young people. There are twice as many or more youngsters under fifteen than in the overdeveloped countries. Even if each woman were to have only two children, the population would continue to grow rapidly. This effect has been likened to putting on the brakes of an express train: the faster the train, the longer it takes the brakes to stop it. Will it stop in time?

The consequences at least for the forthcoming decades are likely to be tragic and, combined with spreading environmental degradation, could trap hundreds of millions in a downward spiral of falling incomes and growing hunger. On one view population will stabilise at least by the middle of the next century as the long overdue demographic transition occurs and birth rates fall. But it has been estimated that this could double energy needs by 2020, as well as requiring huge inputs of raw materials to create even the minimum supportive infrastructures. On another view, population will start to fall because of the cumulative effects of malnutrition and disease combined with social and environmental collapse. Already the dry tropical areas of Africa appear to be moving towards such a breakdown.

One alleged solution, advocated by the influential Brundtland Report,[10] is that of an industrial acceleration out of the crisis. This is a popular cornucopian cure-all. Since much of the newly created wealth would pay for the technological fix which would, hopefully, contain the eco-crisis, the Overdeveloped World could carry on much as usual. And the rising living standards of the Third World would usher in the long awaited demographic transition and stabilise population growth. 'Development is the best contraception'; 'With every mouth God sends a pair of hands'. In reality the global ecosystem is being tested to destruction as the whole world is led to aspire to the insatiable consumption of an affluent minority which may have already overshot planetary carrying capacity. Moreover it could well be that the kind of development proposed by Brundtland and others would do no more than maintain continued population growth at the present level of wretchedness.

This cornucopian response is sometimes linked with the argument of socialists and others that the problem of world poverty is a problem of the inequitable distribution of land and other resources rather than a problem of absolute shortage. The enormous sums spent on armaments, for example, would alone provide sufficient resources to feed the hungry. Thus in July 1982 the *New internationalist* featured a straight line graph into the next century showing a steadily rising world grain yield. Underneath was the claim: 'Feeding the ten billion: If current trends continue, food production will keep pace with population growth. But feeding the world's hungry depends on better distribution, not just higher yields'.

In fact the so-called 'green revolution' of the 1970s in Third World agriculture is proving ecologically unsustainable, dependent as it is on an economically and socially vulnerable, high cost, petrochemical agriculture. Yields are rising at a progressively slower rate and in some cases are now stationary or falling (as in the case of rice). The UK Parliamentary Office of Science and Technology has reported that food production has now fallen behind population growth in 27 out of 39 sub-Saharan African countries and that by 2025 tropical Africa will be able to feed only forty per cent of its people.

The redistributist half of the *New internationalist* argument is, however, rather more credible than the cornucopian half. In the distributist view overpopulation is a right-wing myth which distracts attention from the need for land reform and a radical redistributive revolution. Authoritarian policies aimed at controlling family size by forced sterilisation and by various penalties and grants are seen as invasive of human rights and disempowering of women and of the poor in general.

There is much truth in all this. Land reform (especially in Latin America) would considerably relieve poverty and population pressure. Moreover, a major redistribution of resources from the Overdeveloped World is essential for any long-term solution of the global crisis. However, in the absence of policies more specifically aimed at creating social conditions which favour smaller families, it does not follow that redistribution would significantly reduce birth rates unless it quite substantially increased incomes per head. Moreover, redistributist policies are radical long-term aspirations which should surely not exclude urgently needed short-term remedies. Is there not an ideologically inspired perversity about refusing to include in the 'poverty package' acceptable population control policies which could readily be implemented and which could, in particular, enhance women's quality of life?

One of the most promising policies is the promotion of equal opportunities for women, with positive discrimination in education, worthwhile jobs, and supportive welfare services, all backed by sufficient overall empowerment to tip the scales against patriarchal values. The correlation between women's education and smaller, better-off families is undeniable yet persistently ignored. A typical study in Thailand showed that women with five or more years of education had half as many children as those who had not.[11]

The above specific population control measures must be set in the context of strategies which address the whole range of problems afflicting the Third World. Such strategies would focus on community empowerment and draw upon the best in traditional values and culture. Population levels in many traditional societies remained stable for centuries, with strong community support in sickness, old age and misfortune, and with security of landholding from one generation to the next. Such conditions could arguably be recreated and enhanced by a radical conservatism where population would once again be voluntarily controlled in order to maintain social and environmental well-being. This would require rolling back the whole dislocating process of 'development'.

Finally, significant reductions in the populations of the industrialised countries would not only be beneficial to them but could also reduce their consumption of world resources. It has been estimated that if 'the impact per unit of consumption were the same in all three countries, the birth of an American baby would represent more than fifty times, and that of a British baby more than thirty-five times, as great a threat to the environment as the birth of an Indian baby.[12]

3 Living as if there were no tomorrow

A SECOND aspect of the ecological crisis is the depletion of the Earth's life sustaining resources: water, soils, forests, minerals and fossil fuels. In the 1970s there were forecasts that it would not be long before our accessible mineral wealth was exhausted and the planet was reduced to a useless shell. The usual straight line graphs all pointed to catastrophe. Subsequently, however, technologies have become phenomenally more efficient in their use of existing raw materials and energy sources and innovative in developing countless new synthetic materials. Nevertheless, continued high industrial growth could still precipitate an energy crisis through pollution rather than depletion, if the hoped for clean up per unit output of emissions were offset by an increasing overall volume. Renewable sources of energy such as wind and water power would not be sufficient to sustain such cornucopian levels of growth.

It is now becoming clear that the most disastrous form of resource depletion is the degradation and loss of topsoil, on which all human life depends, and the associated deforestation and exhaustion of fresh water reserves. This is in large part the cost of employing an unsustainable and ultimately destructive agricultural technology in order to double world food output over the second half of this century.

Deforestation is a global problem affecting climate, topsoil and biological diversity, and is due in the main to large-scale commercial undertakings feeding the insatiable demands of unrestrained industrial growth. Concern has now widened to include the vast temperate forests of the northern hemisphere, but the loss of the tropical rainforests is particularly grievous. Over half the world's plants and animal species depend upon this extraordinary biological powerhouse, and rainforest clearance much accelerates the massive die-off of species which is occurring throughout the world. (The loss of invertebrates and plants could be as high as one per day, and is increasing exponentially). The rainforests also constitute a pharmaceutical laboratory of immense medical and nutritional significance whose lore is fully known only to indigenous peoples who are also facing extinction. The tropical forests are, moreover, important determinants of world climate, circulating moisture towards the poles and cooling the temperate regions. Forests also soak up carbon dioxide, which accounts for half the global warm-up).

Less sensational is a creeping, world-wide desertification, creating recurrent and widespread famine. Between 1970 and 1990 global topsoil losses were equivalent to the whole of India's cropland, and desertification the whole of China's.

The case of the Ogallala Aquifer is a bizarre example of the mindless squandering of water reserves. The farmers of the US Great Plains cereal belt extract 6.5 million acre-feet of water each year from this huge natural reservoir. Nature puts back only 185,000 acre-feet. At present rates of extraction the tap will run dry by the middle of the next century and one of the world's greatest bread baskets will turn to dust.

The third aspect of the ecological crisis is the problem of multiple pollution (in which we include toxic wastes and the denaturing of foodstuffs). Until recently natural systems received the waste products of industrial civilisation on a scale and at a rate which enabled them to be broken down and recycled 'free of charge'. All that was considered necessary was to discharge, disperse and dilute, with the help of tall smokestacks and long sewage outfalls. This natural resilience and absorptive capacity is now being overwhelmed. James Lovelock's Gaia hypothesis[13] maintains that it is only a finely balanced equilibrium which enables the planetary ecosystem to sustain over half a million species of plants and over a million species of animals. Occasionally a species occupying a particularly favoured niche (*homo sapiens?*) will overshoot the carrying capacity of its ecological support system, followed by die-out and eventual restoration of equilibrium at a more modest level. The Irish potato famine in the nineteenth century is an oft quoted example.

Synthetics represent the quietest of various ecological time bombs that are ticking away behind the world's more immediately pressing concerns. In recent decades the scale and pace of industrial growth owes much to the increasing number of chemical compounds in such fields as artificial fibres, pharmaceuticals, paints, building materials, industrial chemicals, pesticides, herbicides and fertilisers. Some 70,000 such synthetics are now in use and over a thousand are added every year. The very qualities which have made many of these substances commercially successful are those which also make them non-biodegradable. They accumulate in the environment with unpredictable long-term effects, and many are now known to be toxic in degraded or decayed forms or through pollution occurring in the process of manufacture.

Dioxins are a startling example. Essential to plastics manufacture, they are integral to modern industrial society. Released during production they are then absorbed into the food chain. According to the German Federal Health Office (BGA), German agricultural land has already absorbed an average amount well above the safety level, but no one knows how to dispose of the contaminated soil safely. People in seriously affected regions have been complaining of chronic head and stomach aches and premature loss of hair. There is no reason to suppose that similar situations do not exist on other industrialised countries.

Some compounds which are harmless in themselves combine with others to produce toxic cocktails. Moreover, it was discovered in the early 1950s that toxic substances like DDD (a close relation of DDT) which are present in minute traces in the general environment tend to accumulate exponentially up the food chain through, for example, plankton, fish and human beings, with a several hundredfold increase in toxicity. In general it is extremely difficult to estimate the *cumulative* effect of specific synthetics and other pollutants and even more so their *combined* effect. Finally, there are difficulties in measuring or even detecting and isolating large numbers of them. Only a fraction of the suspected pollutants in vehicle exhaust emissions, for example, have even been clearly identified.

The denaturing of foodstuffs through the application of chemical technologies exemplifies all that is wrong with an industrial consumerism in which maximum private profit is paramount.

Crops are grown in exhausted soil made 'fertile' by large applications of chemical fertilisers and treated with pesticides and fungicides. Animals are repeatedly dosed with antibiotics, steroids and other hormones and kept under unnatural and confined conditions (for the abuse of animals commonly accompanies the abuse of foodstuffs).

Next the food is processed with artificial colourants, anti-oxidants, stabilisers and flavour enhancers, sugared and salted, and maybe bulked with air and water to increase its volume and weight.

Thirdly, much of the food will have to be stored for long periods and transported over considerable distances, so it has to be preserved by chemical and other treatments whose side-effects are not fully known.

Meanwhile, my country shop cannot afford the additional equipment now supposedly required to maintain standards of environmental health. Bread is therefore no longer baked there and local free-range eggs are no longer on sale. Battery farm eggs have been substituted because legal free-range eggs are not locally affordable. The eggs and the bread have commonly been kept in store and then 'imported' over long distances.

To continue this review of the multiple industrial assault on the functioning of our planetary system (and on our own well-being) the nuclear energy industry provides a remarkable show case of unfounded technological optimism and credulity, and of the power of official, industrial and scientific vested interests. Exposure to commercial accounting (which counts research and development costs, together with reactor decommissioning and long-term waste storage costs) has revealed the gross inefficiency of nuclear power. In the US decline has been spectacular; in the UK electricity consumers pay some ten per cent on their bills to keep the industry in existence.

This is an industry in which any nuclear accident could be catastrophic and yet on its own estimate there is a probability of a major accident every 47.4 years—or, in other words, at any time. Evidence of creeping contamination is also accumulating, like the probability that radioactive emissions may be responsible for concentrations of leukemia cases in the vicinity of nuclear plants. Furthermore there is no satisfactory method for safely disposing of the accumulating nuclear wastes. Plutonium, for example, has to be 'isolated' from the environment for at least a quarter of a million years! Finally, all nuclear reactors produce plutonium, and any country with a civil programme is in a strong position to manufacture its own weapons.

The most dramatic and well publicised of pollution problems have to do with changes in the Earth's atmosphere and climatic behaviour.

The first to come to prominence was acid rain, that is to say, the acidification of lakes, rivers and soils by sulphurous industrial pollution. This damage continues. Still more alarming was the discovery that the planet's protective ozone layer was being eroded by chemical emissions, resulting in an increased incidence of cancers, allergies, eye cataracts and weakening of the immune system, as well as affecting agriculture and fisheries. The international response has proved inadequate and this is an increasingly alarming phenomenon.

More dramatic still has been the arrival of the greenhouse effect. This global warm-up was unanimously confirmed in 1990 by some three hundred leading scientists on the Intergovernmental Panel on Climatic Change. And the previous year twenty-four world leaders meeting at the Hague had concluded that the warmup threatens 'the very conditions of life on Earth'. To date, however, the international response has been uneven and falls far short of what is needed.

Basically, the greenhouse effect is caused by air pollution trapping heat inside the Earth's atmosphere and at the same time letting more of the sun's heat through to the earth. Origins include coal fired power stations (an estimated 10 per cent); tropical forest burn-off (20 per cent); and industrial and vehicle emissions and nitrous fertilisers (38 per cent). Action is thus required over a wide range of issues: energy efficiency, reafforestation, industrial and agricultural policy, and relations between the industrial nations and the Third World.

Widespread public concern over the greenhouse effect has for the first time put in question previously taken-for-granted assumptions about continued large-scale industrial growth. However this concern now seems to have been overlaid by the belief that technological fixes could make present levels of growth environmentally sustainable (Part III of this book). The contrary view, which is the subject of Parts IV and V, remains very much a minority one. But first we must take the search back to the social forces behind the ecological crisis, and then to its origins in the human condition itself.

4 The great powerhouse of superindustrialism

THE NEXT three chapters will review contemporary social forces at work on planet Earth, though by no means in purely ecological terms. Our social system has potentially terminal ecological crisis built into it. It is as if it were designed to self-destruct. However, I do not believe there is anything inevitable about this. But an effective response will require changes that are political, economic—and radical. It is inconceivable that such changes could somehow be governed by exclusively ecological imperatives. They will be no less determined by our experience of social problems as social problems, and by social values and aspirations which have more than ecological significance, but which are nevertheless ecologically informed.

The industrial system is the powerhouse of ecological crisis. The capitalist and communist varieties had much in common, but the former has now clearly proved to be the effective wealth creator. Industrialism has now become an essentially capitalist phenomenon. Indeed, trenchant socialists like Raymond Williams have brushed aside the term 'industrialism':

> The most evident damage [of capitalism] has been the relentless drive for profit and the accumulation of capital, but underlying even this has been a basic orientation to the world—at once its resources and its people—which it defines as raw material . . . What is seen is not life forms and land forms in intricate interdependence, but a range of opportunities for their profitable exploitation.[14]

The first phase of industrial capitalism was characterised by factory mass production. In the late nineteenth century emphasis shifted to the struggle of a monopolistic and colonising capitalism to win control of world markets and raw materials. Finally, we now have a consumer capitalism which creates not only commodities and services but a whole distinctive culture in which to float them.

Superindustrialism is the term used in this book to denote the whole social culture created by consumer capitalism. I endorse Raymond Williams' view that 'the society which is now emerging is in no sense post-industrial. Indeed in its increasingly advanced technologies it is a specific and probably absolute climax of industrialism itself'.[15] The new industrialism is to be understood in terms of its continuities as well as its discontinuities.

In the first place, capitalist industrialism retains its built-in need for limitless growth. But the effects of exponential growth rates (since 1950 there has been a seven-fold increase in manufacturing output) can no longer be naturally absorbed by the ecosphere. Superindustrialism is therefore faced with the need to become ecologically sustainable if it is to survive.

Second, the economy is still dominated by large, monopolistic production and distribution units. But these are now more complex and decentralised and are often surrounded by a dependent network of small satellite contractors.

Third, control is still exercised by an elite, but is now exercised in a more diffuse and implicit fashion. The political stability of superindustrialism depends upon the existence of enough people with enough electoral and other kinds of influence to ensure the indefinite continuation of a culture of consumption which has become an ingrained way of life for them. This is the 'culture of contentment' highlighted by J.K. Galbraith.[16]

Fourth, the economically overdeveloped countries of superindustrialism continue to exploit the other countries of the world, but they now do so through transnational companies and global financial and regulatory institutions. These operate across politically independent states which were formerly colonies.

Fifth, emphasis shifts from the manufacture of commodities to the provision of services (whether shopping malls, package holidays or leisure complexes) and of self-service commodities (like home videos); from wage workers to credit-worthy consumers; from the utility of commodities that are necessary to the skilful presentation of those that are not.

The insatiable hunger to possess in order to confirm the self to the self and to others, beyond the satisfaction of reasonable needs, is a long recognised characteristic of our human condition. This craving, the endless multiplication of wants spurred on by envy and status-seeking, emptyness and boredom, has been reckoned by the world's spiritual traditions as a cause of suffering second only to the denial of basic needs. Their testimony ranges from the Taoist aphorism 'He who knows he has enough is rich' to the response of a native North American to the taunts of the white invader: 'Miserable as we seem in your eyes, we consider ourselves much happier than you, in this that we are content with the little that we have'.[17] In traditional communities opportunities for acquisitiveness (avarice, it was called) were comparatively limited. But there was a wide range of other more socially wholesome satisfactions and marks of distinction, including valued skills and knowledge, integrity and wisdom, as well as a rich and varied popular culture. At a gross level, religion offered a variety of consolations; at a subtle level it celebrated the joy of simplicity and sufficiency.

The everyday reality of superindustrialism is a consumer culture in which this richness and diversity has been so diminished that the commodity market (which now packages experiences as well as things) has to bear a disproportionate weight of the human need for meaning, significance, status and belongingness. 'I buy therefore I am', proclaims the California car sticker. And it is a market that has been deliberately designed to foster and exploit this dependence. The purchaser is offered not only the product but also a sense of personal identity designed into it and reinforced through the media. This 'designer culture' turns on 'the search for that elusive psychological bridge between people as they are and people as they would like to be',[18] or, rather, as those who make money from them would like them to be. Power, prestige, savoir-faire, seductiveness, a caring green image or instant enlightenment can all be purchased as fantasy reinforcements to self-identity and a sense of belonging, consolidated by soap operas and magazine features which support the accompanying advertisements.

How far the designer culture actually succeeds in designing people as well as products is open to question. Most psychological investigations do not reveal consumption to be among the main determinants of happiness in life, among which marriage, family life, friendships and satisfying work feature most prominently for those who are not actually suffering poverty. Consumer- dependency is evidently a rather shallow phenomenon grounded on cultural deprivation rather than having any intrinsic power. But it is a kind of frenzy which the rest of nature cannot sustain indefinitely. That is not the least of the reasons why an ecologically harmonious, steady-state society will need to offer a wide range of wholesome high quality satisfactions which will make the consumer itch look silly and irrelevant.

Writers like Christopher Lasch[19] have maintained that the affluent society creates a culture of 'survivalism', marked by a lack of social responsibility and a loss of faith in civic, state or other corporate expressions of it. The traditional sense of belonging to a 'civil society' (still less to a 'community'), sustained by collective concerns and responsibilities has receded. At the height of her power Mrs Thatcher was able to proclaim that 'there is no such thing as society; there are only individual men and women and there are families.'[20]

Superindustrialism has well nigh completed the destruction of community begun by nineteenth-century industrialism, if we mean by that much abused term a closely knit, semi-autonomous network of reciprocal rights and obligations which are well rooted both economically and socially. Jeremy Seabrook argues that, in place of community,

> Mass markets serve as a focus for illusions of shared and participatory activity. In this process the peer group becomes a kind of substitute for community, and the desire to belong to an atrophied culture finds its principal outlet in shared styles, fashions, heroes, television programmes, brand loyalties, shopping habits and addictions. Controlled and manufactured experience stands us in the stead of more organic involvement in community, neighbourhood or social struggle.[21]

All that having been said, there are encouraging signs that survivalism may not be as pervasive (at least in the UK) as has been proclaimed by writers given to apocalyptic generalisations of this sort. Successive annual British Social Attitude Surveys, as well as other opinion polls, show an *expressed* widespread continued commitment to collective responsibility for social problems. Most people say that they would be willing to forego tax cuts in order to improve funding of the National Health Service. And in communities that have been marginalised but not devitalised, defensive self-help initiatives are to be found. Eventually, it may not prove, after all, so difficult to find our way back forwards!

Automation and livelihood are other facets of industrialism which must claim our attention, on both ecological and social grounds, and as providing pointers to the future.

As early as 1930 John Maynard Keynes warned that 'we are being affected by a new disease . . . of which we will hear a great deal in the years to come—namely technological unemployment. This means unemployment due to our discovery of means of economising on the use of labour outrunning the pace at which we find new uses for labour'. Technological unemployment has so far been mainly in manufacturing, with the introduction of computer controlled machine tools. Automation is now far advanced in the white collar and service industries, with a widening gap between technological and managerial staffs on the one hand and poorly paid dial watchers and keyboard operators on the other. In the UK in particular since 1981 there has been a sustained improvement in productivity in the economy as a whole. The average annual increase of 5.5 per cent has been bettered only by Japan.[22]

In the late 1970s and early 1980s Bill Jordan, Clive Jenkins, Barrie

Sherman and Tom Stonier made large claims about 'the collapse of work' by the end of the century, with a mere ten per cent of the potential workforce providing all our needs.[23] Nevertheless, the traditional industrial 100,000 hour working life expectation is already being halved in the UK, mainly as a result of early retirement. Technological innovation appears usually to be motivated by anticipated labour savings, rather than a wish to increase production. As the compensatory effect of increased overall production (and employment) is arguably slowed down by increased environmental costs and constraints, the curve of technological unemployment could steepen.

The social and political implications of the coming of the 'post-employment society' have been discussed by writers as diverse as Charles Handy,[24] Bill Jordan[25] and André Gorz.[26] They are largely agreed that the historic political significance of mass technological unemployment lies in its erosion of earnings as the basis of consumption. For if there are fewer and fewer wage-earning producers, how are the products to be purchased? Attention thus shifts from production and wage bargaining to consumption and the politics of the distribution of purchasing power (through a basic income for all, for example).

For radical green optimists this post-employment economy remarkably resembles the conserver, steady-state economy which they believe to be the only viable response to deepening environmental crisis. Full-time employment for life will disappear; part-time work will become the norm (already a fifth of employed workers work fewer than twenty hours a week); the basic income will provide essential backup; and the domestic, informal and small business sectors will become prominent. The ecological crisis and the automation crisis would thus, arguably, *together* shape the future green self-employment society.

If the post-employment society is slow in coming, at least Marx's 'industrial reserve army' of the permanently unemployed has at last arrived on the scene. Since the mid 1950s there have been eight severe recessions, and each has left a higher peak of unemployment than the previous one. The 'official' unemployment figure is currently rising towards three million (or four million, if successive governments' massaging of the figures is discounted). In the European Community unemployment is expected to stagnate around the fifteen million level. And in the US by 1992 unemployment had climbed back to its high level of six years previously, but with a greater proportion in the long-term category.

The pessimistic scenario for the post-employment society is of a large, sullen and demoralised class of permanently unemployed people plus a fringe of poorly paid part-timers, together with the self-employed and numerous small service and contracting businesses scratching a bare living on the margins of the formal economy.

Already there are in the UK some nine million men, women and children dependent on state welfare benefits, together with another nine million struggling to make ends meet on low pay. This nascent underclass amounts to nearly a third of the population and it is growing (the number of families claiming means-tested benefits doubled in the 1980s). In addition to the registered unemployed it includes growing numbers of elderly people, single parent families, the homeless, the physically and mentally ill who have been 'returned to the care of the community', people confined to ethnic and inner city ghettos and dumped in desolate housing estates, together with whole communities in the north of England and in Scotland, Wales and Northern Ireland which have to all intents and purposes been written off by mainstream society. Most of these people are disempowered by the multiple deprivations of chronic joblessness or poverty trap wages, junk housing, poor diet, ill health and inadequate healthcare, low levels of literacy, lack of information and know-how, broken family life, and so on.

Professor David Donnison, a former Chairman of the Supplementary Benefits Commission, has drawn attention to the characteristics of this 'new poverty'.[27] Unlike their historical predecessors, the new poor do not constitute a recognisable social class, with an acknowledged place in society ('The poor are always with us') and a strong sense of solidarity which could be politically significant. The new poor are not a mobilisable political force; they are relatively powerless; they are stigmatised as failures who have proved unable to claim their share in the affluent society and may suffer humiliation and even guilt. Moreover the rising tide of general affluence has tended to push the low waged into real poverty: the disappearance of many local facilities and the decline of public transport forces them into the car culture; the shopping mall, geared to free spenders, has replaced the corner shop offering neighbourhood credit; the pool of decent rented housing on demand has dried up; even the central heating system may be too expensive to use. Struggling to hold on to luxuries that have become necessities, the new poor find themselves hard put to afford traditional essentials like adequate food and clothing.

There is a sense, however, in which superindustrialism implies a poor quality of life across the whole social spectrum. F.E. Trainer has assembled a remarkable range of studies indicating the absence of any significant correlation between material well-being and a sense of the quality of life. According to several of these, in the US and Western Europe people's assessment of their quality of life (or 'happiness') has progressively declined through the increasingly prosperous 1960s, 70s and 80s. Trainer concludes that not only is our present level of affluence ecologically unsustainable; it is also 'undermining crucial non-material conditions that make for a healthy community, a sense of purpose, fulfilling work and leisure, supportive social relations, peace of mind, security from theft and violence, caring and co-operative neighbourhoods, and satisfying day to day life experience'.[28]

5 Socialism: 'the great sustaining myth'

VIEWED from beyond the era of pre-ecological innocence we can now see more clearly how far capitalism and socialism share similar values and assumptions. For both, 'the environment' is an open frontier for heedless exploitation (though nowadays masked by the fashionable 'sustainable growth').

Lenin proclaimed that electricity + Soviet power = socialism (with the 'communist stage' of true abundance lying beyond). Since Boris Komarov wrote *The destruction of nature in the Soviet Union* in 1978 it has become increasingly evident that communist industrialism has been even more environmentally destructive than the capitalist version. Here is the chillingly authentic voice of Stalin's industrialisation of Siberia in an ode by Vladimir Sasuburin:

> May the taiga be turned into ash,
> May it be logged and the tundra trampled.
> So be it, because it is inevitable.
> Only on foundations of concrete and girders
> Can the comradeship of all humanity.
> The brotherhood of man,
> Be erected![29]

The communists were latter-day Cartesians who tried to bypass Adam Smith by pushing that rational, structural-functionalist tradition ('scientific socialism' they called it) to impossible extremes. Conceived as 'social engineering' by Stalin, it was the most ambitious attempt ever to translate a social ideology into reality, and the most disastrous. The calculative and centralising command economy did in fact achieve considerable success in laying the foundations of an industrial economy, both after 1917 and again after 1945. But in the end it failed, and was too inflexible to evolve into a consumer culture. And the human cost was, of course, enormous.

The reformist, parliamentary socialist tradition ('social democracy' or, latterly, 'democratic socialism') shares much of this top-down social engineering ethos. In Britain it was Herbert Morrison who was the typical architect of the Brave New World, with its nationalised corporations, the vast housing estates of municipal socialism, and the welfare state which 'delivered' services and benefits. There is no doubt that institutions like the National Health Service have relieved an ocean of suffering and still struggle to do so. But in Britain and elsewhere this tradition of corporate care is being overwhelmed by problems of size, inflexibility, complexity and cost-effectiveness.

The collapse of communism has been paralleled by the swing in the West towards an uncompromising free-market capitalism and the end of any remaining vision of a parliamentary transition to anything that could be called socialism. All of the foregoing add up to what has been called 'the decay of one of the great sustaining myths of our era—the hope and promise of socialism'.[30]

However, we have not heard the last of the socialist tradition. Purged of communism, purged of welfarism, even, hopefully, purged of romantic ideology, it could well eventually re-emerge in serviceable new forms to challenge its ancient adversary. And Marxist social theory, beyond its ideological vulgarisation, has long been well regarded (at least outside Anglo-America) as an extremely fertile intellectual tradition. The social analysis in this book is itself underpinned by Marxian phenomenology.

David Marquand has observed that:

> Casino capitalism on the Anglo-American model is quite different from the high quality social capitalism of the Federal Germans, the Austrians and the Scandinavians [which] is sustained by an intimate web of co-operative practices, socially responsible institutions and solidaristic values.[31]

This originates in the catholic, as well as the socialist, tradition that the state has a duty to limit the damage which otherwise uncontrolled capitalism would create. However, capitalism will need to be very much further evolved if it is to support a truly ecologically 'safe' steady-state economy, and even more so if it is to provide the social equitability which is a corollary of such an economy.

Most particularly relevant here is the third of the socialist traditions, that of libertarian socialism. But this were better introduced in Part IV when we come to review the state of radical green politics.

6 Problems and possibilities of an unfolding new world

FOR NEARLY four hundred years the global dynamic has come from rapidly evolving, capitalism-powered nation states and particularly from 'the great powers' among them. After they had divided up almost the whole world the balance of power among them broke down in two horrendous world wars. The second of these ended colonialism and exhausted Europe and Japan. Thus the global balance narrowed down to the two great remaining superpowers, with their polarised ideologies and balance of nuclear terror. With the collapse of the USSR the centuries old distribution of power between the great industrial states has come to an abrupt end, pushing the world out into a bewildering new era.

By 1989 it was possible for an obscure US official named Francis Fukuyama to win a footnote in history by proclaiming 'the end of history'. Liberal capitalist democracy could now live happily ever after. There was talk of a New World Order, but in fact the remaining power centres of the United States and its two lukewarm partners, the European Community and Japan, appear to be confining themselves, in effect, to reactive 'peace-keeping operations' where regional stability or key resources and lines of communication are threatened.

1990 saw the the eruption of dozens of small nations across the Balkans and the former USSR (in which a large-scale replay of the Yugoslav tragedy could well be enacted if an aggressive nationalistic government came to power in Russia). But let us not forget that the world public opinion that recoils at ethnic cleansing in Bosnia also cheered on 'heroic little Lithuania' to independence and democracy. Beyond Europe, the continued integrity and stability of many of the artificially created Third World states is also increasingly in question as they are subjected to a wide range of pressures (including the widespread militarisation fostered by the free market in arms). Many of the westernised, post-colonial elites are becoming insecure and unreliable; the tightening economic and financial squeeze by the rich countries creates potential crisis conditions, pointing, particularly in

Africa, to local political, economic and ecological collapse. The world of tidily imposed order is rapidly receding in what, from *that* viewpoint, appears as a threatening miasma of balkanisation and disintegration. (According to an American defence journal, US targeting is now directed at 'that swirling pot of poison, made up of zealots, crazies, drug runners and terrorists'.[32]

In the long run there can be no really legitimate and effective interventions so long as the rich and powerful nations (and notably the US) continue to play at God, vigorously representing a reluctant and half-hearted 'international community'. Their impartiality is too compromised by their own strong vested interests and past self-seeking record. The underlying global reality is that a genuine international community of free partners cannot emerge so long as a clutch of powerful countries is busily bleeding a relatively powerless global majority of nations. This is the problem we must examine next. Its resolution would create the possibility of a worldwide pattern of federations and confederations of small peoples and nations, nesting vertically into global and regional regulatory bodies (like a reborn United Nations and European Community), with a constitutional requirement to uphold human rights, national identities, and ecological integrity. Such a new world order may be riddled with problems and still a long way off, but it is the only hope that we have beyond the difficult new era that is opening up. The fag end of great power politics in a peacekeeping role simply will not do.

For four centuries the world's rich and diverse cultures were variously plundered, exploited, disrupted, marginalised or totally obliterated by the soldiers, missionaries, traders, administrators, and settlers of the colonising powers. One fifth of the world's population now controls and uses three-quarters of the world's resources. That is the Overdeveloped World, where consumption so far exceeds any reasonable definition of human need as to have become socially pathological. The United States, for example, with six per cent of the world's population consumes one half of the world's income. This is the outstanding moral issue of our time, upon which so much else turns and which has the same origins as the ecological crisis with which it is intimately connected.

Even most anti-colonial revolutionaries have assumed that the former colonies must become 'modern', 'developing' countries, hastening to wipe out historical injustice by catching up with the former colonisers. Hundreds of millions of people aspire to the ownership of a television set, to the glitter of urban life, to a Western-style education, to a prestigious job in the local bureaucracy. This is progress. What other goals could there be? Yet this is a sad and threadbare fantasy. For the whole world's exploding population to achieve American living standards would involve wrecking the planet by increasing output a hundred times or more—and without even necessarily eliminating great social injustices.

The scale of Third World exploitation and disempowerment, from the military and economic to the cultural and psychological, is immense. The gross and readily observable fact is that most Third World countries are systems for the often ruthless exploitation of the peasants and labourers who constitute the overwhelming majority of the population (one half of the population of the Third World is landless). The main beneficiaries are transnational companies, which have developed and distorted these economies for the low-cost mass production of a small number of foodstuffs, minerals and raw materials needed to sustain the affluent societies. Many Third World countries are dependent on just two or three basic export commodities.

The two hundred largest transnational companies together have a turnover equivalent to a quarter of the annual production of the whole world. They have influential connections with the world banking system and with the governments of the industrialised countries, and enough power to bend many sovereign states to their will (Unilever has an annual turnover greater than the combined GNP of twenty-five African states). Most Third World 'aid' actually reinforces dependence, with big, export boosting schemes which sooner or later impoverish the poorer sections of the population and the environment on which they depend. They have also provided local bureaucrats, landowners and speculators with the trappings of a Western lifestyle—token national airlines, grandiose public buildings, luxury apartments, inappropriate and short-lived technologies and pot holed two-lane highways to nowhere.

Some Third World governments are little more than well rewarded (and well armed) agents for the exploitation of their own people. Those which have sought greater autonomy, self-reliance and social justice (like Cuba, Ghana, Nicaragua and Tanzania) have been blocked or defeated by a crushing combination of adverse circumstances, including deliberate coercion and destabilisation.

The Washington-based Worldwatch Institute reported a steep increase in Third World destitution in the 1980s, and claims that almost a quarter of humanity are now unable to satisfy basic food, clothing and shelter needs. Africa is particularly badly hit, being the only continent to show an annual increase in infant and child deaths. Economic decline is due in part to higher prices of imported manufactures combined with falling prices of Third World exports. The big fall in Third World commodity prices in 1985, for example, saved the consumers of the Overdeveloped World some

$65 billion—more than twice as much as was given in 'aid'.

These adverse terms of trade have plunged Third World countries deeper and deeper into debt. Even to keep up with the interest payments the desperately poor of the world have to pay some $95 billion a year to the desperately rich. More is being lent so that these payments can be maintained, but only on condition of the kind of 'structural readjustment' fashionable among free-market ideologues. The GATT (General Agreement on Tariffs and Trade) has been used to bring down import barriers (with little reciprocity in evidence) and to outlaw export controls, price supports and subsidies whereby many Third World governments have been trying to protect their peoples and their natural resources. They have been required to divert even further resources to foreign exchange earning exports, together with cuts in imports and public spending. These policies have rapidly translated into lower standards of living and more oppressive government. It is claimed that in Costa Rica incomes were so rapidly depressed that the number of children suffering from malnutrition doubled within a year.

Growing indebtedness has accelerated the short-term exploitation of natural resources, building up towards catastrophic conditions of soil exhaustion and loss of tree cover in some countries. The Brundtland Report conceded that 'environmental degradation, first seen as a problem of the rich nations and a side effect of industrial wealth, has become a survival issue for developing nations . . . Despite official hope on all sides, no trends identifiable today, no programmes or policies, offer any real hope for narrowing the gap between rich and poor nations'.[33]

The latest form of Third World exploitation is 'ecological imperialism', that is to say, economic pressure and conditional aid to induce Third World countries to make inequitable sacrifices to protect the planetary ecology which the industrial countries are doing most to undermine. This was very much a not-so-hidden agenda at the largely abortive Rio de Janeiro Earth Summit in 1992. Even such a well informed and sincere politician as US Vice-President Al Gore can pose an implicit threat of ecological imperialism. It is good to know that Gore believes in 'making the rescue of the environment the central organising principle for civilisation'. But the means is to be a Global Marshall Plan, which Gore conceives as a mission inspired by American values and perspectives, and analogous to the 'free world's' struggle against communism.[34]

The most important requirement for a response that gets to the roots of Third World crisis is that of radical institutional and attitudinal changes in the Overdeveloped World itself. The crisis of the Third World is a crisis of the whole world. It is not just an item—even the main item—on the agenda of the Overdeveloped World which can be shrugged off by massive injections of aid against a background of business as usual.

1 The Third World countries need to become more economically self-reliant. As the Economic Commission for Africa has put it: 'If hunger is to be averted, Africa must start producing what it consumes and consuming what it produces'. The peasants of Uganda and Tanzania have been better off when foreign trade was depressed, since land was then temporarily available for growing food for their own needs. The industrial countries will therefore need to negotiate and adapt their trade policies according to the diverse needs of each Third World country, tapering off their heavy imports of foodstuffs and raw materials, paying more realistic prices, and selling their own products more cheaply. There is plenty of slack to be taken up. Halving the world's arms expenditure would go far to eradicating world poverty and disease. And if a *real* green consumerism of simply reducing needless consumption caught on, further big diversions of resources could become possible. The millions who die of malnutrition each year could be adequately fed by the grain which would be saved if Americans were to reduce their meat intake by a mere ten per cent.[35]

2 Within these favourable terms of trade, debt repayments should be deposited in development funds managed by genuinely representative bodies in each country.

3 Sensitive aid would be needed to help overcome the social and economic distortions of the era of post-colonial 'development', so that each country could determine its own future. Typical of the alternative development strategies that are now coming to the fore is the Dar-Es-Salaam Declaration of 1990, which called for 'planned disengagement from international capitalism, regional food self-sufficiency, satisfaction of basic needs for all, [and] development from below through the termination of the anti-rural bias as well as concentration on small and medium-scale enterprises'.[36]

4 The industrial countries must make environmental reparation, through assistance in restoring and regenerating the exhausted soils, depleted woodlands and fouled rivers of the post-colonial era. They must assist, if invited, in the reshaping of truly sustainable Third World economies—though there is much that the post-industrialising world might itself learn from the reclamation of traditional, ecologically harmonious production methods.

5 It will be necessary to subsidise, without strings, those states which have
   to carry the burden of conserving resources of outstanding global
   significance, such as the rainforests.

The above implies a veritable world revolution which would require
most of the international and economic regulatory bodies and all the
transnational companies to become totally different animals from what
they are now or else to be replaced. Fortunately, the changes proposed
would tend to knock away the various props on which most Third World
post-colonial elites depend, and the more so if much of the support is
channelled through legitimate local non-governmental organisations, well-
known to their opposite numbers in the industrial countries. The most
promising development, however, is the emergence of a growing number
of autonomous, democratic and community-based development projects
and organisations in many Third World countries, a theme to which I shall
return in the final part of this book.

In conclusion, the Overdeveloped World must commit itself to two
historic tasks and must do so in ways which really do support the empowerment and self-determination of others, instead of binding them into new
and more subtle forms of dependence. It must truly, and at last, *let go!*

In the first place it must redeploy its huge surplus wealth and technology to support the planetary life support system which it is at present
undermining.

The second, and intertwined, task has to do with social justice.

There is the moral obligation to the new poor of the affluent societies.
And there is also the *real* Third World debt, which is owed to the great
majority of the world's people—'the wretched of the Earth' who have been
so heedlessly oppressed and exploited for so long in order to help bring
affluent societies into existence elsewhere for a fortunate minority.

The third task is to respond to the plight of the peoples of the Second
(ex-communist) World. Hopefully it will be out of common humanity,
but also not least because ecological well being, like peace, is indivisible
and some of the world's most threatening examples of ecological breakdown are to be found behind the former iron curtain, where the resources
to remedy them are so inadequate.

Any concern to develop an ecologically stable and harmonious society
from out of the present one will need sensitively to come to terms with
these several requirements, which lie beyond the immediate problems and
concerns of our present affluence. Mere self-reliance and isolationism are
probably not a workable option, and certainly not morally defensible.

7 Progress, cornucopia and the social fallacy

IN retrospect, we now begin to see how an all-pervading sense of progress has diminished the past to a cast-off launching pad serving only as a measure of our present so much higher achievements. And it has made of the future just a bigger and grander version of the present. When no longer spellbound by progress we see earlier cultures with a fresh eye. They have their own validity and can maybe even offer worthwhile pointers for us, as we confront our future with a more appropriate humility and uncertainty.

Before the four hundred years of boundless economic and social development in the West, answers to the fundamental questions Why is it so? and, What might be done about it? were sought in the contemplative investigation of the God-given human condition itself (What is the nature of humankind?). The social order was experienced as no more than a relatively changeless context for the cultivation of this perennial wisdom. Social theories were based on assumptions about human nature rather than on the study of social phenomena, and were concerned with the maintenance of a stable social order wherein everyone had a well-regulated place and whose ultimate purpose was to nurture spiritual salvation. The evidence of this was everywhere. In France alone, in the period from 1170 to 1270, the construction of some eighty cathedrals and five hundred cathedral-sized churches was undertaken. It has been estimated that this activity absorbed at least one third of the gross national product, comparable with present-day military expenditures.[1]

However, by the late eighteenth century a sense of 'progress' was sufficiently well established for Edward Gibbon to proclaim that 'every age of the world has increased and still increases the real wealth, the happiness, the knowledge and perhaps the virtue of the human race'. A hundred years later, buoyed up by the scale and rate of human growth, the prospect of unlimited progress had begun to sustain the hopes of millions for a better future. It surely held the one sure promise of social justice, as its benefits trickled down to even the poorest. This was vividly demonstrated in North America and other 'empty' continents, where the frontier seemed to offer enough space and resources to swallow up every problem. Go West, young man! Traces of this naive and idealistic optimism still endure . . .

In Erich Fromm's words: 'We were on the way to becoming gods, supreme gods, who could create a second world using the natural world only as building blocks for our second creation'.[2] Belief in cornucopian progress is still widespread, though now it claims to be ecologically sustainable, or at least for long enough to usher in the era of global prosperity and social justice to which the Brundtland Report aspired in 1987. Caught up in ecological crisis, the cornucopian is like a bank robber who pleads to be allowed to commit just a few more raids and then he will have enough to live on and can go straight. In 1930 J.M. Keynes speculated about the day when everyone would at last be tolerably well-off and we could 'once more value ends above means and prefer the good to the useful'. Unfortunately, however, 'for at least another hundred years we must pretend to ourselves and everyone that fair is foul and foul is fair, for foul is useful and fair is not. Avarice and usury must be our gods for a little longer for only they can lead us out of the tunnel of economic necessity into the daylight'.[3]

Not only is the natural environment finding it increasingly difficult to sustain Keynes's final hundred years of this undertaking, but the very achievements of cornucopian techno-social rationality are leaving us with less and less that confirms our sense of identity and keeps us sane. For the past two or three hundred years Westerners have been widening their freedom and individualism, but at the expense of traditional stabilising beliefs and institutions like, for example, marriage, the churches, the authority of tradition, the continuities of skills and knowledge. These have been demythologised, stripped of enduring value, made irrelevant, or reduced to matters of mere functional convenience.

Speed, convenience, choice, time saving, instant access, the supremacy of presentation over substance (and the confusion between them) have all contributed to increasing disorientation and feeling of meaninglessness. More and more doors open more easily, but the rooms are more and more empty. We feel launched upon an ocean of relativity from which the absolute horizon has disappeared. This mood has been processed by academics into an intellectual perspective (it largely ignores emotions) called deconstructive post-modernism.[4] This believes that we each construct our own arbitrary, rootless and transient reality, nothing outside of which can have meaning or, apparently, make moral claims upon us. Deconstructivism denies a shared and responsible reality of any meaningful kind, in contrast to ideology, which abstracts, distorts, solidifies and fortifies our sense of reality. It implies a bleak, nihilistic survivalism in a disintegrated world and it is seeping out into a 'minimalist' fiction and into art, architecture and design.

Associated with this psychic breakdown is another phenomenon of the Age of Progress which I call the 'social fallacy', and which is particularly relevant to the purpose of this book.

In the nineteenth century the unprecedented dynamics and complexity of social development stimulated classical economics, utilitarian liberalism, Marxism and a whole emergent range of social sciences. Religion was privatised and marginalised, though still for a time considered ethically serviceable. The new sciences of the mind concerned themselves with those maladjusted to the norms of industrial society. These burgeoning social sciences, backed by immense cornucopian optimism and technological triumphalism, combined to create the social fallacy. This is a rational-functional preoccupation with exclusively techno-social explanations and remedies for almost all human ills, whether war, social injustice, old age, ignorance or even existential insecurity. Even evil can be conditioned out of existence by socially engineering a better society, a notion which Mahatma Gandhi was fond of ridiculing—'systems so perfect that no one would need to be good!'

The social fallacy is ingrained in almost all of us. Although a fallacy in terms of its absolute claims, it owes its plausibility to very real achievements. (And we shall need such achievements no less in the future, but stripped of the follies associated with the social fallacy). Consider, for example, how the experience of old age has been transformed for those able to benefit from modern medicine and hygiene and a healthy diet. In the pre-industrial society in which, in Thomas Hobbes' words, life tended to be 'nasty, brutish and short' (as it still is for many Third World people), literature and legend bear witness not only to the wisdom of sages but also to the fear, pity, loathing and mockery aroused by the multiple miseries of old age experienced by those few who lived that long. We do not need the myth of progress in order to value progress of the kind that can still be ours.

Since the social fallacy is preoccupied with fixing things 'out there', the mind 'in here' only requires attention when it fails to do things out there which right thinking minds are supposed to do. One's mind is a private matter unless it becomes a public nuisance. The social fallacy implies not only a mind/feelings split, but also as total a separation as possible of the personal from the public. The former is a second-class realm inhabited by the emotions, the feminine, spirituality, art, literature and, of course, psychiatry. The occasions when it gets out into the public domain are commonly 'embarrassing', if not worse.

As the hollowness of the social fallacy becomes more apparent, there is a growing concern to take investigation of our present ills down to deeper levels. What is there about human beings that appears certainly to impel them to vast and repeated self inflicted suffering, and possibly also to their extinction? And whatever it may be, can we do something about it? There appears to be a growing and convergent movement of opinion here. The following sequel to the Club of Rome's historic doomsday pronouncement of the early seventies, *Limits to growth*,[5] in fact strikingly paraphrases what E.F. Schumacher was already saying at that time:

> The components of the corpus of society and of the individual's being are out of balance: the emotional, spiritual and even the intellectual elements have been overwhelmed by the weight of our physical triumphs. The establishment of a sane equilibrium can only come through a deeper understanding of the individual human being; the problems lie deep within human nature[6]

The authors conclude that 'we need to reorientate research and development programmes, and radically reorientate priorities.' The first of these should be 'fundamental research: investigations concerning the human individual, his nature, motivations, potentialities and limitations—and the social, educational and other structures which project human qualities and defects'.[7]

The social fallacy has attracted the attention of the American psychiatrist Roger Walsh:

> Almost all discussions [of the global crisis] have focused on political and military factors [whilst] the underlying sources—our minds—of both problems and solutions were usually overlooked. Much anger, blame and attack was therefore directed out at the world, thereby often exacerbating the very emotions that caused the problems in the first place. In other words, the failure to appreciate the psychological roots of our global situation appeared to reduce the depth and effectiveness of our responses and even to make them counterproductive.

Walsh concludes that there is need to develop a 'psychology of human survival' which emphasises two fundamental tasks:

> One is to work to relieve suffering in the world. The other is to relieve the psychological causes, starting within ourselves, which

contribute to this suffering. The challenge is not only to contribute, but to learn and mature in the process.[8]

Walsh's book demonstrates the weaknesses as well as the strengths of an exclusively psychological approach to an understanding of the human condition. He draws upon several different schools of psychology, but each is rooted in different presumptions and is more or less unrelated to the others, thereby fragmenting our understanding. Moreover, cognitive psychology and behaviourism appear to be secondary levels of explanation, and much of what they have to offer is quite commonplace, like the behavioural conditioning of the mass media.

The psychoanalytic schools go more to the root of the human condition, emphasising existential insecurity and the consequent will to pleasure (Freud), to power (Adler), to have (Fromm) and the will to meaning of the existentialists. Erich Fromm, in particular, has persuasively demonstrated the interaction of psychological, ideological and socio-economic factors. The spiritual, and particularly the Buddhist, diagnosis of the human condition which is offered in this book is hospitable to much in humanistic, Jungian and transpersonal psychology as well as in the psychoanalytic tradition. Together with phenomenological sociology, they offer valuable elaborations and extensions of traditional Buddhist analysis in respect, for example, of the ego defence mechanisms of repression, denial, projection and rationalisation.[9] However, for the most profound and potentially transformative insight into what it is to be a human being and to have created the world we have created, I believe we must base ourselves ultimately on the major spiritual traditions validated across widely different cultures and fundamental in the evolution of civilisation.

8 Diagnosing the human condition

SPIRITUALITY is not a body of knowledge, not a metaphysic. It claims that the way we ordinarily experience life is delusive and inauthentic and results in behaviour that can cause much suffering to ourselves and to others. It proposes an unimaginable personal transformation which will free us from our lifelong and futile lawsuit with reality, enabling us to 'get out of our own light'. This Buddhist way of putting it is nicely paralleled by Thomas Merton, one of the most celebrated of socially engaged Christians:

> The life of the spirit, by integrating us in the real order established by God, puts us in the fullest contact with reality—not as we imagine it, but as it really is. It does so by making us aware of our own real selves, and placing them in the presence of God.[10]

This insight is cultivated through meditation, prayer and other established practices.

Traditionally, spiritual practice and testimony have been embedded in religion, though arguably this does not necessarily have to be so. Religions are complex phenomena, evolved to meet a wide range of psycho-social needs. The inner, spiritual search for self-transcendence is only one of these, and its relationship to religious institutions and dogmas has often been uneasy.

'Spiritual', 'mystical', 'esoteric' traditions are found in all the world's great religions—Gnosticism in Christianity; Hasidism in Judaism; Sufism in Islam; Vedanta in Hinduism; and pervasively in Buddhism. After making allowances for differences in vocabulary, symbolism and other cultural refractions, their testimonies have much in common, and constitute what has been called a 'perennial philosophy'. Moreover, in recent years there has been a steady flow of publications from reputable physicists drawing attention to the striking parallels between the quantum revolution in subatomic physics and mystical revelation in the world's great religious traditions.

Each spiritual tradition has its own particular strengths and emphases, and in this they may be seen—and even experienced—as complementary to one another. This idea, which is very much in the spirit of this book, has been developed by Charlene Spretnak in her book *States of grace*, to which the reader is strongly recommended.[11]

The spiritual tradition upon which this book is grounded is Buddhism. This is partly because it is the only one of which I have direct personal experience. But it is also the one which can most readily contribute to bridging the gap between socially engaged spirituality and activists who have a secular, humanist, rationalist background. For many it has the merit of lacking the transcendent saviour of the monotheistic religions, although its response to the ultimate questions of existence is arguably essentially similar to that of the Judaeo-Christian mystical tradition. It can thus offer a second bridge, in that opposite direction. Buddhism is non-dogmatic and non-authoritarian, inviting experimental verification through personal experience based on a wide range of psycho-physical practices, and with guidance readily available. It avoids philosophical speculation and its intellectual analysis is grounded upon meditative insight. Less well known is the Buddha's concern with social issues as well as personal salvation. For D.T. Suzuki, perhaps the best known Zen Buddhist in the West, 'the most important point to remember is that all the Buddhist teachings are the outcome of a warm heart cherished towards all sentient beings and not of a cold intellect that tries to unveil the secrets of existence by logic. That is to say, Buddhism is personal experience and not impersonal philosophy'.[12]

The autobiography of each of us will have one common underlying theme—the need to build up a strong sense of identity. Depending on personality and the culture into which we are born, this may tend to be a group identity, a merging with the crowd, or, especially in our modern high egoic western culture, a standing out from the crowd by making our personal mark in some way.

Belongingness is our biggest ego-confirming prop. It embraces all the things on which we are more or less dependent (like our workplace identity, social class, family, nation and the various other roles we play out), and also all the things which belong to us and help to make us feel who we are. These include not only material possessions but also our self-confirming public persona (if we have one!), our beliefs and past experiences, and even our 'possession' of other people. As to making our mark, the pursuit of power, wealth, prestige, love and sex have been recorded as constant concerns throughout history. It can be a sobering reflection on how much of a long life has in fact been lived out of anxiety, ill-will and lust when someone called 'me' was really supposed to be directing operations.

But note that what is significant is not the forms of belongingness or the objects of desire *in themselves* (many of which may be beneficial). What is important in the long run is the urge, the need, the impulsion, that *underlies* these feelings and behaviours, which in themselves may be trivial or needless and mere instrumentalities of the strength of our desire (or aversion). And these in turn reflect the frightened need to affirm, affirm and affirm our sense of self. We can never begin to find real freedom and peace until we realise that it is the underlying fixation which is the root of the problem and not its object. 'Hit the horse, not the cart', as the Zen proverb has it. Of the majority of patients that he observed in therapy, Eric Fromm remarked:

> They complain about being depressed, having insomnia, being unhappy in their marriages, not enjoying their work, and any number of similar troubles. They usually believe that this or that particular symptom is their problem, and if only they could get rid of this particular trouble they would be well . . . These patients do not see that these various complaints are the only conscious form in which our culture permits them to express something which lies much deeper and is common to the various people who believe they suffer from this or that particular symptom. The common suffering is the alienation from oneself, from one's fellow men and from nature; the awareness that life runs out of one's hand like sand, and that one will die without having lived; that one lives in the midst of plenty yet is joyless.[13]

Whatever the object happens to be, the sheer speediness of the hyped-up life is very evident in some people. It may be the life of disputatious zeal, highly tuned rationality and the insatiable achievement of the driven personality. Or it may be the all-singing, all-dancing kind of life, helped on with alcohol or other dope, romance or just insatiable sex, and dollops of fatalistic humour. Being busy and on the go confirms that we are alive, well and here. But sometimes we momentarily become aware of our self-deception, out of the corner of our eye:

> As, when an underground train, in the tube, stops too long between stations
> And the conversation rises and slowly fades to silence
> And you see behind every face the mental emptiness deepen
> Leaving only the growing terror of nothing to think about.[14]

We each have our own way of coming to terms with life or, in other words, of convincingly masking and evading what we are. Most of us, most of the time, are hardly aware of this process; we *are* the process. One way or another, we get by, and a fundamentally different way of living may scarcely be imaginable. However, as we shall see, the *social and historical* translation of this human need for massive self-confirmation has been disastrous.

This insatiable need originates in our deep sense of vulnerability, impermanence and the threat of all that is other. When, through meditation, we allow the mind to become still we can contemplate in its lower depths more buried rage and frustration than we ever imagined, and then, underlying that, the fear from which it arises. And underlying that again is a devastating emptiness and meaninglessness. This is the pit from which we have been trying to escape all our lives. This is the pit from out of which history is made . . .

The self even cuts itself off from the body as a vulnerable, alien and frightening thing which aches and bleeds. So 'my body' becomes a carefully maintained and exercised possession of 'my mind'. And herein is the paradox in which lies the human predicament. In Ernest Becker's words, 'man is out of nature and hopelessly in it; he is dual, up in the stars, [with a] self-consciousness which gives him the status literally of a small god in nature, as the renaissance thinkers knew . . . and yet housed in a heart-pumping, breath-gasping body that once belonged to a fish'.[15] This paradox poses a question to which each of our lives is some kind of response.

Absolute acceptance (which cannot be merely willed) of our fragile and transient humanity is the only way in which we can find inner peace and release. This is the emptying of the wants and aversions of the clinging and opinionated self so that the world is experienced undistorted by them. Things then become 'beautiful, but not desirable; ugly, but not repulsive; false, but not rejected; a task may be boring and trivial, but we do it without anxiety and alienation'.[16] The physical and emotional sorrows of life, bereavement and poverty, war and sickness, do not disappear. But in the profound and unreserved acceptance of their pain we are freed through a clear-seeing compassion to act the more effectively to remedy all those pains which it lies within our power to remedy.

Note the Buddhist distinction between pain—physical, emotional, existential—on the one hand, and suffering, angst, unease, on the other. Suffering, in the sense used here, originates in our compulsive *evasion* of pain, and particularly of the painful underlying truth of our human condition. This evasion is the prime mover, and it can take the form of immensely destructive personal and collective behaviour which flows from trying to prove we are something other than what we are.

To see spiritual liberation as a personal matter that has nothing to do with politics and economics is thus as intrinsically absurd as is the opposite viewpoint. On the contrary, this is the only perspective that really can make the personal political and vice versa, because it is the only one that goes deep enough to dissolve our defensive alienation. To be moved to take the search back to the most fundamental questions about human nature because of despair at the fate of the planet or of incomprehension at some people's gratuitous brutality to others, or of sorrow at the immense plight of the people of the Third World, is no less valid than when we are likewise moved by personal failure, loss or anxiety.

In whatever form we experience most intensely the problem of being human, it is there at that personal level we must start. But the individual and personal response is also the prime mover of history. It is the interactive and cumulative force which shapes societies and imparts their historical momentum. It is there that the final explanation lies of our ecological, social and existential predicaments, though without necessarily invalidating explanations at any of those three levels. The following, by the great thirteenth-century Japanese Zen Master Dogen, on the way of liberation, is worth pondering:

> To study the way is to study the self.
> To study the self is to forget the self.
> To forget the self is to be enlightened by all things;
> To be enlightened by all things is to remove the barriers between
>   one's self and others.

When the Buddha offered his diagnosis of the human condition 2,500 years ago in northern India, social evolution still had a long way to go before it could support adequate social science. We are now in a position to couple the prime mover identified by the Buddha to compatible contemporary social theory. That is the purpose of the next chapter.

9 The social dynamics of the spiritual diagnosis

WE ARE each born into a society in which previous generations have already created everything we need in order to enable ourselves to be a somebody or, for most people for most of history, a nobody who at least belongs to something or somebody somewhere. All societies are engines for perpetuating at great human cost the fundamental evasion described in the previous chapter. Our own, however, surpasses all previous ones in the scale on which it stokes the ancient Buddhist 'fires' of greed, aggression and ignorance. Social revolution is necessary for three reasons. First, to restore ecological harmony; second, to enable all of the world's people to attain well-being and social justice; third, to create positive social conditions for liberating ourselves spiritually, that is to say, to free ourselves from self-obstruction in order to address ourselves more effectively to the first and second tasks.

History is driven by a subjective hungering which goes far beyond material need. Wars have been waged on no more than points of honour and other pretexts. The poor and oppressed have commonly accounted it a great honour to be able to make their lives meaningful by dying gloriously in the service of their rulers. And the rulers have rarely been satisfied to expropriate from their subjects just sufficient to be comfortably off. They must also have their conquests, their grandiose public works and memorials, their pomps and majesty, their conspicuous luxury, to confirm to the world and themselves who they are. Similarly, the living standards which are regarded as indispensable in the overdeveloped countries are far beyond any reasonable need and are sustained at considerable cost to the underlying quality of life.

From out of the interweaving of material (objective) and existential (subjective) needs, the members of a human society interact to create meanings which are shared, enforced, and also challenged (such as the supremacy of an individual or group). Out of these meanings are shaped social structures and institutions which embody them (such as the state).

Moreover, the meanings, the beliefs and values take on an objective reality themselves, and may come to be experienced as standing over and against their creators. Authority, for example, is seen as a *thing* which is intrinsic to government, instead of a belief in the heads of the governed and which they can withhold (though at the risk of being coerced by power). Similarly, in personal life, out of fear or anger or aggressiveness we enlarge, shape and colour problems and then objectify this subjective overlay so that they appear even more threatening.

This is how we experience a reality whose meanings are socially constructed. Note that this contrasts with the postmodern 'deconstruction' whereby social reality is an individual experience which has no shared objectivity. It also contrasts, on the other hand, with the conventional Marxist view of individuals as essentially social constructions. However, my own Buddhist view, whilst emphasising the individual struggle for self-affirmation as the social prime mover, would nevertheless also give very considerable *secondary* weight to the process of interactive social conditioning.

The principal means of collective self-affirmation is *antithetical bonding*. This is group bonding which affirms and and exalts belongingness-identity by emphasising the differences and the otherness of one or more other groups, which are opposed, rivalled and possibly subordinated. The antithesis may be economic, political, ethnic, religious or, most persistently, by gender. History very much revolves round 'us' and 'them'. 'They' provide a legitimised (and often well researched) target for the projection of all the fear, anger and self-aversion of which we may normally be scarcely aware ourselves. In times of stress and crisis all this denied emotion can be embodied in and unburdened upon the other side with a gratifying sense of release that can amount to blood lust. Vaclav Havel observed of the people who have 'hated him personally or still do' that 'their hatred always seems to me to be an expression of a large and unquenchable longing . . . it's an active inner capacity that is always leading the person to fixate on something. It has a lot in common with love'.[17]

Once set in train, polarisation and antagonism (which might have quite insignificant beginnings) may feed upon themselves in a tightening spiral. The middle ground is excluded, total loyalty to one side or other is demanded, self-censorship of any deviation from the assumed group consensus becomes habitual, and nothing but evil can come from the other side. Party politics well exemplify this sterile and destructive phenomenon, and acceptance of such adversarial systems (of which our culture bristles with examples) makes it difficult to avoid being sucked in.

What I shall call 'ideology' is the characteristic intellectual manifestation of antithetical bonding, and is a transparent example of how a subjective need can shape a seemingly objective view of the world. For ideology exists as much to confirm and legitimise the identity of those who uphold it as it does to provide a comprehensive explanation of social or other reality. 'Fundamentalism' is a particularly narrow and uncompromising expression of one or more dogmatically held basic principles. It may be the sharp end of an ideology or it may be no more than some obsessional belief like 'small is [invariably] beautiful'.

The fact that ideology is usually, at least in part, a credible *intellectualised* expression of the root evasion described in the previous chapter gives it a certain plausibility. However, as Thomas Merton has remarked,

> The intellect is only theoretically independent of desire and appetite in ordinary, actual practice. It is constantly being blinded and perverted by the ends and aims of passions, and the evidence which it presents to us with such a show of impartiality and objectivity is fraught with interest and propaganda.[18]

It is not difficult to recognise the tell-tale emotional clatter of the ideologically driven intellect when it is in overdrive. Thus a reader complained to the editor of one of the most fundamentalist of British green magazines that 'though in complete agreement with the substance of what you say, there is a spirit of aggression emanating from the pages which makes me recoil from it. I can understand this—there is good reason for anger; the anger appears to have curdled, however, and become vengeful and spite ridden. This is to move from the constructive to the destructive'.[19]

Ideology contrasts with what I term 'meta-theory'. Meta-theories are broad cognitive representations of reality, enabling us better to understand, forecast and actively relate to phenomena. Scientific and philosophical meta-theories are contingent on our present state of knowledge, and are helpful investigatory perspectives which have no absolute authority *in themselves*. The Buddhist perspective introduced in the previous chapter is of this kind. Its validity will depend on whether it finds any confirmation in the reader's experience, and the whole Buddhist edifice ultimately depends upon meditative insight, (which is as legitimate a form of investigation as scientific method and certainly more accessible to the lay enquirer). Whereas meta-theory attempts to define the view, ideology more defines the viewer. Meta-theory is always in danger of going stiff with ideology, and some of the great intellectual systems of our time can be traced across the spectrum from meta-theory to ideology. Marxism, for example, extends from the 'vulgar Marxism' of communism and the hard left to, say, the Frankfurt school, with its open-ended and continual self-critical development of the Marxist tradition.

It is an historic tragedy that movements for radical social change commonly hunger after ideology and are blinded by it. It seduces by its heady sense of empowerment—a quick fix with ultimate failure built into it. Buddhism is very much an ideological solvent, and the critique of ideology, particularly in its radical, green, new age manifestations, is a major concern of this book. This raises the question of how it might be possible to develop a movement for radical change whose members for the most part were content with no more than an unfreighted *awareness identity*, plus skilfully used meta-theory and directional values instead of having to burden the movement at every level with their own unresolved personal needs.

To help the reader become familiar with the animal, the characteristics of ideology and the antithetical bonding commonly associated with it are summarised below.

1 Ideology solidifies useful contingent theories and concepts into articles of faith. The classic green example is Schumacher's emphasis on small is beautiful as against the current obsession with bigness. After the creative thinkers come the ideologues to proclaim their panaceas: 'Whenever something is wrong, something is big'.[20] Similarly, traditional cultures are idealised without reservation, and bioregionalism, decentralisation and other useful green principles are treated as cure-alls. And on the left-hand side of the page the new age paradigm is reassuringly contrasted with all that Cartesian wrong-headedness in the adjacent column (that old classic, *Zen and the art of motorcycle maintenance* is still the best antidote to that kind of dualism).[21]

The founding fathers and mothers, and even the current upholders of the orthodoxy, are beyond criticism, which is reserved for 'the other side'. Genuine internal debate is rare, for ideology is about building walls, not bridges. If you are not green then surely you must be grey? The ambiguity, uncertainty and inconclusiveness which characterise most controversial social phenomena could weaken resolve and therefore find no place in ideology. 'If the trumpet soundeth a hollow note, who shall prepare himself for the battle?'

2 Ideology seizes upon a key issue and makes it into a simplistic and exclusive organising principle—whether it be the class struggle, patriarchy or ecology—which explains everything else and which is subordinated to it, or else marginalised or simply ignored if it cannot be fitted in. By contrast, meta-theories are not necessarily mutually exclusive.

They may be different ways of looking at the world, in terms of a different set of 'facts'. The discoveries and formulations of science are explicit in its own methodology and on these terms they can be 'proved' and shown to work. On those terms spiritual healing and homeopathy may arguably be 'unscientific' but nonetheless effective and valid on their own terms. Similarly, this book draws together a wide spectrum of differing perspectives to which a Buddhist meta-theory is hospitable.

3 No ideology is complete without its millennial vision, whether it be the Second Coming, the Revolution, or Ecotopia. Although models of a future society are proposed in this book (with even a fanciful News-from-nowhere included) these are used simply to illustrate guiding values to be embodied in our practice as of now, or as simulations for dissection. For ecotopians, on the contrary, the 'transition' is as debatable and fuzzy as the 'goal' is clear and detailed. History teaches that the goal invariably turns out to be a mirage.

4 To hold the support of the faint-hearted, nothing less than inevitability will do. Thus, the paradigm shift to the new age is already under way— the Great Turning—thanks to the workings of the Aquarian conspiracy.[22]

5 Ideology appeals so powerfully to our root need for self-assurance that its followers can feel as if they have been reborn into a whole new reality. As Susan Griffin explains, 'an ideology holds the promise that one may control reality with the mind, [and] *assert the ideal as more real than reality*'.[23] The Russian language has a unique word for ideological reality—*pravda*. This is official truth, or the movement's truth. It contrasts with *istina*, which is informal truth, awkward realities, the way things are, beloved of investigative journalists and rockers of boats, the truth which always sooner or later comes out. And how grateful we are at such times for its bitter, salty, liberating taste!

6 Ideologies and their movements tend to be fissiparous. They breed factions which brandish mini-ideologies, seizing hold of either one or the other end of the stick, like the deep ecologists and the social ecologists we shall encounter later.

7 Ideological movements provide complete identity kits, not just the badge and car sticker, but a whole new wardrobe, lifestyle and circle of acquaintances. The weight we give to these will indicate whether they are simply enjoyable incidentals or whether they are lures for our project of yet again evading the question of who really we are. And there is The Magazine which will open so many new windows

for us—all with the same view.

8 Finally, as Oscar Wilde reminds us, 'life is too important a thing ever to be taken seriously'. But ideology takes itself very seriously. Irony, black humour and playfulness are 'out of place', since it is unclear whether they are 'really to be taken seriously'.

How long will it be before workshops on unilateral ideological disarmament become a feature of radical movements, and the dismantling of ideological mentalities (ideological audit) becomes something which is checked out (and made fun of) as a matter of course in meetings and magazines?

The following reminders, when thinking, speaking, writing and acting, may be helpful.

1 Be on your guard against sliding into the seductive mind sets outlined above. Beware of the triumphalist itch: your truth will be more acceptable if you don't rub people's noses in it. This is one of my own favourite bad habits! George Orwell warned about our 'subjective contamination' of reality: 'One cannot get away from one's subjective feelings, but at least one can know what they are and make allowances for them' so as to avoid falling into a 'sort of masturbation fantasy in which the world of facts hardly matters'.[24]

2 When presenting what you hope are objective conclusions from particular experiences or research, it may be appropriate to add some information about your assumptions, personal background, feelings, prejudices and anything else which might help the reader to form her own opinion of the validity of your findings and conclusions. Taking readers or listeners into your confidence will give you an authentic credibility.

3 Where possible, try to find out how it is and tell it how it is, without mixing in your own wishful overlay. Could we not risk more public space for *istina* rather than *pravda*?

4 Ideology is about answers in search of questions and questions in search of problems. It is not unknown to end up with the wrong answer to the wrong question to the wrong problem.

5 It is not necessarily a sign of weakness to avoid coming up with firm conclusions. The evidence may not justify *any* conclusions that are firm. It may be best simply to present it and warn about the danger of jumping to conclusions.

6 Beware the edginess of ideologically inspired communication which so easily tips over into waspish and provocative language. I know it is sometimes difficult to resist the opportunity to 'have a dig' at an adversary. But this is a self-indulgence which will usually be counter-productive in terms of more long-term goals. If you really want to grow vegetables, there is no point in including a few weeds just for the hell of it.

7 Ideology fixates on things; it reifies. Processes are no less important. How something is written, said or done, and by whom, when and where, may say more than what it is.

8 It is said that Aneurin Bevan would sometimes open with 'Tell me your truth and I'll tell you mine'. By trying to bear scrupulous witness to another's truth something may be learnt which could be more valuable than simply trying to 'disprove' them. Could not the editors of magazines like *Resurgence* interview factory farmers, property speculators, chief constables and religious fundamentalists as well as poets, saints, healers and green business consultants *ad nauseam*? The purpose would not only be to discover what makes these aliens tick but also sensitively to reveal how our differences unite us. It is a mistake to suppose that empathy with adversaries diminishes the will to eliminate the situations they perpetuate. The experience of nonviolent activists like Gandhi suggests quite the contrary. A contemporary Zen master (who happens also to be a well informed critic of the Japanese nuclear power industry) offers the following pointer: 'Even if we continue our discussion with another person for one thousand years we may not reach final agreement. But we should try not to get rid of our differences, for these are the very things that teach us and enrich our lives'.[25]

Using my definition of ideology as a basis for assessing a succession of contemporary movements and beliefs is bound to produce a strongly critical and disturbing book. This is because ideology is a characteristic and pervasive (though not invariable) social expression of our human condition itself. And so if any reader were to suppose that all this fault finding is no more than bloody-mindedness, then I have failed to clarify my central argument.

Some may be upset by a book which is not only often ambivalent in its treatment of 'the other side' but which is also concerned with the creative destabilisation of beliefs and affiliations to which the reader may be deeply attached. I would ask such readers please to take time and emotional space to observe the place from which their strong feelings and convictions arise. For the inside view needs to go together with the outside view like the inside and outside walls of a dwelling. Most of us are more or less caught up in the ideology trap; most of us have a profound need for things to be how they usually in fact are not.

This book also illustrates a paradox of the critique of ideology. The logical nature of language requires that the *this* of my critique be set dualistically against the *that* of some ideological phenomenon, initially thereby setting up (at least formally)the very kind of polarisation which is the subject of the criticism! Usually, however, the argument has been subsequently carried forward to a third, non-polarised (if paradoxical) position. Many illustrations will be found of this.

The Prince of Peace proclaimed 'I have not come to bring peace but a sword'.[26] The Madhyamika Buddhist tradition out of which I am writing is no less incisively paradoxical. And for Zen Buddhism also, 'grandmotherly compassion' is ultimately unhelpful. For any shortage here of the real stuff I can only plead my exasperation at the way in which, time and time again, promising radical social movements prostitute valuable ideas and thus disable themselves so needlessly and yet so compulsively.

Finally, the fate of St Oran, a friend of St Columba, is offered as a warning to would-be critics of ideology. As well as a great worker of curses and miracles, Columba was amongst the most astute of Celtic saints and knew the value of orthodoxy and not frightening the horses. But one day he was moved to wonder whether heaven and hell really were as he preached. Oran, a fearless mystic, volunteered to go down and find out. Dug up after three days, Oran reported that in fact heaven and hell, good and evil, were by no means as simple and opposed as religion would have us believe. A shocked Columba immediately ordered his friend to be reburied. His cry, 'Earth, earth, in the mouth of Oran that he may blab no more,' passed into Gaelic folk wisdom, as a terrible warning about allowing too much truth . . . [27]

10 'We're all environmentalists now!'

PART III is about a range of responses to the ecological crisis which accept either an environmentally reformed version of the established industrial culture or else futuristic variants of it founded on the same expansive and acquisitive assumptions. In other words, they range from pragmatic adaptations (or muddling through) to high-tech cornucopian utopias. It is assumed that environmentally friendly technologies, coupled with some modest regulation of the free market economy, will enable continued substantial industrial growth to be ecologically sustained. 'Environmentalism' is the term used here for this essentially reactive response to ecological pressures which sees nature as a manageable resource 'out there'. Environmentalists believe it is sufficient to hit the cart rather than the more sensitive horse. Thus, the 1992 Rio de Janeiro Earth Summit agenda was about limiting the threat to biodiversity, forests and climate, and not about restrictions on automobiles, agribusiness and free trade.

Rejecting the doomsday predictions of the 1960s and 1970s, environmentalist optimism was characteristically expressed in the much acclaimed 1987 Brundtland Report: 'What is needed now is a new era of economic growth—growth which is forceful and yet at the same time socially and environmentally sustainable'.[1] Over and beyond lies the visionary science fiction wing of environmentalism. Although numerically insignificant, its founders include such commanding figures as Richard Buckminster Fuller, with his manual of planetary management,[2] and Teilhard de Chardin, who believed that the destiny of mankind (*sic*) in this generation was 'to grasp the tiller of creation'.

The alternative radical, dark green response to ecological crisis has been termed 'ecologism', and is typified by the Green Party (meaning in this book the 'England, Wales and Northern Ireland Green Party'). Radical greens view humankind as an integral and dependent part of the natural order and not somehow outside it and able to transcend it. Continued substantial industrial growth cannot be ecologically sustained and will inevitably lead sooner or later to the breakdown of global society as we know it. It is therefore necessary to evolve an alternative social order based on a stable 'steady-state' economy, whose pollution levels are modest enough to be absorbed by the ecosystem and whose energy and other needs would as far as possible be supplied from renewable resources. The social implications require such a society to be fundamentally different from the present one and radical greens are, in effect, nonviolent social revolutionaries. Their numbers have been put at under five per cent of the green movement.

There is, by contrast, a huge environmentalist campaigning movement typified by organisations like Greenpeace (with more members than the Labour Party) and the rank-and-file activist Friends of the Earth. They work for the substantial reduction of all kinds of pollution and the conservation of energy and raw materials. Campaigns range from banning the dumping of raw sewage in the sea to promoting urban cycle tracks; from preventing a wood being cut down to make way for a motorway in southern England to sending letters to a transnational corporation to induce it to halt some vast logging project somewhere in the Third World. Included in this movement there appears to be a small, ill-defined but possibly influential radical minority which sees these campaigns as contributing to the growth of a new, green, social culture very different from the present superindustrial order. Public articulation of such assumptions, however, would be seen as divisive and 'political'. Most environmentalists do not sympathise much with the visionaries of dark green politics, and may well not even vote for the Green Party. There are no tidy distinctions here. It is, for example, possible to come across both radicals who are realistic and pragmatic and fundamentalist environmental campaigners for whom the most modest road improvement is a first step to perdition.

Although the evidence of ecological crisis continues to accumulate, many indicators suggest that public interest in the environment appears to have declined in the past year. The 1992 edition of *British social attitudes*[3] reports a mere two per cent strongly agreeing that 'for the sake of the environment people should use less home heating' (a modest enough sacrifice!). However, thirteen per cent strongly agreed that 'the government should do more to protect the environment, even if it leads to higher taxes;

industry should do more to protect the environment even if it leads to lower profits and jobs; and ordinary people should do more to protect the environment, even if it means paying higher prices'. But in view of the recent evidence of the disparity between respondents' expressed intentions and what they actually do (as when in a polling booth), even these modest figures may lack credibility.

Certainly the global recession has concentrated many people's minds on their own immediate livelihood. But I suggest that waning environmental concern may also stem from two characteristics of the green movement itself.

In the first place, much of the campaigning has been negative—about stopping things happening, and sometimes even putting the frighteners on the public. (In their 1992 election broadcast the leaders of the Green Party sought votes by solemnly counting down to Armageddon as a doomsday clock ticked loudly in the background). Much more cheering for everyone is the widely canvassed notion of 'sustainable growth'. As Liberal Democrat leader Paddy Ashdown put it, 'The beauty of this agenda is the way it synthesises all the things you want to do and all the things you have to do'.[4] In other words, you can have your cake and eat it . . . There has at the same time been a quite vengeful (if not wholly undeserved) backlash against the Green Party as killjoy eccentrics and closet authoritarians. A waspish editorial in *The Independent* newspaper of 11 September 1992 complained:

> There are elements in the Greens' programme that are offensively as well as unrealistically authoritarian. Zero population growth and zero economic growth are policies that would have to be imposed by force on most of the world's population. The people's democracies of Eastern Europe very nearly achieved both . . . If human greed is ruining this planet, it will be checked by self-interest, not superhuman virtue.

In the second place, with its narrow, short-term and compartmentalised perspectives the environmentalist movement, amidst all the good work it is doing, may also be encouraging a restricted and complacent view of the ecological crisis, whether it be illusions about the impact of an individual green lifestyle or the belief that 'saving the planet' is all about a dozen crucial campaigns to defeat a dozen 'threats to the environment'.

The limitations and vulnerability of campaigning exclusively about the environment have been exposed by the recession. Most environmentalists have tended to be accepting or indifferent about other aspects of the social order and sufficiently well off as to see the environmental threat as the only remaining threat to their own well-being. Redundancies, bankruptcies and mortgage repossessions are making them think again. A successful 'post-environmentalist' movement would need to focus on a whole better way of living our lives than the way we have to live them now. Across the spectrum of everyday concerns it would need to spell out realistic steps to a whole future, and not just 'saving the planet'. The radical political mileage is in that wide credibility gap that lies between the recycling of cans and the vision of ecotopia . . .

The greening of consumerism

Green consumerism nicely exemplifies the strengths and weaknesses of environmentalism. It is about the use of consumer preference to induce business to offer less environmentally damaging goods and services. Examples are additive-free foodstuffs, recycled paper, lead-free petrol, minimum packaging and ethical investment opportunities. And environmental concern has to some extent been extended to exclude support for oppressive regimes, military links and so on.

There is no doubt that green consumerism offers a ready means for many individuals to take some environmental and social responsibility and to experience some sense of empowerment. And it gives green campaigning organisations a powerful means of bringing pressure to bear on producers to behave more responsibly, right from the day that Friends of the Earth first hit the headlines by dumping throwaway containers on the steps of Schweppes' London office.

On the other hand, green consumerism implies that consumer pressure could alone be sufficient to make profit-based organisations both willing and able to 'save the environment'. It assumes that most consumers enjoy wide freedom of choice, that cradle-to-grave information is available for most products, and that consumers have enough time and expertise to evaluate it. Can the shopper insist, for example, on buying products that have only been transported by rail and sea? Who, moreover, is manipulating whom? In terms of resources to influence and control, the big business which manages the consumer culture clearly has the upper hand. More than one business expert believes that 'the selling of the environment may make the cholesterol craze look like a Sunday picnic'.[5] However, according to a survey undertaken in 1991 by Mintel, the market research group, the customers are not readily deceived. Only ten per cent believed that the supermarkets' caring campaigns are primarily aimed at bettering the environment, whereas seventy per cent suspected that manufacturers use the green issue as an excuse for charging higher prices.

Green consumerism, moreover, contributes to the whole comforting belief in 'green growth'. Joel Makower, responsible for the American *Green consumer*, gave the game away when he wrote that 'by choosing carefully, you can have a positive impact on the environment without significantly compromising your way of life. That's what being a green consumer is all about'. Another observer offers a very different view of what it is all about:

> Because the message is so terribly diluted, so distressingly cosmeticised and prettified and commercialised and sanitised and legitimised, only the slimmest idea of the real crisis is conveyed and only the thinnest range of necessary solutions to it offered. And at the worst end, the ecological crisis is made into such an opportunity for selling products and personalities that it ends up reinforcing the very worst features of the civilisation that caused the crisis in the first place.[6]

Perhaps green consumer magazines could shift their emphasis to the challenging task of *reducing* consumption and demonstrating how that can actually lead to a higher quality of life. This has more to do with becoming acquainted with what is going on in one's head than what one is supposed to be looking for in the shops.

The fundamental shortcoming of green consumerism is that it fails to address the structural changes which will need to be made in society if we are to get through the ecological crisis in good shape. Consumerism has itself so atomised society that it is not always easy to get that idea across. Giving up your car is a real contribution, but only when others do likewise will the *solution* come into view. But they will only follow suit if you and they insist on an adequate public transport system and a radically different approach to the planning of communities.

Let us wield our green consumerism (and anti-consumerism) for all they are worth, but always mindful of the limitations. Here as elsewhere environmentalism is fine so long as we can use it to move beyond environmentalism . . .

11 The credibility of the great tech fix

HOW likely is it that superindustrialism will be able to continue to maintain present growth rates and at the same time resolve the attendant problems of environmental degradation and pollution, resource depletion and over-population?

As an authoritative and widely endorsed manifesto for sustainable development the Brundtland Report is worth quoting again here. 'Experience in the industrialised nations has proved that anti-pollution technology has been cost-effective in terms of health, property and environmental damage avoided, and that it has made many industries more profitable by making them more resource efficient'. Moreover, it is not only claimed that continued high growth rates are possible, but that they are now necessary to solve the environmental and social problems that they have created. 'There is no choice of either/or . . . We can only achieve sustainable growth providing we manage to protect the environment and we shall only succeed in protecting the environment if we accomplish sustainable growth . . . building another world on top of the one we have and doubling, at least, our demands on the planet's ecosystems'.[7]

New and lean technologies

The development of technologies which are more efficient in their consumption of energy and other resources is proving to be the most successful part of technologically fixing the eco-crisis. Some seven years ago ICI chairman Sir John Harvey-Jones proclaimed 'the industrialist's mission' as being 'to get more and more out of less and less . . . And actually we are getting pretty good at it. Incidentally, too, that's not because we are boy scouts. It's for bloody good business reasons'.[8]

By 1990 the average amount of energy needed to produce one extra unit of gross domestic product was a quarter of that needed in 1973. Over this period of unparalleled economic growth, Japan actually cut its energy consumption by six per cent. The development of lean technologies between 1980 and 1990 enabled American cornucopian Julian S. Simon easily to win his bet with catastrophist Paul Ehrlich that the prices of five key metals would fall over this period. 'As soon as one predicted disaster doesn't occur, the doomsayers skip to another', quipped Simon, the scourge of environmentalists. 'We need problems so that we can come up with solutions that leave us better off'.[9]

Even the old smoke-stack industries have made remarkable progress. US Steel cut its production of hazardous waste by half in five years, as well as halving the labour needed to produce a tonne of steel—and from a smaller tonnage of poorer quality ore. Forty per cent of steel production is now from scrap metal, which requires only twenty per cent of the energy needed by virgin ores.

More significant is the emergence of a new generation of 'clean and lean' technologies like quantum electronics, information technology and the new high performance ceramics. The last will enable a switch to be made to an abundant raw material and is in many respects superior to plastics and metals. It can, for example, be used in the manufacture of engines which can operate at very high temperatures, giving cleaner burning and greater energy efficiency. Again, the substitution of fibre optics means that one tonne of coal can be used to produce 80,000 miles of fibre in lieu of 90 miles of copper wire.

One observer has speculated that with these developments 'it may be technically feasible to enjoy the civilising benefits of industrialisation at a per capita level of material consumption little more than one fifth to one tenth of the existing level'.[10] But what is really on offer here? Is it a superindustrialism which we are somehow taming and transforming so that it marks time forever, content to go on satisfying much the same modest material needs from less and less with ever increasing ecological and technological elegance? Or is it to be still the same voracious beast, whose continued overall growth rate could destroy the environmental benefits of its increasing economies per unit of growth?

Genetic engineering: the synthetic future

From these still comparatively conventional technologies there is a qualitative jump to biotechnology, and particularly to its sharp end—genetic engineering. This is less a technology than a vision of a synthetic future wherein nature (including human beings) has been refashioned at a fundamental level to meet virtually all human needs.

Genetic engineering aims to resynthesise 'biological resources' (microbes, plants and animals) so as to combine genetic material across natural boundaries in order to provide 'economic utilities'. Such transgenic manipulation is being used, for example, to create giant farm animals as more cost-effective bio-machines than could be obtained by traditional breeding from nature. Here, as elsewhere, if animals then why not people? With the current hostility to radical and purposive *social* change, eugenics is making a come-back from the inter-war years. Eminent scientists are once more speculating about programming 'good' and 'bad' traits into and out of babies at conception, to create superpeople.

As nature becomes too poisoned and worn out to sustain the demands made on her, the synthetic vision of an artificial, substituted environment becomes more credible. We are, after all, already accustomed to living in increasingly artificial conurbations (with lifestyles to match), separated by petrochemical deserts wherein a few scattered nature reserves, 'country parks' and the like do themselves appear somehow contrived and artificial. This is undoubtedly the direction which sustainable growth would have to take if it did turn out to be possible. But do we really want that kind of success? Would it not make our humanity itself somehow no longer sustainable?

Unresolved problems of the tech fix

Given selective reading, it is not difficult to build up quite a head of tech fix optimism. Green capitalism can offer page after page of neat and ingenious technological solutions which soon make the reader feel better about our planetary prospects. But this feeling may not survive subsequent exposure to the no less plausible doomsday literature. Unless in a hurry to take sides, the reader will begin to reflect on the many uncertainties and imponderables in this hugely complex problem.

As we have seen, there are many promising developments in the more cost-effective use of energy and raw materials. The loss of topsoil and forest cover continues apace, however. And the former, together with the rainforests, can only be replaced over centuries rather than decades. Moreover, the effective long-term treatment and 'disposal' of pollutants and toxic wastes remains an intractable and growing problem.

In an earlier section on the synthetics revolution (Chapter 3) it was noted how difficult it can be to detect, analyse, predict and remedy the effects of many pollutants. And in some cases the problem may already have become too big for our technological and social resources, as with the global warmup and the accumulation of nuclear wastes. Other toxic wastes have either to be incinerated at very high temperatures (which can create further problems) or else stored indefinitely in landfill sites which, with hindsight, have to be increasingly sophisticated and expensive to prevent their contents leaking into the soil and underground water courses.

Some treatments which attempt to simulate nature do achieve considerable success. The pollution of water supplies by nitrate run-off from fertiliser can be treated with special bacteria which produce an innocuous gas and which do not themselves come into contact with the water. This Dutch system is claimed to be self-sustaining and reusable. This is in fact a typical *quasi-solution* in that if applied on a large scale it would, combined with other similar achievements, give a new lease of life to petrochemical agriculture, with its immense capacity for environmental degradation and the production of unwholesome foodstuffs.

Moreover, the foregoing could give the misleading impression that the ecological crisis amounts to a shopping list of problems which might hopefully be crossed off one by one. But ecosystems are holistic phenomena which are more than the sum of their dynamically interacting parts. The properties of water, for example, cannot be predicted from those of hydrogen and oxygen. Similarly, over periods of time phenomena may develop unpredictably and cumulate into qualitatively different forms. The character of the ecological crisis is defined by William Ophuls as 'not a series of discrete problems [but] an ensemble of interacting problems that exacerbate one another through various kinds of threshold, multiplicative and synergistic effects . . . entrained in an exponential rate of development'.[11] It is from this rich, bubbling ecological stew that the tech fixer attempts to distinguish, isolate, process and predict specific phenomena.

In the holistic view all tech fix solutions are inherently quasi-solutions in that, *given the present economic system,* they remove some impediment to ecologically unsupportive rates of growth. More specifically, the solution of one problem tends to create further problems, which may be unpredictable, more serious than the original problem, may proliferate, and may be detected only after a considerable time lapse. The 'green revolution' in Third World agriculture is perhaps the biggest ever quasi-solution, now beginning to contribute powerfully to the ecological, economic and demographic crisis that grips the Third World. Similarly, a breakthrough in nuclear fusion would be a quasi-solution to our energy problems. For so much cheap, abundant, and (arguably) safe energy, given our present primitive level of ecological awareness, would, in Paul Ehrlich's words, be 'like giving a machine gun to an idiot child'.

So far we have been discussing the likely effectiveness of various technological responses to the ecological crisis intended to make present rates of industrial growth sustainable. If these proved inadequate to protect the environment (or were successful but at the cost of creating an increasingly intolerable synthetic environment), then many such technologies would nevertheless remain essential to the alternative steady-state, minimal growth, conserver economy proposed by the radical greens. This would entail phasing out high polluting industries (like petrochemical agriculture) and emphasising clean and lean technologies increasingly powered by renewable energy. The ultimate aim would be to reduce pollution once more to a quality and quantity which would enable it to be processed by the ecosystem with only modest technical assistance. In the meantime, sophisticated pollution technology which did not simply move problems around would be indispensable. Particularly important would be the production of durable products which were reliable, readily repairable, whose life could be extended by reconditioning and whose materials could eventually be recycled. It has been estimated that the life of many manufactured goods could be extended by thirty to fifty years.

The problem, however, is not so much to develop appropriate technologies as to evolve an economic and political system in which they would not be used to legitimise unacceptable levels of growth.

12 Green capitalism and the management of sustainable growth

HOW likely is it that superindustrialism will prove able and willing to fund environmental technologies adequately, and to regulate and manage its impact so that the ecosystem can continue to support a substantial growth rate? And how can 'impact' and 'adequacy' be measured anyway? And can it, moreover, broaden its imperatives to include social justice for the peoples of the Third World?

The radical view is that for global big business environmental and social needs are comparatively marginal and open to manipulation anyway (as in the treatment of Third World debt). Its main thrust is to sustain the dynamics of power and maximum profitability. Thus, Ted Trainer offers the following dark green indictment:

> It is an economic system that depends on continuous growth in order to survive and prosper. In order to crank up consumption we are having to resort to more and more fantastic contortions, such as astronomical loads of debt, advertising, military expenditure and sheer wastage.[12]

Nevertheless, for some years books have been appearing that are full of glowing accounts of industrialists for whom environmental care is one of their prime business goals.[13]

Many would-be green businesses have shown considerable interest in wooing those environmental organisations which have long ago put catastrophist scenarios behind them and are now keen to be seen as sufficiently 'responsible' as to be given the ear (and perhaps the money) of prestigious business interests. This co-operative spirit is reflected in the emergence of bridging organisations like the UK Centre for Economic and Environmental Development, established in 1984 in order to 'reconcile the needs of business and industry with the overriding imperative of conserving our irreplaceable natural resources'.

For radical greens, 'The polluters' plan is clear. They cannot win head-to-head battles with the grassroots environmental justice movement, so they court mainstream environmental groups with money'. That, at least, is the conclusion of the US group Citizens' Clearinghouse for Hazardous Waste. The magazine *Green line* goes on to give 'details of only a few questionable donations and sponsors in the US: The World Wildlife Fund/Conservation Foundation lists as donors Chevron, Exxon, Dupont, General Electric, Shell, Ciba Geigy, Kodak, American Cyanamide. Procter and Gamble, Union Carbide, Mobil and Texaco. Earth Day 1990 celebrations were so heavily underwritten by corporate polluters that even *Time* magazine called the day "commercial mugging"'.[14] Moreover in the last year or two the big corporations have been taking a much more hostile and even ruthless line towards their more implacable green critics.

The foregoing highlights the spectrum which ranges from dark green ecologism to pale green environmentalism. For adherents of the former, continued 'growth mania' is the heart of the problem, and behind that is the economic and social system which needs it to survive. And behind that, again, lie deeply ingrained mentalities and attitudes (in the understanding of which green spirituality and green feminism are relevant). At the other end of the spectrum, and welcomed by business, are the 'integrators' who 'attribute environmental damage not to unalterable selfish attitudes and interests but to defects in scientific analysis, in appraisal of costs and benefits, and above all in education and training which can and should be remedied in the ranks of many large scale agencies both public and private'.[15]

However, to see the problem as one of polarisers versus integrators is itself polarising and simplistic. It is possible to be highly critical of mainstream business on grounds of ecology and social justice without locking oneself into a whole anti-business ideology. There *are* at least some genuinely environmentally orientated businesses which radical greens can and do need to support, and particularly where small and medium sized enterprises are involved. And there are plenty of people who are in business as much to do some good in the world as to make money. The question is whether the mainstream business system is itself frustrating of such aspirations, a problem to which I shall return later. There are even semantic difficulties, as one green consultant reveals: 'Companies get very embarrassed talking about concepts like right and wrong; they're not part of the marketing jargon'.[16]

The radical green damper on the need to grow and grow is the sticking point in relations with industry. For example, IBM, a company with an exceptionally good environmental reputation, requested the Centre for Economic and Environmental Development (CEED) to assess how far its

UK policies conformed to the concept of sustainable development. In virtually every respect IBM was doing its best to follow a policy of 'being continuously on guard against adversely affecting the environment and seeking ways to conserve natural resources'. Nevertheless, the CEED report felt obliged to conclude that, although these policies were directed to sustainable development, 'clearly an open ended objective of continued rapid growth cannot be sustained indefinitely'.[17]

There have been no subsequent developments to invalidate the considered conclusion of Jonathon Porritt and David Winner in 1988:

> British industry remains for the most part lacking both in the imagination necessary to seize hold of new opportunities and in the determination genuinely to clean up their act rather than just clean up their image. The exceptions to this, however important, remain exceptional'.[18]

Can growth be kept within ecologically sustainable limits?

Purists maintain that if the market is completely free it will be ecologically self-regulating.[19] As we have seen, there is some truth in their contention that the depletion of scarce resources will encourage the development of alternatives, (but potentially fatal omissions include the planet's topsoil, water supplies and rainforests). It is also claimed that the high cost of anti-pollution equipment will be sufficient to deter industrialists from polluting. The evidence suggests, however, that many will tolerate pollution if they can get away with it, and particularly if their business is under other pressures. The long history of industry in respect of public health and the conditions of its employees demonstrates that with few exceptions even modest standards of ethical behaviour have had to be enforced by the state.

An energy campaigner, Jeremy Leggett, experienced 'a sense of shock' at the reception he received at an oil industry conference late in 1991. Instead of the expected 'denial, accusations of exaggeration, and aggressive counter-arguments', Leggett found that 'few questioned the premise, [and] all were interested . . . in whether or not it was possible for the fossil-fuel juggernaut they were aboard to be slowed or turned. And if so, how'. However, although, in the words of a man from Conoco, 'there's an environmental consciousness revolution going on in the industry', a 'sideways shift of responsibility was a common theme':

'Our company can't change unless our competitors do, simultaneously,' said one very senior American. 'Governments must make the
first move, and put pressure on us.' I told him that I regularly heard
the exact opposite from governments. 'We need to get re-elected,' say
politicians of all nationalities. 'There's only so much you can do in
five years, unless industry gets proactive, instead of endlessly reactive.' 'I would guess a lot of people would agree with you here,' said
a Marathon man. 'But there's just no easy way to break the chain'.[20]

Pollution and other environmental damage may be controlled not only
by regulation (including outright prohibition), but also by graduated taxes
and subsidies which, ideally, would reflect the actual cost of the damage
done to the environment. This principle is well established in the USA,
Sweden and elsewhere and has been popularised in Britain by the Pearce
Report.[21] These are no more 'licences to pollute' than are regulations
which (except where they are absolute prohibitions) permit pollution up to
a limit, and without paying. The strongest objection is that they are
socially regressive in that they ration scarce resources by price. A carbon
tax, for example, would need to be accompanied by regulating petrol price
differentials in terms of occupation, disability, rural residence and so on.
The relative merits of regulation and financial incentive are complex and
suggest that optimum results would be best achieved by a judicious mix.

More fundamental than these instruments of control are their purpose
and context. The goal must be an ecologically steady-state economy, that
is, one in which environmental impact can be sustained indefinitely
(through renewable energy technologies, technologies which enable pollution to be absorbed naturally, the more cost-effective use of raw materials,
sustainable use of the soil, and so on).

Present levels of economic activity and growth are clearly too great to
enable such a steady state to be maintained. It should be noted, however,
that growth itself is not the problem but the amount of environmental
impact created by growth. While new technologies are certainly reducing
this impact per unit of economic activity, they would be unable to do so
within the foreseeable future to the extent of creating a steady-state equilibrium. In other words, economic activity is becoming 'cleaner', but
overall it is still so 'dirty' that there is an urgent need to curb its growth.
But to what extent would growth, and even present levels of economic
activity, need to be cut back?

To answer this question requires the identification of different environmental impacts, defining the tolerable limits to be set upon those impacts
and calculating the instruments of control (regulation, financial incentives

and disincentives, and so on) needed to achieve those limits. Much of the Pearce Report was about theoretical constructs to define the meaning of sustainable growth; it did not adequately address the problem of under-taking a cost-benefit analysis of the effects of economic activity upon the global ecosystem over a period of time. This bizarre notion was dismissed in the answering Bowers Report.[22] The most that is practicable is a patch-work of pragmatic and piecemeal international schemes like those which are being proposed to cut the various emissions which contribute to the greenhouse effect. Such cuts are desperately needed, but scientists are unable to predict their climatic consequences and no one can begin to guess how far they will make our present levels of economic growth sustainable. What is happening at the economic/ecological interface is altogether too vast, complex and unpredictable to be measured except in the broadest terms, yet it is certain that it could be serious enough to destroy our civilisation.

Economist Michael Jacobs has maintained that, although 'uncertainty is endemic within environmental science' so that 'environmental targets will often be ranges rather than points', nevertheless such uncertainty 'does not render sustainability meaningless . . . The fact that we do not under-stand the environment perfectly does not mean that we cannot use what understanding we do have to make decisions about it'.[23] Few would dissent from this; but what is crucial is the *extent* to which such measure-ment and control is deemed practicable and accurate. Optimism for Jacobs implies a controversially mechanistic and calculative understanding of eco-economic phenomena. It also implies a similar unproblematic perception of the long-term effectiveness of technology in reducing envi-ronmental impacts. Both kinds of optimism make for confidence in a higher sustainable level of growth than would be acceptable to sceptics. Jacobs apparently believes that significant growth would be possible— 'sufficient to support a global population of eleven billion', extending the so-called 'green revolution' with 'modern irrigation methods and mecha-nisation' and 'planting faster growing or higher yielding crops'. Yet a reduction of overall environmental impact per unit of GNP by only 65-75 per cent over the next fifty years is the most commonly quoted estimate.[24] But a global economy growing at two to three per cent annually implies a quadrupling over the same period.

The contrary view is that although we must indeed do our best to measure and control environmental impact in order to achieve and hold in a steady state the level and kind of economic activity, our ignorance and uncertainty are necessarily so great that our safety margin must be very wide—so wide as to amount to no more than minimal growth rather than some modification of present levels of growth. David Pearce himself subsequently expressed an 'aversion to risk arising from our ignorance about the nature of the interaction between environment, economy and society'.[25] However, a steady state *would* increase the incentive to improve the environmental efficiency of the economy (that is, to achieve greater ecological—including human—welfare through diminishing energy and material inputs). Thus at least some continued growth would be possible in that its environmental impact could actually be diminishing. There is no necessity for the zero growth upon which some green fundamentalists have been insistent. And to provide an adequate standard of living for all of the world's peoples within the steady state we shall also clearly have urgent need of highly sophisticated clean, lean and renewable technologies.

Above all, minimal growth has fundamental social implications which distinguish ecologism (with its radical political imperatives) from environmentalism (business almost as usual). These include ecological and social management of the market and beyond the market which would change the whole character of the economy; the need for redistributive political policies (like basic income, ceilings on income and wealth, and the satisfaction of basic needs as of right); and a veritable revolution in the nature of livelihood, work and employment. The question of sustainability is thus of central importance in the radical green rationale.

If sustainability turns out to be unsustainable?

If environmental technologies and governmental restraints turn out to be ineffective to protect the ecosphere from the effects of continued growth or to damp it down sufficiently, and the mounting costs of environmental protection prove unsupportable, then some kind of social and demographic decline or collapse will become inevitable. Eugene Schwartz[26] has argued that the residue of quasi-solutions and unresolved global social problems could cumulate and converge to the point where, with rising costs and diminishing resources, further technological remedies became difficult to apply. The scope for positive economic and social adaptation would also narrow, mortality rates would rise, health services would no longer be equal to the rising demands made upon them, and the whole culture would begin to break down. Schwartz believes that a typical ecological overshoot of planetary carrying capacity may already have occurred, with irremediable damage yet to be felt.

Certainly cancer rates have been rising alarmingly. Between 1968 and 1988, in the US, Japan, the UK and three other industrialised European countries, rates of bone cancer and bone marrow cancer in people over the age of sixty-five increased by 50 to 600 per cent depending on the country selected, and kidney cancer, breast cancer and lymphoma by 10 to 50 per cent. Statistical distortions arising from greater longevity and better reporting and diagnosis were taken into account in the authoritative report from which these figures are taken.[27] Epidemiologists attribute such rises primarily to environmental factors (notably air pollution and toxic waste) and unhealthy diet. It has been argued that synthetic chemical compounds account for between one and ten per cent of all cancer deaths—and it usually takes from twenty to forty years after exposure for cancer to develop. More generally, it has been claimed that low-level radiation plus a wide range of environmental toxins and exposure to ultraviolet rays will have genetically irreversible effects from one generation to the next, with increasing infertility and early mortality combined with a sharp fall in the overall health of the population.[28]

Decline could steepen into ecological crash, with economic growth eventually resumed in some form or other, setting the whole tragic ecological cycle once more in train. Alternatively, the cornucopian addiction may become discredited before decline has proceeded too far, and an ecologically stable economy might begin to take shape, together with the kind of social and political culture that would be compatible with it. As Professor John Bowers concluded in his critique of the Pearce Report, 'To get an economic system which is sustainable, environmentally friendly and non-polluting will require a massive mobilisation of resources and, since current social systems are not based on sustainable development, fundamental changes in the social structure'.[22] More recently, Pearce himself conceded that sustainable development 'may even require systematic changes in social values'.[29] This sociopolitical reconstruction could take various possible forms, from the authoritarian to the libertarian (Ecotopia at last?) and from massive pragmatic adaptation to revolutionary upheaval.

The positions which people take up on the pale to dark green spectrum of environmentalism to ecologism will probably have at least as much to do with personality, background, and beliefs as with some dispassionate weighing up of the tangle of claims, counter-claims and speculation available as evidence. At the least, however, the latter will be important in articulating our root inclinations and giving them a rationale. So it is not only necessary to look into the evidence but also to spend time looking into the habitual reality which we have each created for ourselves in our lives and through which, largely unaware, we give meaning to the evidence.

Those of us who are, in any case, inclined to be profoundly critical of the industrial and acquisitive society will tend to a darker shade of green.

The same applies to people who have an instinctively holistic feeling for things, or believe that our problems originate deep within us but that nevertheless we do have the potential to do something about them. And unfortunately the radical green stance also has powerful appeal for the many who have strong fundamentalist and ideological hungers. It is now time to move on to examine the many variant inputs to this radical green alternative.

13 Radical green politics

THE STABLE, ecologically harmonious society which is the radical green goal has been described as follows by William Ophuls, one of the most penetrating writers on this subject:

> A steady state society is essentially one which has achieved a basic long term balance between the demands of a population and the environment that supplies its wants. Implied in this definition is the preservation of a healthy biosphere, the careful husbanding of resources, and a general attitude of trusteeship towards future generations. The exact nature of the balance at any time is dependent on technological capacities and social choice, and as choices and capacities change organic growth can occur.[1]

In this part of the book we assess a variety of different trends and movements relevant to the ideal which Ophuls outlines. This chapter is about specifically political ideas and movements and highlights problems and opportunities.

Authoritarians, reluctant and zealous

Before the second world war ecologism, or dark green political ecology, was typically authoritarian and conservative, though of the soft, populist or paternalistic variety. Rejecting 'modernism' it was anti-capitalist, anti-urban, opposed to large, centralised institutions of all kinds, and sought to bring back a romantic rural golden age. Its folksy nationalism, however, tended to spill over into racism and the eugenics of ethnic purity. Traditional, conservative values would be nurtured (and enforced) by self-sufficient, self-governing communities, rooted in the soil.

It has been argued that the Nazis were the first authoritarian greens to nearly win control of a state. There is little doubt that, in the words of one researcher, 'there was a strain of ecological ideas among the Nazis', fully expressed in the 'ministerial planning and personal archives of the Third Reich'.[2] Evidently, however, this was more a German than a Nazi phenomenon, since it finds no parallel in the other contemporaneous fascist movements. (One of the more obscure causes of the second world war was the Nazis holding the Poles responsible for the outbreak of pine bud mite along the frontier in 1937, which adversely affected the Germans' huge afforestation programme). With the outbreak of war the 'hard' wing of the Nazi Party, led by Heydrich and the technocrats, got the upper hand and put an end to the National Socialist vision of a greening of the Third Reich.

After the war there was a remarkable and historic shift in the predominant politics of ecologism from soft right to soft left. There are, however, still some significant contemporary green right-wing thinkers.

Classic right-wing authoritarian political theory assumes that man (sic) is by nature self-centred, aggressive, disorderly and greedy, to the point now of threatening to destroy his environment and himself. Strong government is required to keep him in order, to inculcate social habits and to sustain a civil society of general benefit to its citizens.

Some advocates of a conserver society, like Garrett Hardin, are reluctant authoritarians who are pessimistic about the practicability of making such a society democratic and consensual. Following the seventeenth-century political theorist Thomas Hobbes, they believe that a stable society must depend on 'mutual coercion, mutually agreed by the majority of people affected', who compact together to abandon such individual liberties as 'the freedom to breed'.[3] Similarly, William Ophuls has little doubt that, 'whatever its specific form, the politics of the sustainable society seem likely to move us along the spectrum from libertarianism towards authoritarianism'.[4]

Ophuls is evidently another liberal who, after pondering the political imperatives of a conserver society, reluctantly advocates a qualified authoritarianism. He optimistically claims that 'there seems no reason why authority cannot be strong enough to sustain a steady state society and yet be limited. The personal and civil rights guaranteed in our constitution, for example, could be largely retained'.[5] In Ophuls' view the conserver society would require a shift away from egalitarian democracy towards 'political competence and status', evidently vested in some constitutionally licensed paternalistic governing class. Less controversially Ophuls believes it will also be necessary to move from individualism to communalism, whereby the interests of the community take precedence over those of the individual. This is a view taken by a wide spectrum of writers, many of them in no sense authoritarians.[6] It should be added that Ophuls believes that his ecotopia would be a diverse and holistic society whose people would be 'relaxed, playful and content, [enjoying] personal fulfilment spiritually, intellectually, esthetically, scientifically'. However, the experience of communist societies reinforces skepticism about the likelihood of powerful rulers of corporate states long remaining constitutional, benevolent or even competent.

In contrast with this 'reluctant' dark green authoritarianism is a kind sufficiently full-blooded and zealous to attract accusations of 'eco-fascism'. This is commonly based on a fundamentalist ecologism which assumes that the social order must be display the same (alleged) characteristics as the natural order if it is to be in harmony with it. The view which these green authoritarians have of both nature and society is neo-Darwinian. That is to say, their assumptions about the nature of society lead them to an interpretation of ecology (particularly in respect of early evolutionary theory) which they then re-import, with all the authority of 'the natural order of things', into their economic and political thinking.

For a green fundamentalist like Edward Goldsmith, following the natural order 'competing individuals eventually arrange themselves so as to constitute a hierarchy and learn to accept their respective conditions within this hierarchy'.[7] No good can come of democracy and welfarism because they empower those who are by nature unfit to exercise power; if they were fit, they would not need such artificial aids! Hence in Goldsmith's ecotopia 'all unemployed people would automatically have to join the Restoration Corps, unemployment benefits being altogether eliminated'. Again, no good can come of feminism either, since it creates 'an increasingly large number of even more maladjusted women who are being forced by their education and other social pressures to struggle against their natural instincts'.[8]

For both green authoritarians *and* libertarians, traditional pre-industrial societies are assumed to provide a 'natural' model for the future. Goldsmith's ecotopia would therefore consist of a much reduced population living in small, labour-intensive and self-regulating family and community units, in which 'only a certain number of foreigners would be allowed to settle'.

Although fundamentalists like Goldsmith fortunately do not—at present—need to be taken seriously, green authoritarian writing as a whole does offer certain pointers and emphases to which radicals need to attend.

First, the reluctant, Hobbesian authoritarians like William Ophuls might prompt libertarian greens to reflect on whether some of their historically inherited ideological baggage of libertarian individualism might really be appropriate to the conserver society.

Second, soft left ecologism slides easily over into the soft right version. To achieve their radical goals even movements dedicated to grassroots democratic and decentralised futures can produce populist, brainwashing elites unable to resist short cuts to power.

Third, some form of authoritarianism at present seems the most likely response to severe environmental crisis. Unless people are well-prepared, confident and united there will be a rush for the lifeboats as soon as they realise that our civilisation really is falling apart. Strong government will be invoked, whether in the name of justice or of privilege.

And finally, there is also in the authoritarian tradition a conservatism which offers a useful antidote to those who are addicted to (almost) instant ecotopias. Founders of modern conservatism like Edward Burke, observing the unfolding of the French Revolution, have reminded us that human societies are more complex and well-rooted in their historical evolution than had been assumed by libertarian romantics like Tom Paine. Attempts at rational reconstruction from first principles commonly collapse in tyranny and disorder (as evident in the 1990s as in the 1790s).

'Bliss was it in that dawn . . . ': The libertarian origins of green radicalism

The libertarian political tradition is the mirror image of the authoritarian. The root concern of libertarian politics is not the maintenance of order but liberation from repression. For the authoritarian, original sin (or its secular variant) is redeemed by the discipline of well-regulated social institutions. For the libertarian, basic goodness is warped and corrupted by the self-same institutions. If they can but be freed from repressive social structures, men and women will be enabled to create a society whose members naturally behave in a public-spirited, peaceable and co-operative fashion.

Although it had antecedents in some of the radical reformation sects, libertarianism originated essentially in the eighteenth-century enlightenment and the American and French revolutions. It was the political expression of a wider romantic movement to which much in the present new age culture can be traced. (Romanticism puts feelings above intellect, reveres nature, exalts the feminine, is attracted to mysticism—though only on its own terms—and believes in the innate goodness of humankind). Prominent founding libertarians included Rousseau, Thomas Paine, William Godwin, Mary Wollstonecraft, and Thomas Jefferson.

The Jeffersonian vision was of a United States of small farmers, crafts-people and merchants in a confederation of self-governing communities. This self-reliant, public-spirited frontier tradition has continued to flourish in American culture and public life and now inspires the United States green movement. Except where it connected with specifically socialist currents, libertarianism has tended to prefer mixed economic systems, blending community, co-operative and private ownership, provided always the undertakings were on a small, human scale that did not divorce owner-ship from personal involvement.

In the nineteenth and early twentieth centuries libertarianism developed as a rich and diverse intellectual and political current of prophecy and protest, as in the anarchism of Kropotkin and, later, of Alex Comfort, Paul Goodman and Murray Bookchin. In Britain it flourished in the decades before the first world war, in the romantic early days of socialism, in the Arts and Crafts Movement and William Morris's *News from nowhere*. The term 'post-industrial' originated with Arthur Penty, an English guild socialist and follower of Morris and Ruskin—all believers in a decen-tralised, artisan, rural society of frugal and upright craftsmanship. In small favoured historical and geographical niches libertarianism briefly got its feet on the ground, as with the Spanish anarchist movement of the 1930s. The last time when it was once more bliss in that dawn to be alive was during the flowering of the late 1960s, a time of tremendous libertarian visionary energy beside which the collapse of communism in our own time has all the excitement of collecting an insurance policy which has fallen due.

For all kinds of libertarians—anarcho-syndicalists, mystics, nature lovers, feminists, pacifists, aesthetes—the coming of the ecological crisis is the ultimate vindication of their condemnation of a greedy and alienating industrialism, itself the culmination of a long historical tradition of outer oppression and inner repression. And so the ancient libertarian utopia became ecotopia, founded, in Murray Bookchin's words, on the 'co-operative, life-affirming tendencies [in] human nature, nurtured through interaction with an appropriate ethical community which is participative and richly differentiated in the stimuli, forms and choices it creates to make for personal self-formation'.[9]

The mutually balanced diversity of ecosystems themselves is seen as a fundamental validation of the ecotopian vision. From out of their own historical tradition, 'social ecologists' looked at nature and found the opposite to the neo-Darwinians. Hence Bookchin welcomes 'the mutualistic attributes emphasised by a growing number of contemporary ecologists—an image pioneered by Peter Kropotkin . . . Ecosystem diversity [therefore] grades into social diversity, based on human scaled decentralised communities'.[10]

From the libertarian tradition a prophetic and visionary green ideology has been fashioned, instilled into an increasingly resistant public at a rate of several books a year. My concern in this book is to strip this greened libertarian tradition of its ideology and romanticism, make it more serviceable, and outline the possibilities for doing our best with the way things are, including the kind of people we tend to be.

For a start, it will be useful to take a closer look at the libertarians' idealisation of human nature. It is this that leads them to believe that, freed of oppressive social structures, we will naturally work together to uphold one another's interests. This belief is the glue that holds together the ecotopian vision.

The green idealisation of human nature goes back to the romantic eighteenth-century idea of the 'noble savage', whether palaeolithic hunter-gatherers or the primal peoples of contemporary social anthropology. They are assumed invariably to live in harmony with nature and with one another. And, as always with ideology, the evidence is selective and quickly assumes the universal validity and absolute power of myth. These half truths find little support even from sympathetic anthropologists. In his very thorough critique of 'green primitivism' Roy Ellen, who 'broadly supports the Green programme of political action', hammers home the point that 'no one human culture has the monopoly of environmental wisdom'.[11]

It is true that the hunter-gatherer cultures which occupy some 99 per cent of human history, together with the present survivors, do afford remarkable examples of a harmonious and sustainable at-oneness with nature, thanks to small populations, isolation, and range of subsistence strategies (including extensive infanticide). It is no less true that, particularly in times of rising population, even hunter-gatherers have inflicted heavy damage on the environment. The first human settlers of North America, for example, left a trail of destruction behind them, driving two thirds of the larger mammals to extinction. Of Europe, Ellen observes that 'there is evidence that the Pleistocene megafauna as a whole became extinct through over-hunting, and the temperate forest of Europe was decimated by early farmers living at low population densities in non-stratified societies using simple technologies. Today, presented with such people face-to-face we would regard them as the very epitome of the primitive living with nature'.

As to the innate peaceableness of primal peoples, the evidence here is biased by most anthropologists' assumptions that they are inherently aggressive, and by the deterministic polarisation exhibited in the academic literature on this question. However, even sympathetic researchers can find comparatively few examples of indisputably peaceful peoples, like the Inuit (Eskimo), Pueblo Indians, Tahitans, !Kung, and Kalahari Bushmen.[12] And even in these cultures high rates of personal violence are found. One exasperated anthropologist exclaims that 'the oft repeated claim that hunters and food-gatherers in general are more peaceful than people at a higher cultural level is certainly false, and so obviously false that one wonders how it can survive so stubbornly in the face of the overwhelming abundance of known facts'.[13]

In short, even on the evidence of sympathetic anthropologists, that primal peoples past and present invariably live in harmony with nature and one another is simply not true.

Beyond this rejection of the green libertarian idealisation of human nature, it will be evident that this book *is* founded on a belief in what Matthew Fox[14] calls 'original blessing', or our 'original nature' or 'Buddha nature' or whatever else it be called, and not on some version of original sin. We are each born, however, with an identity crisis, and all our griefs originate ultimately in a customary human inability simply to accept that identity in full awareness and in a need to establish and confirm it in ways which bring down suffering on self and others.

We have seen earlier how this personal condition is socially and historically compounded and supercharged. But the Buddhist diagnosis here joins only marginally with that of the libertarians for whom the problem is *no more* than one of an oppressive social environment. The argument of this book is that we shall need to start to nudge the evolution of human consciousness itself beyond its present high egoic level in order to build, as from now, the radically different green culture of mutuality on which the steady-state economy will depend. But to this end we shall also need to develop institutions and structures which provide for security, cohesion, restraint and responsibility, as well as freedom and empowerment.

Root problems of radical green politics

What follows is based on the experience of the Green Party of England, Wales and Northern Ireland. Much of what I have to say would be applicable to typical green parties elsewhere in Europe and in North America, as well as to many other small movements for radical social change.

Insignificant though it presently is, the Green Party perfectly exemplifies most of the underlying psycho-social phenomena highlighted in this book, and particularly in the discussion on ideology in Chapter 9. Even if the party were to disappear next year, the libertarian tradition which it exemplifies would still persist, fragile and flawed though it is. For, in one variant or another, it offers the only radical social and ecological alternative to the prevailing social and economic order. This is why constructive critique at a very fundamental level is so essential. We cannot afford yet another false dawn . . .

The Green Party coincides only approximately with the radical green constituency in the UK. Results of a survey of members at the end of 1992 suggest that as many as a fifth were what I have termed environmentalists. Compared with the estimated seven million people associated with the environmental protest movement, membership is no more than 7,000 at the time of writing. In the 1989 elections to the European Parliament, the party won 15 per cent of the vote, but after three years of internecine conflict its vote fell to a mere 1.3 per cent in the 1992 general election. Many radical greens are active elsewhere, mainly in the broad environmental movement, but also in connection with the New Economics Foundation, the Red Green-Network and small fundamentalist sects like the Fourth Worlders and Murray Bookchin's followers in the UK Social Ecology Network.

Of the major UK parties only the Liberal Democrats have actually claimed environmental concern as the cornerstone of their policies. Closer examination of the party's overall policy making, however, reveals a bold rhetoric aimed at the widest possible constituency but resulting in blatant incompatibilities—whether in its enthusiasm for ever increasing material consumption,[15] or for the 'open playing field' of the Common Market, or its nuclear defence policy.

Returning to the radical green vision, the following will give some idea of the immensity of the undertaking.

1   The economy would be ecologically sustainable indefinitely, in that its waste could be absorbed by nature, its energy would be renewable, and its raw materials consumption modest, sustainable and efficient. Populations would need to be significantly reduced, and there would be a shift from consumerism to a more simple, but high quality lifestyle.

2   The human-scale economy would produce goods and services for need rather than stimulating wants, with emphasis on a labour-intensiveness and appropriate technology. Local, regional and national economic self-reliance would be important.

3   Likewise a manageable, human-scale politics would emphasise citizen empowerment, and hence decentralisation and non-hierarchical

organisation. Power would be transferred to local communities, districts, regions and small nations, linked together in confederations. Nothing would be done at a higher level that could be done just as well at a lower level.

4 Extremes of power and dependence, of wealth and poverty, would be excluded from this conserver society, on grounds of both social justice and socio-ecological stability. Capital and income differentials would be low, with a guaranteed basic income for all. Fundamental economic and civil rights would also be guaranteed.

5 Global solidarity would replace allegiance to the nation-state. Nonviolence would be a fundamental principle, and social, cultural and species diversity would be encouraged.

6 Since the historic regulators of the market and the state would evidently be marginal, this ecotopia could be sustained only by an historically unprecedented level of social responsibility and public spiritedness (though this is rarely mentioned in green manifestoes).

As Jonathon Porritt has observed, this amounts to 'nothing less than a non-violent revolution to overthrow our whole polluting, plundering and materialistic industrial society and, in its place, to create a new economic and social order which will allow human beings to live in harmony with the planet ... Dark Green thinking offers a radical, visionary and fundamentalist challenge to the prevailing economic and political world order'.[16]

The full version of this ecotopian vision, running to forty pages, first appeared in 1972 as a 'Blueprint for survival' in *The Ecologist* magazine.[17] David Pepper[18] has identified twenty of the twenty-three 'major points' made in this seminal work as having also been made in Peter Kropotkin's 1899 anarcho-communist classic *Fields, factories and workshops*. Whether this was a coincidence or not does not really matter. Plenty of variants of Kropotkin's utopia are to be found in the luxuriant libertarian tradition as a whole, and there can be little doubt about the Blueprint's indebtedness to *that*. These libertarian proposals were originally primarily about demonstrating something different from ecological sustainability, namely how individual liberty might be fully achieved through community responsibility (something still highly relevant to the radical green agenda). It is a remarkable episode in the history of political ideas that the ecological crisis should have been the means of bringing to widespread prominence a utopian vision which, beyond the loyalty of some tiny eccentric sects, had become of little more than historical interest.

Such a policy or 'philosophical basis', as the Green Party would call it, is indeed, as the party claims, above and beyond the categories of conventional 'grey' politics, high flying in its romantic idealism and so far to the left as to be off the usual political scales. The Blueprint's drafters evidently felt that the threat of planetary catastrophe was so total that only such a utopian response could measure up to it (and the subsequent demise of techno-bureaucratic 'hard' socialism and communism has made it also the radical left's only visionary option). If, however, we shift our attention from the utopian perspective of the Blueprint and attend, instead, to how we might begin to cultivate its eco-social values now, then it does begin to appear more credible, as I shall try to demonstrate later. And if it is the very nature of our present civilisation that has precipitated the ecological crisis, then nothing less will indeed do than the seemingly utopian task of creating a new, ecologically appropriate kind of civilisation.

So much for the vision splendid. The problems and dilemmas which plague the parties and movements dedicated to achieving it are much the same as those which have dogged socialist and other radical movements for a hundred years or more.

At the heart of the libertarian political project is the contradictory situation in which a small and relatively powerless group of idealistic intellectuals find themselves (Green Party membership is overwhelmingly middle class, professional and graduate). They are dedicated to popularising the goal of a good society and of somehow empowering the mass of the people to achieve that goal. However, thanks to 'false consciousness' (as the Marxists call it) and an ingrained sense of powerlessness, this appeal of the vanguard commonly falls upon deaf ears. A long period of political education and working at the grassroots is therefore indicated. This, however, is slow, unrewarding work, in which the educators run the risk of themselves being disconcertingly re-educated, and the prospects of even limited formal political power become more attractive. Those of a reformist inclination will therefore turn to the ballot box, which their radical colleagues will see only as an adjunct to 'mass, nonviolent direct action'.

For the British Green Party policy making and faction fighting appear so far to have been at least as absorbing as electioneering, and laying the social foundations of a conserver society evidently has come a poor fourth.

One of Jonathon Porritt's many exasperations with the Green Party has been about its 'footling around with never ending debates about minute policy details, the vast majority of which will either be entirely disregarded or end up as useful hostages to fortune for those who want to bury the Greens under a mountain of knocking copy'.[19] In fact, the Green Party has a whole 'policy making community' whose addiction to drafting the future on their word processors and circulating endless papers to one another acts as an intellectually satisfying surrogate to the exercise of political power. Members will sacrifice much time and energy mastering the party's labyrinthine hyper-democratic policy making procedures in order to enshrine their pet concern in the party bible, the *Manifesto for a sustainable society* or MfSS. The MfSS prescribes in 124 pages of small print all the many things, ranging from policy on cannabis to policy on gypsies, which the party would presumably cause to happen if the queen were to invite it to form a government.

This curious addiction (which still leaves out some important middle range policy areas, as in economics) is not only time wasting but, more importantly, it betrays a disturbing underlying attitude to power and empowerment. For this huge prospective legislative programme, and the powerful central government apparatus presumably required to implement it, are in startling contrast to those passages in the MfSS whereby 'the present system by which policy is determined centrally at Westminster and imposed on the public would be reversed' (para AD110), and nothing should be done at a higher level if it can be done at a lower. This contradiction seems to have escaped many party members, as the following anecdote suggests (from John Papworth, at a Green Party conference in 1989): 'The [education] debate was not on how the party proposed to abolish the Ministry of Education and restore its powers to elected parish or village councils where it surely belongs; on the contrary it concerned the type of sex education the party wanted to direct every school in the country to give to every child'. When Papworth described the rude treatment which would be meted out by his parish council to any official telling them how to run their school, 'this evoked the curious response, to rapturous applause moreover, that this was all very well in an ideal society, but that in the real world we Greens had to get power first, then we should be able to tell everyone what to do, and only after that could we begin to decentralise power'.[20]

The energy which goes into all this paternalistic conceptualisation would surely be better expended working in local communities, work places, councils, professions and everywhere else where there is opportunity for people to make a beginning laying the foundations for a different way of life. Janet Alty, a leading advocate of such a strategy, argues that:

> Power, in the definition of the Green Project, does not lie solely in the legislative process. A great many Green ideas can be made to function here and now (the subversive or indirect route) and do not need to wait for permission (legislation) from elsewhere. If we were to spend more time on locally adoptable policies which do not rely

on national (or even local) legislation, we would make much faster progress in establishing ourselves as electorally trustworthy, while at the same time involving people directly in Green ideas and activities.[21]

The practical difficulties of previous generations of grassroots radicals (as in building up a factory floor industrial movement, for example) have been modest compared with those facing the pioneer builders of a here-and-now green political and economic culture. The Green Party believes that party organisation should uncompromisingly foreshadow that of the society it seeks to bring to birth. Consequently there is a confederal constitution in which the 'local parties' (not 'branches'!) enjoy very wide autonomy. Potentially, at least, this gives them the freedom to get on with the grassroots work in ways appropriate to the locality and to local talents. A few do indeed successfully do so. But in the absence of local *animateurs* little happens elsewhere, since there is little stimulus or back-up from the centre. This is because of the party's extreme decentralist and anti-leadership tendencies, which have starved and restricted the capacity of headquarters (even when in funds) to provide specialist back-up, make media waves, raise wide issues, and put up 'personalities' as household names so that the party has a continual national presence. This is yet another example of the disabling fundamentalism that grips the party.

This is not to say that there is not a real leadership and centralisation dilemma for the Green Party of a kind perennial in radical movements. In a classic study published in 1911,[22] Robert Michels demonstrated that as voluntary bodies like political parties and trade unions grow larger and more powerful and complex, power becomes concentrated in an elite of elected career politicians and professional bureaucrats. Their control of funds, communications, specialist expertise, and complex procedural systems makes them more than a match for rank-and-file dissidents. And yet on paper and to outward appearances the organisation remains democratic. The members of the elite modify the original goals of the organisation to serve their own short-term pragmatic interests. In their own view, however, they are usefully engaged in the politics of the possible, yielding solid benefits in contrast to the sectarian impotence of the fundamentalists who denounce their 'betrayal'. A creative resolution of this problem is required which would enable strong local parties and a strong centre to complement each other. There is no magic constitution awaiting discovery that could do it. The answer has to lie deep in a mutualistic organisational culture. But it is precisely the ideologically charged climate of radical movements that is inimical to the growth of such a culture, notwithstanding all the rhetoric to the contrary.

At the time of writing the Green Party is attempting to consolidate its position around a broader leadership amidst loss of public credibility, falling membership and financial cutbacks. Its future direction is uncertain. Like all radical parties it has its reformists, in the fifth of the membership who see it as no more than the electoral wing of the environmentalist movement. The vulnerability of such a single issue party will be evident. At the other extreme are radicals who seem inclined to give increasing weight to the 'social agenda', which could all too easily slide into strident anti-capitalist rhetoric and complete the Green Party's marginalisation. Such a pull to the sectarian left would also open a gap with the party's mainstream, more inclined to a utopian libertarianism with new age overtones.

It is vital that the social (i.e. non-ecological) agenda should be understood as the political and economic imperative which follows from the requirements of an ecologically stable conserver economy. To do so actually integrates and reinforces the demand for social justice. On this basis much solid progress could be made with policies based on community and regional empowerment, the development of local economies and concern for adequate livelihood and security for all, with the whole well rooted in fundamental environmental policies. There is plenty of scope here for building coalitions around particular issues, with the wider environmentalist movement and with many other organisations with which some common cause can be made at local and regional level. Such moves towards the creation of a green social culture would, and should, accommodate supportive electoral strategies also. I believe there are sound possibilities here for creating an expanding niche in the British political scene.

For the Green Party, its main obstacle to development in that direction is its fundamentalist and utopian streak, erupting in quarrelsome inflexibility. This frustrates both the resolution of its organisational problems and its involvement in an ongoing and practical political process. It is true that the objective conditions are not encouraging; nevertheless much could be achieved. A promising start is, in fact, now under way in developing strategies which have much in common with those advocated in this book

In the final analysis the party's problems are more psychological than political. They are problems of ideology and of organisational culture, which are personal problems of political import. Sadly, they remain largely unrecognised.

Red to green: part of the problem or part of the answer?

Stranded by the receding tide of history, left socialists have sought to associate themselves with the new 'social movements'—the peace, the black, the feminist, and now the environmental movements, seeking to radicalise them and somehow draw them into what they see as the historic, overarching socialist project. In the majority of cases their response to the ecological crisis, ranging from the leadership of the Labour Party to the hardest and furthest left, has been environmentalist and opportunistic in character, simply tacking on some environmental concerns to existing policies. However, some socialists have been strongly attracted to the radical green movement and are concerned to develop a constructive dialogue. In 1990 a Red-Green Network of individuals and small groups was established.

Raymond Williams has declared his belief 'that the only kind of socialism that now stands any chance of being established, in the old industrial bourgeois-democratic societies, is one centrally based on new kinds of communal, co-operative and collective institutions . . . this is really the only road which socialists in these countries have left to travel'.[23] This belief is evidently shared by most radical socialists seeking to free themselves from the discredited tradition of corporate state socialism, whether of Herbert Morrison or Joseph Stalin. Similarly, there was nowhere else the radical greens themselves could have gone other than up much the same libertarian road (though the greens tend to be more reticent about their historical antecedents). On the face of it, the two movements do seem to share a broadly similar vision of the good society.

There are, however, some significant differences. Following the Marxist tradition, radical socialists attribute the ecological crisis (and most social ills) to the workings of capitalism and they see social processes primarily in terms of class and class struggle. Mainstream greens have taken the no less simplistic post-industrial view that capitalism and class are no longer relevant. All that really matters now is how green or grey you are. For them the greening of society will not come through the conquest of power by certain sections of society. It will be achieved by overall changes in lifestyle, the development of alternative initiatives and institutions which will bypass the old order and make it irrelevant, and the creation of a cultural and social climate which will turn greys green comparatively painlessly, with the whole process topped off legislatively.

More important still are the differences in political mentalities and styles. Petra Kelly explains:

The conflicts which the West German Greens have experienced have much to do with the clash of interests between those coming from a rather dogmatic, old, leftist political perspective which shares so many anti-capitalist insights, and those who come from a holistic New Age perspective . . . The clash of interests is often not so much in what we are aiming for, but how we can get there and what strategies we should pursue towards our common goal.[24]

There are hard left socialists for whom the green phenomenon is just a new operational terrain, like feminism or the Third World movements, to be incorporated into their ideological world view, and another political constituency to be co-opted to the socialist movement. They have developed faction fighting and 'entryism' to other organisations to a fine art, and their abrasive, dogmatic and peculiarly arid polemical style can make dialogue difficult.

Nevertheless, socialism asks important questions which need to be answered about the future society outlined in radical green manifestoes. What kind of political system could best balance overall social and environmental justice and equitability against the substantial local autonomy which such manifestoes celebrate? What kind of economy could offer the flexibility and responsiveness of free market capitalism without its social and economic exploitativeness and seemingly inherent expansiveness? What socially responsible but economically efficient forms of public ownership are feasible? In short, how are political and economic empowerment to be made socially and ecologically responsible? On these and other questions relevant to the credibility of ecotopia there is contemporary socialist writing which finds few counterparts in the radical green movement, where it goes largely unheeded.

A socialist presence also makes it more difficult to reduce the world's problems to ecology. Socialists have a refreshing concern for old-fashioned economic exploitation which today flourishes as grossly as ever. Such concern, particularly if smacking of class consciousness, can still cause a ripple of embarrassment in company where protest against the harm done to trees, dolphins and primal peoples is assured a warm glow of unanimity. Barry Commoner makes the point:

> When an environmental issue is pursued to its origins, it reveals an inescapable truth—that the root cause of the crisis is not to be found in how man interacts with nature, but in how men interact with each other—that, to solve the environmental crisis we must also solve the problems of poverty, racial injustice and war; that the debt to nature which is the measure of the environmental crisis cannot be paid,

person by person, in recycled bottles or ecologically sound habits, but in the ancient coin of social justice; that, in sum, peace among men must precede peace with nature.[25]

14 The new economics

THE 'new economics' is another radical green current, and one that is none too easy to define. It has particularly centred on The Other Economic Summit (TOES), which shadows the annual meetings of world government leaders to discuss the economic state of the planet and presents its alternative perspective. TOES is one of many projects associated with the the New Economics Foundation which, according to its prospectus, was 'set up in 1986 to develop and teach a New Economics which satisfies the whole range of human needs, social justice and the sustainable use of resources—and conservation of the environment . . . The New Economics is fundamentally concerned with the nature of *wealth*: money or material affluence is part of wealth—but not if it is at the expense of people's health, creativity, freedom, personal relationships and environment'.

The new economics, as presented in books like James Robertson's *Future wealth: a new economics for the 21st century*,[26] offers a familiar mainstream radical green picture of a future conserver society. Like earlier libertarians Robertson proposes an economy of small private, co-operative and community enterprises, together with networks of 'decentralised entrepreneurial units' in place of large centralised business organisations. He is at pains to point out that this vision 'cannot come from socialism or communism in their conventional forms, nor from conventional market based capitalism, or from the conventional compromise between them known as the "mixed economy".' According to a prospectus for another book, by Paul Ekins and Manfred Max-Neef,[27] the essential economic component would be good work (satisfying, useful and ecologically sound) in 'co-operative structures' with appropriate technologies. 'Co-operative structures' imply 'democratic participation and control, responsible ownership and non-exploitative social relations'. These principles are to be realised in a '"Living Economy" [which] will comprise a competitive, informed market sensitive to the full implications of economic life; a state strong enough to enforce the conditions for such a market and to remedy its inevitable shortcomings in such areas as distribution, concentration of producer-power, social costs and the provision of public goods; a local planning network able to match local needs and resources with a view to developing the necessary diversity and flexibility for local self-reliance; and a means such as a basic income for enabling and rewarding productive but unpaid work in the domestic and voluntary sector.'

The new economists' proposals for building the future conserver society are usually well-considered and thought provoking. More problematic are their assumptions about the economic origins of the ecological crisis and about the transition to the 'New Economy'. Unlike the ecosocialists, they have little to say about anything called capitalism and commonly they do not specifically identify it as the prime mover of global ecological and social crisis. It is conventional economic theory that is seen as the root of the problem, as if it were the theory that shaped the economy, rather than vice versa. Green socialists have given short shrift to this evasive inversion. Martin Ryle has pointed out:

> 'Conventional economics' is not a mistaken theory/ideology; it is the institutionalized practice of a system with particular agents and beneficiaries . . . Its ideas are not only false (they don't constitute the only or the optimum basis on which economic life might be organised), but true (they reflect, because they institutionalize, the exigencies of capitalism). It follows that if we reject the ideas, we must be prepared to confront the institutions which embody and enforce them.[28]

Similarly, the proposed transition to the new economy is as extreme in its consensualism as is the classic socialist fixation on confrontation, struggle, and overthrow. There is at most only passing reference to the resistance of vested interests, the inertia of established institutions and structures, and ingrained values and attitudes. Nevertheless, certainly James Robertson's books offer a valuably wide range of activities for building a green society as from now, ranging from reconceptualisation to physical obstruction, involving many different kinds of people, and building up to an 'unstoppable momentum'.

From the above it is only another short consensual step to assuming that the main problem is simply that top people are muddle-headed and require more talking to. This is reminiscent of the *philosophes* of the eighteenth-century age of reason, who believed that it was sufficient to appeal to the logic and good sense of rulers and they would straightway mend their ways, issue the decrees and sign the cheques. And so for Paul Ekins 'the tantalising fact about the Economic Summit series is that the leaders round the table *could* decide, as The Other Economic Summit has urged them to do, to set a programme in train that would achieve health and food for all on this planet by the year 2000'.[29]

Furthermore, although the movement is staunchly uncompromising in its steady-state and social justice principles, it is nevertheless a very broad church, embracing holistic financiers and capitalists of every shade of green, and working with a wide spectrum of environmental bodies, from the World Wide Fund for Nature to the politicians' Green Alliance and the Council for the Protection of Rural England. It is not surprising, then, that in a candid assessment of its strengths and weaknesses, the New Economics Foundation (NEF) identified its two main weaknesses as a 'lack of clarity created by different assumptions on what the new economics is', and the fact that 'greater clarity about what the new economics is may divide the organisation'.

On the other hand, these weaknesses do have the merit of enabling the NEF and TOES to maintain a very open and inclusive forum, in which a radical green economics can be widely publicised, refined and developed. Basic principles do appear to remain uncompromised and yet useful dialogue is promoted across many different constituencies. It must be remembered also that the NEF is a charitable foundation concerned exclusively with research and education, and it cannot undertake lobbying or campaigning. Although, on the one hand, its green businesspeople and consultants tend to slide into environmentalism and, on the other, the prophetic wing sometimes sounds naive and dogmatic, in general there *is* a refreshing openness and absence of ideology. The new economics movement is an important and promising contributor to the radical green project, and particularly in view of the problems which dog the politicals.

15 Spiritual resources for the green project

A tarnished 'new age'

At first sight the new age movement might appear to be the major contributor to a spiritually informed radical green politics. It proclaims the coming of an age of unprecedented ecological and social harmony; it emphasises personal transformation as the means; and (at least in the Overdeveloped World) it embraces hundreds of thousands of people and has considerable influence. In David Spangler's characteristic new age language: 'The Aquarian Cycle' is stimulating 'the emergence of a new kind of consciousness, an intuitive-mental awareness, attuned to a level of knowing and power unlimited by space and time'.[30]

Perhaps the most solid new age achievement has been the popularisation of a paradigm which challenges the assumptions of the scientistic industrial culture. (A paradigm is an historic mind-set of values, assumptions and ways of feeling and doing). New age writing commonly pairs off characteristics of these two paradigms, setting holistic and organismic perceptions of reality against reductive and mechanistic models of it. The feminine is paired against the masculine; the implicit and intuitive against the explicit and the rational; the fluid and dynamic against the fixed and static; the responsive against the imposed; thinking in terms of process against structural-functionalist thinking; the synthesising approach to problem solving against the analytical approach.

Since it is the mentality which is reflected in the mechanistic paradigm that has brought us to our present ecological and social dead-end, the popularisation of the organismic and holistic alternative is essential if we are to recover our balance and get to the root of our problems. The new values and perceptions are already at work in many different fields, from complementary healthcare to subatomic physics, and from holistic education to alternative Third World development strategies.

Unfortunately, in new age writing the two paradigms tend to be conceived ideologically. Each of the holistic attributes is set moralistically against its counterpart in the Baconian baddies' paradigm. The holistic paradigm does indeed manifest a higher level of consciousness than the reductionist, just as an organism is higher than a mechanism in the sense that it is more complex and evolved. But it is reductionism itself to conceive the pairs as dualistically exclusive, thereby making a mere half truth of the holistic paradigm. To claim, for example, that all things are one is no truer than to claim they are many. This is typical ideological polarisation: creating a dualism and identifying with this against that. As Ronald Laing puts it: 'It was all a machine yesterday; it is something like a hologram today. Who knows what intellectual rattle we shall be shaking tomorrow to calm the dread of the emptiness of our understanding?'.[31] Thus we disable helpful ideas because of our greater need of them as consolations or weapons.

The techno-scientific paradigm in fact epitomises a valuable and even essential level of consciousness, providing it is used appropriately and not as if it were exclusive truth (scientism). Even the construction of a new age chicken coop would benefit from a little Cartesian calculation.

The holistic paradigm, moreover, is not in itself 'spiritual'. It is no more than a conceptualisation, whereas spirituality implies a direct and unmediated encounter with reality. This occurs at the third level of consciousness, the so-called 'higher third' which subsumes both paradigms. Each of the opposed paradigm pairs manifests a whole but seemingly contradictory truth. The one is the many *and* the many are the one. And again, wholes can and cannot be reduced to their constituent parts. The higher third can only be made fully serviceable by being actualised at a higher level of consciousness, a 'spiritual' level at which paradox disappears, as a trick obscuring how things really are. The higher third is the simplest and most fundamental of spiritual doctrines. But it is not accessible by parroting a paradigm; mysticism is qualitatively different from simply acquiring a new world view. Knowing the recipe doesn't make you a cook; too many new agers may be mistaking the menu (and the accompanying floor show) for the meal.[32]

The actualisation of the higher third is most dramatically exemplified in a Gandhi-style nonviolent protest movement. Such a movement acknowledges a separateness of interest from that of the adversary in that it refuses to compromise fundamental principles and, if all else fails, is willing to enforce sanctions (non-cooperation, boycotts, obstruction, strikes and so on) against an obdurate adversary. At the same time it acknowledges its shared humanity with that adversary, avoids confrontational provocation, seeks to empathise, maintains honest communication, is willing to compromise and bargain on non-essentials, tries to resolve the conflict to some mutual advantage, and presents the adversary with a strong moral imperative. This is the sharp end of an engaged spirituality which seeks out the higher third beyond confrontational violence (which compounds the problem) or a false consensualism (which condones continuing social injustice or ecological abuse).

New agers also celebrate ideology's customary millenarian certainties about the new world just round the corner. It is as if, writes Patrick Rivers, 'some miraculous intervention will implant Earth awareness in our collective unconscious without our having to lift a finger to achieve it'.[33] An example of the more modest kind of annunciation is this from Guy Dauncey (with unintentional black humour in the tail); 'We are in the midst of an awesome awakening into some new kind of reality, of which we have but vaguely dreamed. We are on the verge of a whole new level of existence. In the process we have run into some massive problems . . . '[34]

However, new agers generally eschew the robust and aggressive antitheses in which ordinary ideologues rejoice. For does not the new age celebrate *unity* consciousness? And so, in its classic form, the new age movement simply denies the reality of 'the other side' and withdraws into subjective quietism. 'Let's change ourselves and we'll change the world' was the characteristic message from the 1990 Gothenburg new age conference. Beyond personal and lifestyle change and a fashionable and uncontroversial environmentalism, new agers typically show little concern about eco-socially exploitative and oppressive institutions and structures. They claim that we make our own reality and if we are unaware of the boundless love and well-being inherent in it then we are stuck in 'negativity', at 'the level of forms' (to which social action is relegated). There is really no such thing as right and wrong: only negative thoughts. If life seems to be treating you badly (perhaps terminally ill or trapped in poverty) this can only be a reflection of your 'victim consciousness'. The origins of personal and collective misfortune are to be found in our karma. New agers understand this to be an impersonal judgemental mechanism which rewards or punishes us according to our behaviour in previous lives. (It is noteworthy, however, that in Buddhism karma has no retributive significance, and refers simply to the inertia of rooted and habitual biographical and historical mental formations). In all of the foregoing psychotherapy has itself got a lot to answer for, as an incisive critique by James Hillman has demonstrated: 'Therapy introverts the emotions, calls fear "anxiety". You take it back, and you work on it inside yourself. You don't work psychologically on what the outrage is telling you about, [say] nuclear waste, or that homeless woman over there with the sores on her feet'.[35]

One of the more down-to-earth new age writers, J.L. Simmonds, does indeed acknowledge that two-thirds of the world's population 'are living more or less downtrodden lives', and that excitement about the forthcoming new age 'might seem cold comfort to someone languishing in a Central American prison or a woman on her own trying to raise two children on a subsistence salary'. However, 'the bottom line assertion of the new age is that things don't have to be as they are . . . Everyone who stirs or awakens spiritually alters the collective vibrational patterns of the planet, thereby lightening the intensity of the Earth trance with its coarser wavelengths . . . As the process continues it eventually reaches the point where it becomes difficult for anyone to remain asleep'.[36]

Since a socially engaged spirituality is at the heart of this book, it will be useful to pause here to explain how the classic, mainstream spiritual tradition contrasts with new age other-worldliness.

Out of reality we create our own experience of reality from out of our inner needs and fears (but with a lot of help from our social inheritance). Different people each 'make' something different of reality. Reality is thus paradoxical: we do and do not make it; it is given and yet it is not. As we 'cleanse the doors of perception' (as William Blake puts it) and begin to see reality in its own light and not in ours, it appears *more* vividly than previously, and we are *more* exposed to the pain of planetary existence. If we can stay with that pain and despair (and 'despair and empowerment' workshops are now available for activists) we begin to accept, and to see without self-obstruction, how it is. With this comes also, as Morris Berman explains:

> The ability to tolerate ambiguity, to hang out in a space of uncertainty without frantically searching for answers and explanations all the time. Installing a new paradigm in place of the old one, nailing down a new belief system as fast as the old one crumbles, will surely prove, a hundred years hence, to have been a big mistake. We did that before; why do it again?[37]

Wholehearted acceptance brings not passivity but empowerment. When we are at one with the situation rather than battling against it we are freed to respond to its requirements with the whole of our being. No longer impelled to cling to this as against that, we can deploy our emotional and intellectual resources as the situation demands and not as *we* need. This awareness can come of a sudden, sometimes when we have hit rock bottom. From Easterhouse, a huge squalid housing estate on the outskirts of Glasgow, Jeremy Seabrook reports the following example of despair and empowerment into the here and now of how it is:

Cathy McCormack, a passionate woman in her thirties, is committed to the kind of radical change which is believed, in more fashionable areas, to have been struck from the agenda. She speaks with an energy and authority which comes from having known despair during the seven years that she and Tony, her husband, have been out of work. 'I was so broken by it that I felt there was no point in living. I wanted to go to sleep and never wake up again. Then one day something happened. It was a kind of awakening; almost a spiritual experience.' Cathy realised that nothing was ever going to happen, that no one was going to rescue them. 'I understood that my life is here in this place, and no fantasy of escape would help. This is where the wains must grow up and make their lives; here we must survive or perish together.'[38]

Returning to new agers' subjective preoccupations, social context doubtless goes some way to explaining these. The affluent society has thrown open a whole enticing supermarket, culled from cultures worldwide, of 'ancient mysteries', 'secret teachings' and 'esoteric wisdom', painstakingly evolved over many centuries. These have been eagerly and undiscriminatingly appropriated, and unconsciously refashioned, by our speedy and spiritually unsophisticated culture. Thus, as well as being a movement of ideas, the new age is also a fashionable, self-conscious consumer culture among the white middle and upper classes of the most overdeveloped parts of the Overdeveloped World (California accounts for twelve per cent of even the United States' gross national product).

The new age has been packaged and promoted to support a thriving business sector, ranging from spiritual dentistry to deep caring real estate management. Business, at least, is excluded from the social quietism mentioned earlier, and a third or more of the pages of many new age magazines are full of advertisements for a bizarre range of products and services.

Life has become so well-provided, with so many conveniences, and so much historical and social cohesion has dropped out of it, that for many there is nothing left but a narcissistic personhood, stuck in an existential dead end and wondering where to go next. Such a self is quite relieved to be told by no less a new age authority than Marilyn Ferguson that 'the separate self is an illusion'. It is delighted to learn that (prepersonal) emotional release—masquerading as (transpersonal) 'liberation'—is not only OK but infinitely superior to intellectuality.[39] A whole range of burdensome problems, both public and private, can be dismissed as so much negativity and replaced by a new world of fascinating things to play with—earth mysteries, myths, magic, shamanism, astrology and, of course, the occult (with much confusion of spiritualism with spirituality). Too many new age centres purvey an all-singing, all-dancing, fast food spirituality which is superficial, self-centred and self indulgent. Kate Thomas, one of the growing number of seasoned new age critics, concludes that 'the new age entrepreneurs have demonstrated a preoccupation with nurturing the ego, not sublimating it . . . New age workshops and courses do not produce enlightenment, they predominantly produce fantasy, singularly resistant to self-discipline and self-analysis'.[40]

The conclusion of one of its most influential founders, David Spangler, is that 'the image of the New Age may well have died as a useful tool of the imagination for anyone seriously attempting to work with civilizational change and betterment . . . The vulgarization of the New Age indicates that the New Age is over . . . and that now is definitely the time for its degradation'.[41] But is it recyclable? For it is a diverse and contradictory phenomenon. It *has* enabled many to live more fulfilled lives, and it *does* include at least some well-evolved people dedicated to a profound and inclusive spirituality and to radical work for people and planet. Cannot at least parts of the movement be weaned away from consumerism to the ancient spiritualities of self-surrender and transcendent empowerment? Can significant elements of the new age become a resource for the radical green project?

Green spirituality and deep ecology

The impetus to develop a distinctive green spirituality comes in part from a reaction against much in the established world religions which is perceived as anthropocentric, socially regressive, oppressively hierarchical, dogmatic and punitively moralistic. The green new age response has been to turn to the older, biocentric, shamanic, feminist spiritualities. This is an important and valuable undertaking, but the reclamation of an earthed consciousness more remote from our high egoic culture than even the medieval mystical tradition or the oriental spiritualities is bound to be problematic. In the opinion of one critic (who has done his time in Tibetan and Korean monasteries) the assortment of earth and goddess cults, North American Indian lore, witchcraft, 'Ancient Mysteries', and bits of Buddhism, Taoism, Sufism and gnostic Christianity amounts to 'a confused mix of unrooted thoughts and unfocused feelings'. He concludes that 'if a spiritual dimension is truly fundamental to the green movement, as is fervently claimed, then spiritual truths need to be established with the same degree of critical rigour as the economic and ecological truths they are supposed to support'.[42]

A valuable point of entry to wider questions of green spirituality is provided by deep ecology. This maintains that non-human life has value in itself quite independent of its instrumental value (or otherwise) to human beings. In particular, specific life forms are enriched by ecological diversity, and humans have no right to reduce this except to satisfy vital needs. Such interference is at present excessive, and deep ecologists particularly emphasise the need to reduce human populations in the interests of other life forms. In John Seed's words, 'We are but a "plain member" of the biotic community [and] must come to understand that life forms do not constitute a pyramid with our species at the apex, but rather a circle where everything is connected to everything else'.[43] Deep ecologists are therefore critical of the anthropocentric attitude of all those who see man (it usually is 'man') as the lord of creation, whether as Christian steward, technological master, or benevolent conservationist. They would argue that such attitudes maintain our sense of separation (and ultimately our unease, fear and anger) from other beings, from the earth, and from our own bodies and 'unowned' parts of our minds.

Even as no more than an idea, deep ecology has great potential transformative power. It can help us to examine deeply ingrained mentalities, like seeing wilderness conservation as ultimately serving this, that or another *purpose*. However, intellectual acceptance of this idea is not enough; this knowledge must permeate us and become part of our identity. John Seed believes that humanity can only be saved by 'an incredible spiritual revolution, a new wave of consciousness that more or less sweeps through humanity in one generation . . . I believe that individuals can have the same incredible spiritual experiences through ecology and nature as they do through Christianity and Buddhism and so on'.[44] Some of the ways in which we can change our identity are indicated in a manual of practice by John Seed and other deep ecologists entitled *Thinking like a mountain: Towards a Council of all Beings*,[43] This sets out one or two day workshops enabling participants to become more deeply aware of their rage, helplessness and despair at what is happening to our planet and its non-human life forms, and ultimately to experience a profound sense of empowerment. Skilful use is made of rituals, drama, guided meditations, invocations, and body movements, drawing upon the earth wisdom of primal peoples to provide a rich and powerful experience.

Deep ecology is clearly an invaluable contributor to bringing about the shift in consciousness which will be essential to underpin the radical green transformation. Nevertheless there is a biocentric one-sidedness about it which limits its claim to be an *inclusive* spirituality and eco-social transformer.

In particular, the understandable concern to swing the pendulum strongly away from anthropocentrism has laid deep ecologists open to charges of being indifferent to global social injustice and even of being misanthropic authoritarians. These charges stem from the ecological egalitarianism in deep ecology which would accord the same value to parasites and malarial mosquitoes as to human beings. Everything has an 'equal right to live and blossom' (Arne Naess). Barry Commoner has argued that where an ecological perspective is not mediated by strong social concern and understanding it naturally tends to be politically authoritarian. He quotes Garrett Hardin as typical of this kind of thinking: 'How can we help a foreign country to escape over population? Clearly, the worst thing we can do is to send food'.[45] And deep ecology's most intemperate critic, social ecologist Murray Bookchin, charges that 'it has no real sense that our ecological problems have their ultimate roots in society and in social problems. It preaches a gospel of a kind of original sin that accuses a vague species called humanity, as though the people of color are equatable with whites, women with men, the Third World with the First, the rich with the poor, the exploited with the exploiters'.[46]

The underlying reason for deep ecology's biocentrism and failure to develop as a socially as well as ecologically informed spirituality is to be sought in its failure to come to terms with the central paradox around which all spirituality turns. It is that we are animals able to reflect on our finitude and fragility, and to be the embodiment of the 'higher third' in which the biocentric and the anthropocentric are not opposites but one and the same. All this appears to be lost on deep ecologists like John Seed: 'Human beings may have this consciousness and so on, but decomposing bacteria can take the detritus of things decaying and turn it into new life. Now that's a useful thing to do. But what use are human beings ?'.[47] Humankind does have a unique responsibility for the well-being of other creatures and for the whole ecosystem, yet is at the same time a dependent and integral part of that system. The all-inclusive spiritual project is to become fully human, which means to accept wholeheartedly the being separate *and* yet wholly at one with all phenomena; to be aware and responsible *and* yet at the same time a force of nature: in short, to transcend the human paradox. But usually out of root fear we cleave either to being one with the lords of creation or just to merging gratefully with the Council of All Beings.

The biocentrism of deep ecology is no more than an inversion of anthropocentrism. It has still to escape from the perennial ideological trap. Stephen Batchelor has observed that 'in the West we are still caught in a struggle between the theocentric and anthropocentric visions which some greens now seek to resolve by a notion of biocentrism. Such thoughts are alien to the Buddhist experience of reality which, if anything, has tended to be 'acentric'. For ultimately nothing in the universe deserves pride of place . . . Paradoxically, however, placing nothing at the centre is tantamount to placing everything at the centre'.[48] The one-sidedness of mainstream deep ecology has also been addressed by Warwick Fox, whose 'transpersonal ecology' refers to a sense of self which has become ecologically all-embracing.

Thus green spirituality may be directly inspired by deep ecology. Or it may draw upon the biocentric traditions of primal cultures. Or again, as we shall see in the next section, it may take the form of a corrective to the inherited anthropocentrism of the world religions.

If we are to be here and whole, we *do* need to be earthed, instead of minds dangling on the ends of our bodies or suspended in some romantic spiritual evasion. Apart from a few fortunate 'naturals', most of us have to work at learning how to let go, so that, as it were, the water can buoy us up, our feet are freed to find their way in the darkness across the boulder field, and the mountain lightly to lift our steps to her summit.

But there are different routes to the heart of the matter that lies beyond words. Some practice of green spirituality is one such path—though not in itself a destination. Another might be a devotional theistic path. My own has been a path of meditative enquiry into mind (see the Dogen quotation at the end of Chapter 7). All of these paths begin as partial views, with limitations as well as strengths. But as we work and evolve along these paths they begin to converge and to give a more complete, all-round view. Human and non-human become one; feminine and masculine are joined.

Thus the wayfarer who set out on a path of green spirituality will, so long as she does not cling to it, open fully to what it is to be uniquely human—in compassion, creativity, friendship, grief—as well as 'a plain member of the biotic community'. She will pass through the paradox of our animal humanity. Gary Snyder, referring to the need for a 'dialogue among all beings . . . towards a rhetoric of ecological relationships', emphasises that 'this is not to put down the human':

> The 'proper study of mankind' is what it means to be human. It's not enough to be shown in school that we are kin to all the rest: we have to feel it all the way through. Then we can be uniquely 'human' with no sense of special privilege . . . The Grizzlies or Whales or Rhesus monkeys or *Rattus* would infinitely prefer that humans (especially Euro-Americans) got to know *themselves* thoroughly before presuming to do Ursine or Cetacean research. When humans know

themselves, the rest of nature is right there. This is part of what Buddhists call the Dharma'.[49]

That, at least, has been my own experience in latter years, homesteading and politicking here at the head of Cwm Rheidol:

In the damp autumnal woods
The reek of my chain saw
Hangs in the still air.

Christian ecology

The world religions are being subjected to the same green clean-up as everything else. Unrepentant anthropocentrists are, however, still numerous and in high places. Thus Cardinal John O'Connor of New York thought it fit to celebrate Earth Day 1990 with a homily denouncing all this attention to 'snails and whales': 'The earth exists for the human person and not vice versa and is God-given for our use'.[50]

Of the spate of new books demonstrating the inherent greenness of Christianity, some—like Ian Bradley's *God is green*[51] and Tim Cooper's *Green Christianity*[52]—amount rather to special pleading than deep questioning. The troublesome passages in Genesis have been repackaged, and the image of the patriarchal creator who made man in His own image (and woman as an afterthought) has been subjected to extensive damage limitation. In such books there is now a general presumption that, in Tim Cooper's words, 'we are to be caretakers of the "Earth community" rather than autocratic rulers. Our authority should be exercised with passion and concern for future generations'. Although such assurances are welcome, they do not go to the heart of the anthropocentric/biocentric dilemma discussed in the previous chapter. As Matthew Fox observes, 'the theology of stewardship builds a morality instead of a mysticism. You cannot really move people with morality—you can only keep them in check. Stewardship is, by definition, dualistic, as if God were an absentee landlord and humans were serfs hired to do the divine work'.[53]

Although anthropocentrism has been dominant throughout the history of Christianity, there have also been movements and individuals bearing witness to an alternative perception and now reclaimed by a contemporary Christianity which celebrates ecological harmony. There is, for example, the current upsurge of interest in a down-to-earth Celtic spirituality, which comes from the heart of lives lived quite naturally in a state of prayer, in small communities in close communion with nature wherein God's *friendship* is everywhere manifest. In the Outer Hebrides little more than a hundred years ago a woman recalled how, at the start of each day, 'my mother would be asking us to sing our morning song to God down in the back-house, as Mary's lark was singing it up in the clouds and as Christ's mavis was singing it yonder in the tree, giving glory to the God of the creatures for the repose of the night, for the light of the day, and for the joy of life'.[54] However, it is only necessary to read the Irish penitentials to dispel any illusion that this Celtic tradition—harsh yet joyful, ascetic yet flowing—might be serviceable as some cuddly new age Christianity.

Similarly the Franciscan tradition, indwelling with creatures and plants, wind and rain, Brother Sun and Sister Moon, has long provided a refreshing alternative which, unlike Celtic Christianity, has managed to survive within the bounds of orthodoxy. And particularly inspiring for our own time has been the reclaiming of the mystical tradition of the early middle ages in figures like Hildegard of Bingen and of the later spiritual flowering in the crisis-torn fourteenth century, when our high egoic culture was coming to birth, in mystics like Eckhart.

In the twentieth century, Teilhard de Chardin, a towering figure from out of the Darwinian revolution, has exercised a powerful influence on green Christians like Sean McDonagh.[55] Teilhard saw in evolution a 'cosmogenesis' wherein increasing complexity progressively dissolves the distinction between matter and spirit. This yearning and striving evolution is a pre-ordained expression of divine purpose, heading towards the 'omega point' where love will be all. Teilhard died in 1955, and his Darwinian optimism about God working His purpose out to some evolutionary apotheosis has been overtaken by the prospect of an eco-Armageddon. Even McDonagh admits to Teilhard's 'somewhat uncritical belief in the goodness and inevitability of technological progress'.[56]

Periodically theology is revitalised by spiritual transfusions from out of the experience of historic new situations. Thus liberation theology developed in response to oppression and resistance in the Third World, and creation theology (which claims to be inclusive of the whole previous alternative tradition) has been brought to birth by the ecological crisis.

Five years ago Kenneth Leech felt able to maintain that 'many Christians would be able to agree that any theology which is indifferent to the theme of liberation is not a Christian theology'.[57] In refreshing contrast to much green thinking, Christian ecology is much less likely to omit the 'social environment'. The flavour of liberation theology is well conveyed by the following, from two of its best known exponents:

> Underlying liberation theology is a prophetic and comradely commitment to the life, cause and struggle of these millions of

debased and marginalised human beings, a commitment to ending this historical-social inequality . . . In this field, more than in others, it is vital to move beyond a merely intellectual approach that is content with comprehending theology through its purely intellectual aspects . . . We have to work our way into a more biblical frame of reference, where 'knowing' implies loving, letting oneself become involved, body and soul, communing wholly.[58]

In the writing of Aloysius Pieris, Helder Camara, Ernesto Cardenal and others, liberation theology is now reaching out beyond its former anthropocentric and patriarchal limitations. However, as Matthew Fox has demonstrated, the Overdeveloped World, whilst drawing upon liberation theology, needs to develop its own equivalent (which Fox identifies as creation spirituality).[59]

Today the different threads in the radical alternative Christian tradition are being drawn together, and most notably in the creation-centred spirituality of Thomas Berry and Matthew Fox. Fox is a Dominican scholar and imaginative populariser who had the distinction of being silenced for a year at the request of the Pope. He rejects the emphasis which many Christian greens give to the Fall as the beginning of humankind's destructive history, and charges that ninety-five per cent of the attention of both Catholic and Protestant churches has been focused upon 'an exaggerated doctrine of original sin [which] divides and therefore conquers, pitting one's thoughts against one's feelings, one's body against one's spirit, one's political vocation against one's personal needs'.[60] This has created a bleak, punitive religious tradition and provided theological leverage for all manner of oppression and repression: 'It has gotten us . . . into sexism, militarism, racism, genocide against native peoples, biocide, consumerist capitalism and violent communism. I believe it is time to choose another path'.[61]

For Fox the Fall/Redemption emphasis is the most destructive manifestation of a whole dualistic theology 'which has haunted us for 300 to 400 years in the West, and it basically says that I'm here and God is somewhere else, and prayer is about getting to God or getting God here. Carl Jung said there are two ways to lose your soul, and one is to worship a God outside of you'.[61] As the title of his first bestseller *Original blessing* indicates, Fox invites us to rejoice in the open, innocent experience of the cosmos, wherein the preoccupation of human sinfulness gives way to the celebration of divine grace, and suffering is not the wages of sin but the birth pangs of a new creation. And *Original blessing* is, not least, a brilliant but extravagant bringing together of many contributory currents—medieval mysticism, Celtic spirituality, feminist spirituality, Zen and Sufism, and much else.

Matthew Fox has become something of a cult figure and the founder of a movement with some uneasy ideological overtones. Although his creation-centred theology is free of biocentrism, in pitting it against the Fall/Redemption polarity Fox has created his own dualism, and a skewed theology. In *Original blessing* are lists of goodies and baddies (St Augustine & Co), opposed paradigmic columns, and little attempt to soften the polarisation by elaborating the underlying complexities. Moreover, Fox is so busy throwing a party to celebrate that we all do indeed have God's grace, the Buddha nature, Original Innocence, or whatever, that he fails *equally* to illuminate the tragicomedy of a human condition which deceives us into being so much less than what we really are.

There are some curious omissions from the dazzling guest list at the end of *Original blessing*. I refer to the radical, post-dogmatic theology which originated with Kierkegaard a hundred and fifty years ago and which has Paul Tillich and Dietrich Bonhoeffer among its best known exponents. This is relevant here for two reasons.

First, from an existential starting point it continues a perennial spiritual tradition of doubt, questioning, meditation, despair and revelation. Holding the balance between our fallen condition and our original blessing, it urges us to take heart, keep faith, and persevere with our life's work on the human riddle (in whatever form it may take for each of us), with the ultimate promise of realising our full human potential, in both the personal and the planetary sense. In meditative terms the nature of this work has been described as follows by the German poet Rainer Maria Rilke:

> PATIENCE. To let each impression, each kernel of feeling, to come to completion wholly in itself, in the dark, in the inexpressible, the unconscious, beyond the grasp of your own intelligence, and to await with deep humility and patience the birth hour of a new clarity. . .
> Be patient towards all that is unresolved in your heart and try to love the questions themselves, like locked rooms or books written in an unknown script. Do not seek the answers, which cannot be given to you now because you would not know how to live them . . . Live the *questions* now.[62]

This is not only a meditative path, however, and clarity can unfold no less through action that is meditatively informed, as Bonhoeffer demonstrated throughout his life and in his death at the hands of the Nazis.

In the second place, this is a Christian agnosticism which could be accessible to many radical greens who are on the edge of Christianity and attracted thither. It was first popularised in Britain in the 1960s by Bishop John Robinson, and subsequently kept in the public view by Don Cupitt and David Jenkins, Bishop of Durham. They see in Christianity a body of faith, guidelines, myths and ritual enabling us to open more fully to the paradox of human existence and to the suffering experienced by humankind and the whole of creation. They endeavour to interpret the faith in terms of experience and action rather than theological doctrines and cosmological dogma. Thus Bonhoeffer sought 'to live before God as if God did not exist'.

Clearly, Christian ecology offers rich spiritual resources for the achievement of the radical green project, and particularly if bridges of some kind could be extended to the secular, humanistic constituency. But in the excitement of affirmation and celebration it is as well to recall Thomas Merton's reminder:

> [Although] action and contemplation are fused into one entity by the love of God and our brother in Christ . . . the trouble is that if prayer itself is not deep, powerful and pure and filled at all times with the spirit of contemplation [i.e. meditation], Christian action will never really reach this high level.[63]

16 Feminising the future

FEMINISM has much in common with other mass social protest movements, all of which are having to come to terms with the ecological crisis and make some kind of response to the green movement. In turn, all are formative influences upon it. And feminism, whilst providing a different and immensely valuable way of understanding the world, can, like other 'isms', solidify into aggressive and deeply divisive ideology, and the sole organising principle whereby everything else is to be explained.

The various currents in feminism feed successively into one another, with a cumulative relevance to the feminist green project.

Liberal feminism is the feminism of 'women's lib' and the Equal Opportunities Commission. It is a pragmatic movement to create conditions which will enable women to move out of the traditional roles to which they have been confined. It campaigns, therefore, for equal education and training opportunities, for the removal of discrimination against women in employment, for ready access to abortion, for free nursery facilities for all, and so on.

Socialist (or Marxist) feminism offers an historical analysis of the social construction of women's oppression (patriarchy). It argues that this, like other similar forms of oppression, is maintained by the creation of a 'false consciousness' whereby the oppressed accept or even deny their oppression. For Marxist feminism gender is itself a social construction, beyond biology, with the assumption that the discriminative differentiation between the sexes can be ironed out by radical social engineering which destroys patriarchy and the structures on which it depends. Exclusive forms of liberal and socialist feminism both, therefore, exemplify the 'social fallacy' described in Chapter 7.

Thirdly, there is a radical (or separatist) feminism. This exalts all that is female, celebrates sisterhood, seeks to empower women as women, and tends to devalue all that is male. At its best it is a powerful force for positive discrimination and for establishing the presence of the feminine in the countless areas of human existence where it has been suppressed, distorted, ignored and driven underground. At its worst it is a militant ideology which is the mirror image of that patriarchy which it sees as the source of all evil.

In the opening chapter of this book we saw how the rise of the first great warrior civilisations was associated with the emergence of a new, self-conscious individualism from out of the earthbound era of the great mother. But with this new-found freedom came a new existential dread and an overpowering need to fortify the vulnerable ego. There was thus psychic need as well as techno-social possibility for the development of the masculine faculties of aggression, control, dominion, conceptualisation and formal organisation. The ultimate response to the new-found dread was the 'god project'—the quest for immortality by man created by God in His own image, beyond the ancient flow of coming to be and passing away, and tearing apart the unities of the old ecologically founded religion.

This development of masculine qualities in the new high-profile ego was not paralleled by, and integrated with, a corresponding emergent female side of personality. Such a development was both (subjectively) repressed within the male psyche and (objectively) was blocked by the oppression of the female sex, confined still to the role of earth mother and denied that of 'goddess' challenging the new machismo deity. There is much mythic evidence of how strong was the patriarchal fear lest the dark female forces of birth, death, chaos and desire should swallow up the fragile, new-born sense of identity.

The process of patriarchal dominance was completed in the Europe of the high egoic era (AD 1500 onwards), climaxing in the sixteenth- and seventeenth-century witch hunts in which hundreds of thousands of women perished. A strongly masculine mechanistic rationality triumphed as scientific truth, and protestantism and capitalism between them dissolved the medieval institutions and beliefs which had to some extent aimed to mediate and soften man's oppression of man, of woman, and of mother earth, and his repression of rejected parts of his own psyche. Upon women men projected all the feared and unlived parts of their being, making of her the temptress, the frivolous, irrational and emotional creature. At the same time women were required to support a whole range of male inadequacies, nurturing and mothering generation after generation of Peter Pans and Christopher Robins.

For 'nature feminists' the feminist project is the recovery of the ancient earth mother tradition from subsequent patriarchal distortions and diminutions. Some feminists have pointed out, however, that such a feminism emphasises a continuing and immutable dualism of separate and exclusive male and female roles, thereby emphasising, instead of healing, the split between nature and culture.

This brings us to post-feminism (also more accurately termed 'cultural feminism'). In the first place, this shares the radical feminist concern to recover the feminine (though not only for women, but ultimately for men also). In place of earth mother regression, commitment is to the (historically blocked) 'goddess project', that is to say, the development of a mature, self-conscious feminine principle, different but no less evolved than its masculine counterpart.

Goddess spirituality is a movement of renewal which celebrates female and bodily affinity with nature. It draws attention to the crucial importance of the feminine in any spirituality, green or otherwise. Its myths, symbolism and ritual may be derived from whatever is recoverable from the goddess religions of Crete and other lost civilisations, or from the still living cultures of primal peoples, or from submerged but persistent cults like European witchcraft. Its flavour is splendidly conveyed in the following passage by Charlene Spretnak:

> When woman—who has been told by the patriarchal culture that female power is somewhat shameful, dirty, and downright dangerous if unrestrained—immerses herself in sacred space where various manifestations of the Goddess bring forth the Earthbody from the spinning void . . . then the woman's possibilities are evoked with astoundingly joyous intensity. *She* will create the ongoing completion of each mythic fragment. *She* is in and of the Goddess. *She* will body the myth with her own totemic being. *She* is the cosmic form of waxing, fullness, waning; virgin, mature creator, wise crone. She cannot be negated ever again. Her roots are too deep—and they are everywhere.[64]

But beyond the full development of the feminine principle (and depending upon it) lies a second concern of post-feminism, which is the balanced integration of male and female qualities in both women *and* men. This I shall call the androgyny project, whilst making it clear that this does not necessarily imply any muting and merging of female and male characteristics but rather a dialectical sharing and balance, both playful and challenging. Following Carolyn Heilbrunn's definition, androgyny is understood here to be 'a condition under which the characteristics of the sexes, and the human impulses expressed by men and women, are not rigidly assigned . . . . Androgyny suggests a spirit of reconciliation between the sexes; it suggests, further, a full range of experience open to individuals who may, as women, be aggressive, as men, tender'.[65]

Like other facets of psycho-spiritual empowerment this requires a totally open and accepting investigation of who we are. Christina Feldman, a Buddhist meditation teacher and feminist, explains:

> We need to be strong not so we can be invulnerable, but so we can
> be vulnerable . . . Both strength and vulnerability are essential ingre-
> dients in coming to inner wholeness, in discovering freedom without
> fear. In Western culture, women learn to display our vulnerability in
> negative dependency, in helplessness and paralysis. Because these
> very expressions of vulnerability spell danger to us, we learn to call
> vulnerability weakness. We have learnt to misname vulnerability and
> devalue this very quality which is so essential to a life of inter-
> connectedness and sensitivity.[66]

Such empowerment is freedom from over-dependence on either the
male or female sides of our nature. And it is freedom from ideology and
the projection of blame and anger on the other sex, which wastes time and
energy and creates alienation and confusion. It brings freedom and clarity
in breaking the 'mind forg'd manacles' of patriarchy which bind *both* sexes
and for dissolving the social culture and structures which affirm it.

The corresponding male project similarly involves both the recovery
and integration of female qualities and freeing the male qualities from
patriarchal distortion. Specifically, it means men freeing themselves of
brittle, competitive, achievement-hungry, workaholic ways of living, and
of their use of women to compensate for the rejected and underdeveloped
parts of themselves. It means opening to deeper awareness of the violent
and aggressive masculine streak, instead of being either locked into it (hard
macho man) or evading and denying it (soft wimpish man). The men's
movement which has appeared in recent years is about developing this
masculine awareness (which can be a source of positive and creative
energy), reinforcing gestalt therapy with helpful myth.

Edward Whitmont has written of the male project in a passage which
strikingly parallels the words of Christina Feldman, illustrating the conver-
gence of the masculine and feminine in the classic spiritual perspective.
What is required of men is the courage

> To let go of their firm ego position over self and others . . . They will
> have to learn a measure of 'letting be'. This is essential if they are to
> become genuinely affirming of what they really are, rather than what
> they wish to be. This requires a new type of courage: namely to live
> not only with strength but with vulnerability . . . That means
> mustering the courage to enter the abyss by allowing oneself to be
> enveloped, temporarily, by the chaos of subjectivity, the old enemy.
> It means to lose oneself in order to find oneself eventually.[67]

Fundamental to this book is the conviction that the immense human revolution required to overcome the planetary crisis will only be practicable if facilitated by a significant psycho-spiritual shift, implying a change in the general level of consciousness. The androgyny project is one facet of this transformative endeavour.

Feminists differ about the nature and desirability of ecofeminism, which seeks to integrate the feminist and radical green perspectives, and whose most all enveloping expression is goddess spirituality. Most would agree, however, that there is a relationship of some kind between the destruction of nature and the oppression of women, and that these two phenomena can be mutually informing. For some the ecocrisis is just one more indictment of patriarchy, with its alienation from nature and its technocratic fascination. Other ecofeminists make wider connections, as illustrated by these two quotations from Rosemary Reuther:

> We cannot criticise the hierarchy of male over female without ultimately criticising and overcoming the hierarchy of human over nature'.[68]

> Women must see that there can be no liberation for them and no solution to the ecological crisis within a society whose fundamental model of relationships continues to be one of domination. They must unite the demands of the women's movement with those of the ecological movement to envision a radical reshaping of the basic socio-economic relations and the underlying values of society.[69]

Similarly, Sheila Collins argues that 'racism, sexism, class exploitation and ecological destruction are the four interlocking pillars upon which the structure of patriarchy rests'.[70] And other feminists, like Karen Warren, have pushed the argument to its logical conclusion, for an integrative 'transformative feminism' which 'ties the liberation of women to the elimination of all systems of oppression'.[71]

Once oppression is generalised thus, the way is open to examining its roots in the human condition itself, and extending the analysis to an understanding of social processes and structures as a response to that human predicament. And the most common characteristic of those processes is divisiveness, oppression and exploitation by gender, by class, by race, by nationality, and by species. There has been a lot of special pleading and ideological jostling to explain the world from the exclusive standpoint of just one or other of these forms of oppression. But, like the rest, patriarchy is not a force in itself, but one facet of an ultimately *personally rooted* dynamic of oppression as seen from a particular experience of that oppression—that of gender. Nevertheless it is also true that the personal insight and the social analysis of gender, in both its oppressive and liberative aspects, *is* of especial importance because its roots go so deep into the psyche. Hence it has a profound potential contribution to make as a personal and eco-social transformer. The following observations by Alain Touraine were made in a socialist context but they are no less relevant to our present radical green project:

> The women's movement is a movement of liberation not only for women, but of men by women . . . Only women have preserved those personal qualities which male domination has crushed out of men. Since they have been completely excluded from political and military power, women have succeeded in maintaining a capacity for affective relations from which men have been estranged by the structures of power—or have estranged themselves to serve the structures.[72]

Radical green policies have a strong 'women's rights' slant. And in ecotopia a basic income for all would give personal economic independence to women. Recognition of the true economic and social value of child-rearing, housekeeping, and caring for the old and infirm would be accompanied by changing patterns of work (part-time, job share, producer co-operatives) which would give both sexes greater flexibility in lifestyle and life planning.

In radical green politics positive discriminatory measures have, arguably, more often been introduced to give women greater power and representation than is usual in 'grey' political circles. However, the long history of equal opportunities policies has demonstrated that formal changes in public policy, structures and institutions fall far short of expectations in the absence of a strong feminisation of the social (and organisational) culture itself to redress the balance against dominant male values. This is not just a question of social justice. To come to terms with the social and ecological crises, to build the foundations of a socially and ecologically harmonious conserver society, all require a strong expression of female values, ranging from public policy to the daily norms by which people relate to one another. For example, from both women and men in our politics we need much more of the female connective and holistic kind of thinking and feeling, particularly in developing the spirit of mutuality, conflict resolution and consensus building without which no effective radical green counter-culture can make headway.

What is most disappointing about virtually all the strands of the radical green alternative which we have been examining is the failure to make any significant start with the work of feminising the prevailing norms and values, and still less of trying to initiate the androgyny project in some practical sense. Notwithstanding good intentions, typical green politics are hardly less grey and masculine in style than those of the 'grey parties' themselves. There is little commitment to workshop activity (separately and together) and to procedures, guidelines and time allocation which could enable men and women to become more aware of gender roles, and to internalise and balance their feminine/masculine qualities.

In short, feminisation and the androgyny project constitute an important but neglected sector of the inner and the outer work without which there can be no hope for a radical green future.

17 Nationality, community and the periphery

SO FAR the different strands of green radicalism have been comparatively easy to identify. However, this chapter is about more than just splicing a final eco-nationalist strand into our radical green rope. The investigation of nationality brings out also the concepts of *the periphery* and of *community,* which are additional contributory ideas for developing a green politics.

Nationalism, nation-states and 'small peoples'

Definitions of nationhood are notoriously elusive and exceptions can be found to almost every rule—ethnic, linguistic, cultural and so on. 'Pam fod eira yn wyn?' ('Why is the snow white?') sings Welsh nationalist pop star Dafydd Ieuan. Moreover definitions of small nations like Catalunya and Croatia shade off into those of 'historic regions' and culturally distinct 'small peoples', like Corsicans, Flemings, Frieslanders and Galicians.

In Europe, from the fifteenth century onwards, certain rulers with the advantages of geography and an effective army, treasury and bureaucracy, subordinated first their neighbours and then the small nations beyond. The former Counts of Paris, for example, acquired Provence, Brittany, northern Catalunya and Alsace. Republican France became the classic example of these unitary 'nation-states', with the Third Reich as the most extreme manifestation. The European nation-states went on to destroy as much as they could of the world's ancient national cultures, and to precipitate two world wars. The 'empty' continents were settled as white federal nation-states.

After the first world war many small nations emerged as independent states from the ruins of the ramshackle Austro-Hungarian and Ottoman empires. For over seventy years the communists saved the Russian Empire from the same fate by creating a bizarre variant. They also gave a further lease of life to a Great Power fabrication called Yugoslavia.

Trying to keep the lid on with bigger national or supranational structures has always failed eventually. One of the most remarkable historical phenomena is the resurgent resilience of small nations concreted over for centuries by the so-called nation-states. Bohemian independence was extinguished at the battle of the White Mountain in 1620 only to re-emerge three hundred years later (with Slovakia insecurely tacked on) with the proclamation of the Czechoslovak Republic. The three tiny Baltic nations, ravaged by powerful neighbours since the time of the Teutonic knights, enjoyed only a brief twenty years of independence (1921-41) yet fifty years later they have again won their freedom.

The postmodern solution is to allow the attractions of an increasingly undiversified consumer culture quietly to flatten obtrusive national identities. Whether in Welsh Wales or tribal Amazonia, it is amazing what a dual carriageway driven into the heartlands can do in the name of progress and prosperity. The problem is that *that* final solution to the awkward 'national question' is ultimately not ecologically sustainable, which is another good reason for attempting to derail it.

Like socialism, feminism and other 'isms', nationalism offers a social outlet for a whole fistful of half buried personal fear and aggressiveness, as well as for rage, rage, rage against against centuries of oppression and exploitation. Nationalism, whether big or small, can be heady and bloody-minded stuff, whether in two world wars or the more modest carnage in Northern Ireland, Sri Lanka, Bosnia or Azerbaijan. In Eastern Europe national resurgence has awakened dark, ancient myths of land, blood and folk. For nostalgic Russians it is 'Orthodoxy, Autocracy, and Nationality'. This is ethnic nationalism, exclusive and 'cleansing' of all that is other. It contrasts with the inclusive, cultural nationalism, which we need in order fully to celebrate our humanity, to mediate our fellowship as global citizens, and to assist our ecological survival. Notwithstanding the myths of ethnic purity, nations are continually remaking and redefining themselves, both in the perception of their members and through the assimilation of successive waves of incomers. 'Where you're going now is more important than where you've come from,' was the welcome given to incomers by Welsh nationalist leader Dafydd Elis Thomas.

The problem is how to set limits so that more powerful and intrusive social cultures do not overwhelm small nations, destroying their identity and the ecological and community values traditionally tied up with it. Thus, in Wales, the problem arises in miniature whenever a monoglot English person joins the conversation of two or three Welsh speakers. The language has to change to English: a minute but symbolic setback for the rich diversity of human cultural ecology. To learn the language of a small and threatened people is an ecological as well as a political act.

The nationalism of distinctive cultural identity is evidently among the most persistent and indestructible of social phenomena. It is not going to go away. *And undoubtedly its future will need to be increasingly a confederal one,* rather than a replication of either the bloody history of the nation-states and their empires or of Balkan-style 'ethnic cleansing'.

The emergence of the European Community has marked the beginning of the decline of the nation-states and the much less assured rise of eighteen or more small West European nations and historic peoples. (One in six of the Community's citizens speak a language other than the main official language of their state). The Council of Europe's definition would give seventy-eight regions with elected authorities (excluding the UK), each region defined as 'a territory which constitutes from a geographical point of view a clear-cut entity whose population possesses certain shared features and wishes to safeguard the resulting specific identity and develop it with the object of stimulating cultural, social and political progress'. Under the Maastricht Treaty a Committee of the Regions is to be established which could become an embryonic upper chamber of the European Parliament. Its continental membership will be elected representatives from the various regional parliaments and assemblies.

By the end of 1989 the European Parliament was calling for the formation of powerful regional governments, which would be able to bypass the state governments altogether and negotiate directly with Community institutions and with one another. This is already happening. The German Land of Baden-Württemberg, for example, has forged economic, technological and cultural links with Catalunya, Lombardy, Rhone-Alpes and Wales, as a counterweight to the London-Paris-Berlin axis. How long will it be before Yorkshire is able to join in?

Such developments are largely invisible from London, where the question is reduced to whether or not 'we' should go into 'Europe'. For Scotland in the 1990s a legislative parliament now seems inevitable, by one means or another. A Welsh equivalent would certainly follow, and Northern Ireland would surely also be affected. There is thus the prospect of a constitutional crisis, perhaps provoked by some convulsion in UK politics, which could leave the English (and their regions) alone at last to discover who they really are. It is not only Eastern Europeans who are destined to live in interesting times . . .

Radical greens must surely see these as significant achievements and prospects, in view of the importance they attach to the creation of small, autonomous economic and political units with their claimed potential for ecological harmony and social justice. And in 1984 the resurgent

European Green Parties did indeed come up with a *Joint Declaration* which included the following:

> The diversity of its cultures, of its peoples and regions, is one of Europe's greatest assets, to be conserved and developed for the benefit of every European; true sovereignty can only come from a federal structure which takes that diversity into account. Such a structure, which should ultimately consist of regions rather than nation-states, must also be established in a way that respects the dignity and responsibility of all citizens: political, social and economic decisions must be taken by those who have to bear the consequences of them.[73]

Individualism and the nation-state versus community

For over two hundred years the nation-states evolved a concept of republican citizenship, expressed in a range of civil values and principles. This has been spread over much of the globe as a theoretical political and constitutional norm, however much dishonoured in practice. And since it has been substantially inherited by green and other radicals it is worth close examination here.

At the heart of the American and French revolutions was a rationalistic individualism which was part of the more general triumph of reason and order over blind nature and humankind's dark and disorderly past. The latter included a communal or community tradition expressed in a patchwork of small and relatively autonomous peoples and enclaves. But it was self-evident to enlightened liberals like John Stuart Mill that 'nobody can suppose that it is not more beneficial for a Breton or a Basque of French Navarre to be . . . admitted on equal terms to all the privileges of French citizenship . . . than to sulk on his own rocks, the half-savage relic of past times, revolving in his own little mental orbit . . . The same remark applies to the Welshman or the Scottish Highlander'.[74]

By 1887 it was possible for a sociologist, Ferdinand Tönnies,[75] to distinguish between the modern, rational-functionalist *gesellschaft* civil culture and the traditional *gemeinschaft* community culture.

Liberal constitution-making and radical utopias have a Cartesian abstraction about them. This contrasts with the organic, pragmatic, and evolutionary character of community. And whereas the former at best acknowledges religion as an embellishment, the latter is ingrained with ancient spiritualities.

Modern civil society is peopled by 'individuals' who exercise a variety of abstract rights (to representative government, for example), whose private life is their own business, but whose public responsibilities are impersonally regulated by the workplace, the market and the state. In the communal tradition individual identity is much more defined by 'given' membership of family, community, church and other inclusive institutions. Reciprocal rights and responsibilities go with the membership. Community norms and values will be so strongly internalised that sanctions to enforce them may rarely be necessary. Satisfaction comes from belongingness and the respected discharge of one's responsibilities rather than from achievement or acquisitiveness on one's own terms.

Community adapts and accommodates to its own accumulated anomalies and contradictions and even values their antiquity. This is incomprehensible to the rational-functional mentality, where officials value uniformity and consistency, business people demand 'a level playing field', and intellectuals look forward to a global society of individuals freed at last from the dangers and inconveniences of nationality, a Babel of small languages, and irrational notions in general.

Community works not through impersonal contract but through shared assumptions and well-rooted mutuality. Newcomers to Wales, for example, grow restive over 'the socialising' and impatient to get on with 'the business'. But if the first is well-founded, the second follows naturally.

Community lives at home in history, of which the future is no more than a continuation, instead of history being what progress has left behind. In terms of environment and resources, the community economy is cyclical and perennial rather than linear and quinquennial. It values making an appropriate living rather than making as much money as possible from whatever opportunity offers. It values thrift, prudence and moderation within time honoured ecological and economic frameworks. And something of all this still thrives among the small nations and peoples of the periphery—all those 'backwaters' where the solvent of industrialism is still relatively weak.

Radical green politics uneasily bestrides these two traditions. There is explicit recognition that an ecologically and socially harmonious society will need to adopt many communalist values in order to survive. There is the vision of a decentralised society of autonomous communities. And yet much radical green discourse remains implicitly in the enlightenment tradition of rational-functionalist individualism, with the tendency to see the older tradition through a romantic veneer.

A steady-state economy cannot exist without a whole steady state culture to support it. We may be able to abandon affluence but find it hard to discard some of the high egoic baggage which we had previously assumed to be green enough to take with us. Charlene Spretnak has warned of 'an individual-liberationist stance' which 'has little use for the traditional institutions that further human bonding—the family, the church or synagogue, community groups, ethnic associations'.[76] Good resolutions, the 'adoption' of new values, and the erection of structures prefigured in green manifestoes will not be enough to still the momentum of our volatile and restless individualism. Part of the answer will certainly lie in shaping a day-to-day culture which has enough steady-state communalism about it, but with a sufficiently strong blend of modern 'civil society' to enable the best of liberal individualism to flourish (a theme to which I shall return in Part V).

We shall also need to beware of making a romantic fetish of community, ignoring the pettiness, intolerance and personal invasiveness which it can conceal. If we can cultivate the self awareness described in the last chapter of this book we shall be able to see more clearly when rational responses and functional solutions are appropriate. We shall be able to distinguish between an individualism which which alienates both self and others and the bountiful humanism which we need to cherish. Charlene Spretnak concludes that 'what we need now is the maturity to value freedom and tradition, the individual and community, science and nature, men and women'. And in the best of the national movements this radical conservatism is warmly affirmed.

The relevance of bioregionalism

Bioregionalism is a North American green movement which, according to its 1985 Congress, 'seeks to recreate a widely shared sense of regional identity founded upon a renewed critical awareness of, and respect for, our natural ecological communities' (as defined by watersheds and other physical features and distribution of soil types and flora and fauna). It is very much an American perspective founded on what is, by European standards, an historically emptied landscape. The original inhabitants of which it was emptied can now be culturally reclaimed only marginally and inspirationally. The settlers imposed a homogeneous and alien culture, their boundaries cutting straight lines across the topographical features of huge and varied landscapes.

With so little solid history, this American ecocentricity makes good sense. But applied to Europe, where ecological patterns have been modified by layer upon layer of political and economic history, a hamfisted bioregionalism is clearly out of place. Obvious examples are Catalunya and Euskadi (the Basque country) each of which retains a strong sense of identity even though they bestride the Pyrenees and have been partitioned for centuries between two nation-states.

This kind of biocentrism has sometimes been linked with an economic rationality which has ruled out of order, as economically unsustainable, small nations which have insisted on their independence regardless of geographical inconvenience. Arguments of this kind have been used against the Baltic states, notwithstanding their impressive economic achievements during their period of independence between the two world wars.

In short, for 'old' countries like those of Europe an exclusively biocentric regionalism will commonly be found to go too much against the grain of history, language and ethnicity. But if sensitively applied bioregionalism certainly is a criterion which should be taken into account.

Green politics and the periphery

In an earlier chapter we noted how superindustrialism increasingly concentrates power at its metropolitan centres, creating internal as well as overseas colonies on the periphery, impoverished and powerless, dependent and marginalised.

The centre-periphery configuration takes many different forms. At one extreme the people of the periphery may suffer genocide and cultural burial under massive in-migration, with wholesale stripping of their assets down to the bare geology (as with Tibet under Chinese rule). At the other extreme are picturesque commuter villages in the metropolitan heartlands (like London's 'Home Counties') which have been totally destroyed as living communities. Typical centre/periphery examples are: industrialised world/primal, indigenous peoples; Overdeveloped World/Third World; Western Europe/Eastern Europe; Southeast England/West Wales; Rome and Lombardy/Sicily and Sardinia; Turkey/Kurdistan; Switzerland/Turkey ('guest workers').

Elements of the periphery can be found in the metropolitan urban areas themselves, in alienated ethnic and traditional working class communities. There is a community vitality here which is very relevant to the shaping of the radical culture discussed later in this book.

The ultimately marginalised are people 'displaced' and 'redundant' or 'stateless' as a consequence of political, economic, or ethnic circumstance. These include the surviving indigenous, tribal peoples. They represent our primal human cultures, and yet throughout the world they are threatened with extinction.

Some peripheral areas have suffered economic decline due to the collapse of local industries and the exhaustion of minerals, soil and other resources. Produce and raw materials are sucked into the metropolitan centres and returned as value-added goods through towns that have been reduced to mere service and distribution centres. Local people are obliged to seek work in the conurbations, and those who remain suffer low pay, high unemployment and social deprivation (with dependency-inducing handouts). Peripheral regions that remain 'unspoilt' become metropolitan playgrounds. Mass tourism, second homes and preservation orders make local people strangers in atrophied communities surrounded by an enforced and sterile picturesqueness defended by retired incomers from another world.

NOTICE IN ARLES MARKET PLACE

Tourist, you are in famous Provence, a country now colonised, polluted, despoiled, its language forgotten, its ancient traditions betrayed, its soul extinguished.

Where a national or other traditional cultural identity persists it is variously ignored, despised, romanticised or patronised by being stuffed and mounted as 'heritage'. Taffy plays up as the comforting stage Welshman. The Irish Joke provides comic relief from the Irish Question. The people of the Scottish Highlands are now struggling to break free from the kind of image imposed on them in films ranging from *Whiskey galore* (1948) to *Local hero* (1983). Their rich authentic culture has long been overlooked even by their own people, good humouredly accepting the image of the happy-go-lucky opportunist, with a dram in his hand and a twinkle in his eye.

As metropolitan England itself is threatened by a bland Euroculture backed by the Paris-Amsterdam-Frankfurt powerhouse, there is evidence of a confused crisis of national identity, much of it expressed as negative backlash. Raymond Williams has remarked that 'many of the things that happened over centuries to the Welsh are now happening in decades to the English'. And Neil Ascherson reminds us 'that the worst kind of nightmare is when you seem to enter your own home, see all the furniture that was there, and do not recognise it'.[77]

If we move on to consider the positive significance of the periphery for an alternative green future, then there are two kinds of ambivalence with which we shall have to come to terms.

In the first place, there is the ambivalence of people of the periphery who are tempted to pay for the ready livelihood offered by large-scale

metropolitan 'development' with eventual communal, linguistic and environmental loss, including the ultimate loss of any separate identity.
Everywhere among the peripheral peoples there is an urgent need to win
understanding and support for an alternative green regional livelihood
strategy which will protect and enhance cultural and social identity.

Alien development schemes from the centre may expose local greens
(and particularly incomers) to an ambivalence of their own: environmental preservation versus livelihood preservation or, in more sophisticated
greenspeak, deep ecology versus social ecology. Thus many a young Cymro
Cymraeg (Welsh Welsh) is inclined to see the incoming green environmentalist (in the words of a Gwynedd pop group) as 'snob Saes Tori'—an
English Tory snob. The Scottish Green Party has won much local support
with a well researched agro-forestry policy for the Highlands. This could
lead to the resettlement by crofting communities (there is a long waiting
list) of glens 'cleared' a hundred and fifty years ago but now earmarked as
potential wilderness areas.

What is important here is not merely the need to strike a balance. It is
the need to recognise that the aspirations of the periphery and those of the
radical green movement are in fact complementary and mutually reinforcing.

It is a commonplace that national identity rests upon three pillars:
language and culture; community; and the land itself. Different languages
shape feelings and values in different ways. This is very striking in the case
of an ancient language like Welsh. Words like *perthyn* (to belong to, to be
in relation to); *cynefin* (familiar place, habitat); *cartrefol* (being at home);
and *cwmdeithas* (community), have their own peculiar and not quite trans-
latable resonance, earthed to stable, human-scale communities which are
integral with the land and landscape. Even 'nationalism', with its aggressive
overtones, cannot adequately be translated into Welsh as *cenedlaetholiaeth*,
which simply means 'love of one's country'. And the pollution and
ravaging of the land is both a national *and* an environmental issue,
whether it be the stripping of the forest cover by transnational companies
in Thailand or the arbitrary flooding of Welsh valleys to provide industrial
England with reservoirs. The nationalism of ecological sustainability,
economic self-reliance and autonomous, modest-scale communities is
ultimately the only kind that can countervail against the dominant
superindustrial culture.[78]

For greens the periphery is significant because it is the antithesis of the
centre—of burgeoning growth, overpowering complexity and huge organisations. That is why so many greens have moved out there, as small
businesspeople, homesteaders and craft workers (20,000 of these last, the

majority incomers, are to be found in the Welsh county of Dyfed alone).

But empowerment of the periphery needs to be facilitated by legislation which initiates the dismantling of the centre through political decentralisation and through energy taxes and similar measures which tip the odds in favour of regional self-reliance.

Radical greens must aim to bring back to the centre, to the ravaged and overdeveloped heartlands, all that is best on the periphery and which now largely survives only there. A start will thus be made in dissolving the centre-periphery distinction itself. And what is best is the simple, human scale of things, community cohesion, the persistence of values that override the market, a sense of place, a climate of continuity and stability, and a feeling for appropriate sufficiency and right livelihood. True, these qualities may now often be in short supply even on the periphery, but they are still evident enough to give heart and set an example.

The complex interaction of nationality, community and the periphery is thus of considerable relevance to the formation of an effective radical green politics. It is significant that Britain's first Member of Parliament to be elected on a radical green programme is a very green Welsh nationalist, Cynog Dafis. Against all the trends, and in the third biggest swing of the 1992 general election, this achievement was made possible by a close and continuing alliance of the local Green Party and Plaid Cymru, founded on the goals and values set out in this chapter.

18 What kind of green society?

The confederal balancing act

The radical green vision of what governance should be about is well expressed in William Ophuls' picture of a 'decentralized Jeffersonian polity of relatively small, intimate, locally autonomous and self governing communities, rooted in the land (or other ecological resources) and affiliated at the federal level only for a few clearly defined purposes'.[1]

This emphasis on local economic and political autonomy has made Schumacher's dictum 'small is beautiful' a veritable doctrine of faith for many radical greens. This is particularly so for the 'minisculists', as an exasperated Jonathon Porritt has called them: 'There is a romantic—almost illusory—attachment to the notion of complete decentralisation that lurks at the back of a lot of green and alternative thinking and I believe it renders them incapable of serious political and social analysis'.[2]

For Leopold Kohr, a green founding father of the Schumacher era, there is no doubt that 'bigness' is the 'hidden primary cause disturbing the social happiness of man . . . I have tried to develop a single theory through which not only some but all phenomena of the social universe can be reduced to a single denominator. The result is a new and unified political philosophy centring on the theory of size . . . It suggests that there seems to be only one cause behind all forms of social misery: bigness . . . It is always bigness, and only bigness, which is the problem of existence, social as well as physical'.[3] Similarly, for Kirkpatrick Sale, a hardly less influential green thinker, 'economic and social misery increases in direct proportion to the size and power of the central government of a nation or state . . . Size, indeed, might be regarded as a crucial variable in everything'.[4]

Size is, of course, by no means an insignificant social variable, and both writers do indeed make a number of valid arguments along the way. Sale, for instance, notes how consensus democracy rather than adversarial democracy has a better chance of working in small units, where people tend to be 'more politically active, can understand the issues and personalities more clearly, participate more in all aspects of government and regard themselves as having some effective control over the decisions of their lives'.[5]

It comes as something of a shock to find, near the end of Sale's book *Human scale*, the following litany of 'deficiencies to which small communities are undeniably prey':

> Small communities tend to be close knit and homogenous. They are suspicious of outsiders, actually xenophobic on occasion, and not quick to welcome outside ideas and customs, of whatever value. They are conservative, parochial, resistant to change, and accustomed to fixed ways and patterns that do not allow much room for the excitement of novelty or the unexpectedness of variation. They tend to make the individual secondary to the collectivity, breaking down walls of privacy, subjecting all to a kind of tyranny of public opinion. They generally demand conformity, can make scapegoats of those they find threatening, and may force what they regard as 'deviants' into closets.[6]

Indeed, the vices of small societies can be as readily paraded as their virtues. They range through the vicious politics of ancient and medieval city-states, the witch hunting communities of New England, redneck segregation in the States and townships of the American South, the ill-treatment of untouchables in the villages of India, the murderous sectarianism of the communities of Northern Ireland, and the exploitation everywhere by sweatshop employers whose human-scale supervision enables them to squeeze their workers the harder and root out incipient trade unionism.

Where small is manifestly not beautiful both Kohr and Sale are quite happy to introduce other determinants, thereby reducing their master theory to no more than one of many possible, interactive variables which might explain why a particular society is 'beautiful' or not. Sale, for example, explains away the characteristic 'deficiencies' of small communities by claiming that centralisation has drained local talent away to the centre. Again, where big central government has intervened to protect minorities from communal intolerance (as in the American South and in Northern Ireland) Sale argues that popular pressure forced it to act in an uncharacteristic way!

The fall-back position of the minisculists is that where small is incontestably ugly the ugliness is at least on a relatively modest scale—small wars, small-scale injustices, fragmentary environmental damage. For Fourth Worlders like John Papworth 'this is the heart of the matter. We may agree an elected village council may be as amorally motivated as the directors of any international arms company and ready to do as much evil . . . but its capacity for doing harm will be limited in any case not only by its limited size but by the constraints its conceivably better motivated neighbours would be able to impose. (If you don't stop fouling our river we won't let your goods cross our territory)'.[7] Similarly, Schumacher maintained that 'although even small communities are sometimes guilty of causing serious erosion, generally as a result of ignorance, this is trifling in comparison with the devastations caused by gigantic groups motivated by greed, envy and lust for power. It is moreover obvious that men organised in small units will take better care of *their* bit of land or other natural resources than anonymous companies or megalomanic governments which pretend to themselves that the whole universe is their legitimate quarry'.[8]

The *environmental* virtue of smallness is certainly less in question than its social merits, though by no means invariably so. Schumacher underestimates the historic capacity of small communities collectively to bring disaster on themselves precisely because each considers its own, local, demands on the environment to be modest and unavoidable, and fails to appreciate both the overall geographical picture and the cumulative effect over time of its constant nibbling away at some diminishing resource. And as to the social and economic injustices perpetrated in small communities, they have arguably created no less misery than more sensational imperial undertakings. It does seem to be a doctrine of despair to accept that the best we can do to ameliorate social and ecological evils is to tolerate them in penny packets rather than suffer them wholesale.

The final word in this debate can be left to Schumacher himself, who was at pains to make his position quite clear:

> Today we suffer from an almost universal idolatry of giantism. It is therefore necessary to insist on the virtue of smallness—where this applies. If there were a prevailing ideology of smallness . . . one would have to try and exercise influence in the opposite direction . . . Yet people find it most difficult to keep two seemingly opposite necessities of truth in their minds at the same time. They always clamour for a final solution . . . What we wish to emphasise is the duality of the human requirement when it comes to a question of size: there is no single answer. For his different purposes man needs many different structures, both small ones and large ones, some exclusive and some comprehensive.[9]

Thus it is unhelpful to make a useful notion like 'small is beautiful' into an article of faith and a substitute for creative situational thinking. That such a simplistic dogma has gone largely unchallenged within the radical green movement is disturbing evidence of its members' ideological cast of mind.

From the dogmatic simplicities of the minisculists we move on to the convoluted constitution making of the green confederalists. For them also, power must, as far as is practicable, be concentrated in the lower tiers of government, down to district and parish level. The relationship between lower and upper tier governments would rest upon two guiding principles which Schumacher had emphasised. The *principle of subsidiarity* is that 'nothing should be done centrally if it can be done equally well, or better, locally'.[10] The *principle of vindication* states that as long as the smaller and subordinate unit meets certain pre-agreed criteria (e.g. maintaining specific human rights, or remaining profitable) it is free to do what it wants in whatever way it prefers. Schumacher maintained that bigger and higher organisations, whether political or economic, should be created as necessary by the confederal build-up of smaller ones—a building blocks strategy in place of top-down decentralisation. 'The fundamental task is to achieve smallness *within* large organisations. Maybe what we need is not either-or [smallness or bigness], *but the one and the other at the same time*'.[11]

It is noteworthy that the principle of subsidiary function is generally given a confederal (as opposed to a federal) meaning, whereby power resides at the lower level from which it can alone be ceded to a higher authority *and from which it can subsequently be revoked at will*. Similarly it has been argued that the funding of higher level authorities should come from the lower level, from which approval for detailed expenditure must be sought. The Green Party proposes as tiers of government parishes, districts (evidently the most powerful level), and regions, with encouragement of confederal linkages at all levels. With so little power left to central government, parliament would presumably only have enough business to occupy it for a few weeks of the year.[12]

The higher, confederal levels of government would have two kinds of function, relating to the principle of subsidiarity and the principle of vindication respectively.

First, however self-reliant the lower tiers might be, there would inevitably be some economic and technical functions which could be more effectively provided by the higher tier, or at least co-ordinated by it. Examples would be strategic resource management and pollution control, energy systems which require national networking, long distance transportation, foreign policy and defence, international trade and monetary control, and other aspects of international co-operation.

The second function of upper tier government is much more problematic and controversial. It has to do with upholding ecological requirements and social rights and responsibilities between and within the lower tier units, to ensure, in the words of the original text of the Green Party's manifesto, that 'damaging inequalities and practices unfair to other districts do not develop'.[13] For example, what one regional government sees as sustainable growth may be seen by others as a reversion to a growthmania which threatens the future of all.

Environmental responsibilities are linked closely to the upholding of economic and social justice across the confederations. The ending of significant economic growth would create a closed economy and a social climate in which an equitable and guaranteed share-out of all kinds of wealth and advantage becomes essential for social harmony. Upper and lower limits would need to be set on incomes and wealth, what are seen as destructive forms of private and sectional enterprise would need to be outlawed, controversial tax incentives affecting family size might be introduced, and the availability and use of private transport restricted. Even where there had been confederal agreement in enacting such measures, lower tier governments might be reluctant to enforce them. Lower tier financial autonomy implies likely inequalities in standards of public service between one district and another, whether as a result of policy or differences in resources available. Being born into a materially poor district could mean being born into a poor healthcare system. Therefore in its original manifesto the Green Party 'suggests' that the district 'education services, the health service and, initially, the welfare services are financed from provincial funds, each district receiving an allocation calculated on an age related per capita basis. This would ensure equality of service in all areas, regardless of the level of affluence or poverty within a district'.[14]

Most greens are agreed that a bill of rights would still be necessary to protect individuals from the tyranny of majorities. The claims of national, ethnic and linguistic minorities would also figure prominently in the kind of pluralistic, decentralised society which we are discussing here. Such claims already exist in Islamic Bradford and Welsh Dyfed, as well as in more extreme manifestations in Azerbaijan and former Yugoslavia. In Dyfed, for example, the county council's policy that five to seven year olds in many of its primary schools shall be taught entirely in Welsh has aroused the opposition of a group of predominantly English incomers calling itself 'Education first!' If the county had wider powers (or there were a Welsh legislature) it could also restrict housing availability so as to favour local people (whereas the market at present does the opposite), raise other barriers to in-migration, and extend bilingual requirements for public service employment. These are typical conflicts between community rights and individual rights. And they would multiply in a green future as community identity and cohesion, and individual responsibilities as well as rights, came increasingly to be valued as reinforcements to ecological and related social and economic stability.

All of the above points to the conflict-laden implications of a green confederalism. Minority and individual rights and ecological well-being would have to be protected against local abuse and enforced by complex systems of regulation and control, together with fiscal sticks and carrots, operated by a flourishing new-look bureaucracy and appeal judiciary. Weighting the power all at one end of the system (including the power of lower tier units to opt out altogether) is evidently presumed to be the ultimate guarantee of freedom. It could, however, destabilise the whole heavily stressed confederal structure, and increase pressure for more of a top-down *federal* element.

So far we have a suggestive but problematic governmental structure for a conserver society. But it would be no more than an unconvincing constitutional contraption if the argument stopped there. As to getting started at this structural level, the regional option has much to commend it.

As well as the North American bioregional movement, autonomous regional government is already well established in the European Community, though it will take much time and effort to reverse the extraordinary centralisation that has occurred in Britain. For the foreseeable future greens in the UK should postpone any minisculist yearnings they may have and instead strongly commit themselves to the development of autonomous regions, initially within the UK but increasingly in the context of a Europe of the Regions.

Regional governments would, on the one hand, be strong enough to resist the centre, but they would also be well placed to nurture local community initiative. The kind of regions I have in mind would not necessarily have the rationality favoured by administrative draughtsmen or bioregional visionaries. But they would be based on areas whose inhabitants felt a strong sense of identity. There would be no uniform packaging by size and population, and regions in England might range from, say, Cornwall to Merseyside, and Cumbria to Greater London. City regions could be turned around to reverse the traditional urban dominance over rural hinterlands, greening the cities on the one hand and restoring a vigorous, balanced social and economic life to the countryside on the other. The smaller English regions, which might be no bigger than the former shires, might need to associate together for various purposes such as joint provision of services.

The constitution of an English Confederation would enable the regional governments to delegate and partner services to communities able and willing to take on the range of services not uncommon in the rest of Europe at this level: local environmental care, primary education, social services, water supply, waste disposal, management of social housing, public transport, economic development, planning, leisure, fire protection, and the maintenance of public buildings. Such communities would focus on small towns and the hinterlands which depend on them, and populations might be as little as 10,000. Larger communities would be able to shoulder a wider range of services and to administer a higher proportion of them entirely from their own resources. Local economic development would be particularly important.

What is appropriate for England would not necessarily be so for the smaller countries of the Island of Britain. Wales, for example, has a strong tradition of decentralisation, related to linguistic, ethnic and cultural differences, and there is also a generally robust sense of community. Confederation might come more easily here than in England, with smaller, shire regions (*siroedd*) and communities (*cantrefi*).

In exploring the green confederal future as a credible and workable perspective, we must now weave in its economics.

From free market economy to eco-social economy

As has been argued earlier in this book, an ecologically sustainable economy would need to be a steady-state economy characterised by minimal growth. In the first phase it would be necessary both to create the infrastructure for such an economy (like switching to renewable energy and public transport), and at the same time to undertake a de-development programme. This would have the dual object of reducing global consumption to a sustainable level and at the same time redistributing it equitably between the present under-developed and over-developed parts of the world. F.E. Trainer, in his book *Abandon affluence!*,[15] estimated that this would require a one-fifth reduction in the United States' consumption of energy. Some of this could be achieved through changes in lifestyle (like turning down the central heating), but for most of it systemic, structural changes dictated by public policy would be necessary (as with energy efficient appliances and building construction). A one-fifth cut in average 'over-developed' living standards would not in fact involve much hardship: using a bicycle or public transport system instead of a private car and learning to live quite happily without the aid of numerous 'conveniences' and gadgets. And does one individual have some special right to burn 760 litres of fuel jetting from London to Sydney whilst another must walk many miles daily to scavenge firewood because kerosene is too scarce and expensive?

Examples of areas where economic growth would still be desirable are the development of appropriate substitutes for raw materials in increasingly scarce supply, and of ecologically friendly technologies which improve the ecosphere's natural pollution absorption capacity. But because the lessons of quasi-solutions and their unforeseen consequences will by then have been learnt, even such developments as these would be modest and cautious.

The foregoing implies a fundamental shift away from the centuries old culture of wealth creation enterprise. The preoccupation with 'greening business' suggests a misconception about the new directions in which our energies must move. In the first place there will be a more favourable climate for spiritual, psychological and cultural growth—and just play—presently stultified by the climate of industrial civilisation. In the second place, some of that human dynamic would need to go into the rediscovery of the ancient arts of politics, particularly in terms of social justice and conflict resolution. These would be as central to the maintenance of a steady-state economy as wealth creation is to an economy where growth is seen as the all-purpose solvent of a wide range of social problems.

Where there is deprivation people cannot be expected live without the prospect of better times tomorrow. Without an equitable redistribution of wealth, modest income differentials, guaranteed livelihood and other forms of redistributive social justice, most people would still hunger for economic growth, and few politicians would dare not to promise to deliver it. A green economy must therefore be a veritable *political* economy, in which politics are paramount over economics. William Ophuls has observed how difficult this would be, particularly for 'we Americans, [who] have never had a genuine politics—that is, something apart from economics, that gives direction to our community life. Instead, American politics has been but a reflexion of its laissez-faire economic system'. Ophuls coins the term 'economic reductionism' for the use of economic growth as a means of by-passing true politics.[16]

A green economy must be an economy of widespread empowerment in place of widespread dependence. Where there is a dependency culture, whether of employees, consumers, raw material suppliers or other stakeholders, there is a concentration of economic power which has induced it, and such concentrations are a precondition for ecological and social abuse. As James Robertson observes, 'today's economic order and today's economic thinking tacitly assume, not that organisations are for people, but that people are for organisations, as employees, customers, taxpayers, investors, clients and so on . . . By and large the corporate economy is dependency-creating not enabling'.[17] Moreover, existing economic undertakings, whether public or private, tend to grow into large, centrally controlled aggregates—exclusive, invulnerable, self-serving, self-confirming, and co-opting, manipulating and controlling a wide social and geographical hinterland. Even (questionable) economies of scale are negated by exponentially rising costs of complexity, compounded by human and environmental costs which are never acknowledged.

We therefore need an economy characterised as far as possible by manageable, human-scale operations built up within substantial local and regional self-reliance. This would end alienating work by restoring the economic basis of community and hence the opportunity to work directly for the well-being of one another. For a green economy needs to be not only ecologically and materially supportive, but also to meet the basic human needs of control over our life situations, the opportunity to work creatively with others, to make important decisions, to do worthwhile things and to see the results of our endeavours.

Such a green economy would be underpinned by an ecologically hospitable, human-friendly technology, flexible and adaptive to all of the foregoing requirements, and providing, as far as possible, satisfying kinds of work. It would operate on as small a scale as possible consistent with the efficient use of resources, and with the minimum amount of capital commensurate with the necessary added value.

The last of the requirements for a green economy is a spiritual validation which subsumes both the ecological and the social. It must be based on what Schumacher called 'a Buddhist economics', which involves us in an organisation of work such as can only be undertaken in service to others and in co-operation with them, and hence to liberate ourselves from our inborn egocentricity. On the one hand our psycho-spiritual growth is facilitated and, on the other, a mutualistic and integrated economy is consolidated. A steady-state economy can nurture the steady-state people it needs for its survival through norms of mutuality and co-operation rather than conflict and competition. This requirement, even more than the others, is particularly incompatible with free market capitalism.

We must now turn our attention to certain crucial problems to do with shaping an economy which meets the above requirements. The first is about the extent and means of controlling a free market economy, and the second the extent to which the market might be modified or even replaced by exclusively public forms of ownership. The debate—and struggle—

about the extent to which the market's 'economic rationality' should be made subservient to social values which it would otherwise threaten to destroy has been central to the last two hundred years of industrial society. It has found expression not only in the socialist movements but also in the Catholic inspired 'Christian democracy' of the European continent and in liberal humanitarianism and conservative paternalism. Environmental protection has now been added to the traditional countervailing demands for social and economic justice. Social ecologists thus inherit many of the problems with which socialists have for so long been concerned.

The ideal of post-medieval visionaries like Rudolf Bahro and Edward Goldsmith is of an economy of largely *self-sufficient* communities, with family and co-operative undertakings using low technologies and confining their trade (and barter) to very local markets. It is difficult to see how this ideal could be attained except as a consequence of an eco-social breakdown, which would achieve Bahro's 'industrial disarmament' though at terrible cost. And subsequently would we not have primitive accumulation once more and the resumption of Progress?

Mainstream greens appear to favour a strongly regulated and decentralised market economy of small private businesses and co-operatives which would be well rooted in *self-reliant* local economies. Within the confederal framework discussed previously a range of tariffs, subsidies, taxes and controls would be necessary in order to maintain ecological sustainability, social justice, and the breakup of large centralised undertakings.

There can be little doubt about the value of a small business economy in meeting many of the green criteria outlined at the beginning of this chapter. Schumacher, for whom this was 'a very clear-cut matter', strongly favoured small businesses, on the grounds that individually they made little impact on the environment or society and where, with only one or two dozen employees, the unions could readily bring sanctions to bear on exploitative employers. 'Where countries have tried to socialise or nationalise those small businesses, the result was that you just couldn't get the work done any more. Also the urge of many straightforward and honest people to stand on their own feet and do their own thing is frustrated . . . so I have no doubt in my mind that at this level private enterprise is excellent'.[18] However, I believe there are important reservations to be made.

From the green point of view producer co-operatives have more to commend them than small private businesses, but so far they have not multiplied at anything like the rate of private businesses. And like any other business they are obliged to accept the logic of the market, and to consolidate the interests of producers over consumers and other stake holders in the economic enterprise. Generally, a small business economy would seem to exemplify many of the undesirable features of Adam Smith's original competitive economic model if its activities were not channelled and regulated and smallness artificially preserved. Only if society overrode the property laws of the market with ethical legislation could Guy Dauncey's ideal be realised of 'business no longer seen as a means to get rich on the backs of other people, but vehicles through which personal visions can be realised, the local community and the planet as a whole can be served, and fulfilling, meaningful work can be created for all who desire it'.[19]

Furthermore, beyond arcadian autarchy a small business culture would be insufficient to support a green economy deploying the full range of appropriate technologies, many of which would require large-scale, integrated production and distribution systems (as with a strategic public transport network, for example). Moreover, André Gorz has proposed that a range of basic personal and domestic utility goods could usefully be produced by large publicly owned automated factories. They would be simple, durable, well designed and minimally priced. Such an extension of the public sector would enable it to provide most of the citizen's *needs*, leaving the free market to cater for *wants*.

The green benefits of small business would thus only be fully realised if its free market were controlled and included other forms of ownership. It is therefore to these questions that we must now turn.

For green socialists like Martin Ryle the market sector should be both small and tightly regulated. Ryle does, however, acknowledge the need for such a sector, as follows:

> It is undeniable that a plurality of economic powers [the market] is a counterweight to the concentration in the state apparatus of political and administrative power (though, of course, market institutions when they reach the scale of modern transnational companies represent in themselves major and unaccountable centres of control) . . . It is putatively the case that market mechanisms . . . are able to satisfy a vast range of consumer wants more efficiently and less wastefully than the apparently more rational *a priori* methods of 'the plan' . . . Here the feedback of market-type mechanisms is an effective means of allocating social capital to meet demands and of encouraging the necessary expansion and construction of the production and retail enterprises concerned.[20]

Ryle's market sector would cater for *wants* such as books, holiday travel, wine and word processors, as well as providing for all but the 'utility' end of the production of shirts, cooking pans and so on. His market would be so heavily regulated that he calls it a 'pseudo-market'. For the influential green socialist André Gorz, however, this second tier of the economy should be 'the free-for-all, [for] the entrepreneur who works at whatever necessities could be improved upon . . . There is no reason why people should not have an idea and put it onto the micro-market'.[21]

We may assume widespread agreement about the need for some kind of a market sector to produce personal and domestic goods as a second tier of a green economy. Controversy therefore centres upon the first tier. This would embrace the provision of goods and services for social need which were insufficiently profitable to be supplied by the market, plus eco-socially significant categories like the production of major capital goods of importance to a whole region, production and distribution which is still necessarily centralised and large-scale, and other socially and ecologically sensitive production, distribution and service systems. Should these elements of the economy be included in the market sector, though subject to tight control on ecological and social grounds? Or should this first tier be outside the market and vested in various kinds of public ownership?

For writers like John Elkington, author of *Green capitalists*, there can only be one answer: 'Socialism as an economic theory, though not as a moral crusade, is dead. The argument is about what kind of capitalism we want'. Even some radical green socialists of the standing of André Gorz now feel obliged to conclude that:

> There is only one way of managing a business rationally and that is along the lines used by capitalist management. I'm sorry to have come to that conclusion, but all the socialist regimes have come to that conclusion now . . . But what you can do is say that the logic of capitalist management—of maximising efficiency—will be submitted to more important criteria which we will not allow to be sacrificed for the sake of efficiency: people's health, their sleep, the environment, and their way of life.[21]

Similarly, other radical socialists like Alec Nove[22] have felt obliged to accept the need for a predominantly market economy, however strongly regulated.

Traditionally, for a limited joint stock company (which is the conventional business structure) its responsibility to its workers has rested with paying their wages and little more. The market price mechanism is assumed ultimately to take care of its responsibility to consumers, and the company has no particular responsibilities in respect of society or the local community. In fact, legislation, trade unions, public opinion and other forces have considerably modified that picture of a company's responsibilities.

Arguably, *all* kinds of organisation need to develop more democratic and pluralistic structures of ownership and control, embodying the rights and obligations of the various stakeholders, and not only of its workers (in the case of a producer co-operative), the state (in the case of a nationalised industry) or the stockholders (in the case of a limited liability company). But for any organisation which has to survive in a market economy, and particularly for one whose first obligation is to its shareholders, it is extremely difficult to graft such social objectives onto its structure and policies. Its most vulnerable stakeholders, for example, might be people of an overseas country struggling out of neo-colonial dependency and still vulnerable to at least the more subtle forms of transnational exploitation.

There is in fact a certain black comedy in the assumption that capitalism is the only viable economic foundation for an ecologically sustainable society. For, in Jeremy Seabrook's words, 'if it had been the purpose of humanity on earth to bring to the edge of ruin the planet itself, no more efficient mechanism could have been invented than the market system itself, with its prodigious use of energy and materials'.[23] How can an economic system be deemed successful which is both the most efficient engine for wealth creation ever devised yet which has failed to meet the basic needs of most of the world's people, and which has fuelled exploitation, oppression and war on a hitherto unimaginable scale?

The ultimate constraint on the ecological adaptability of capitalism is that undifferentiated growth is integral to it. After years of lobbying business, Jonathon Porritt concluded:

> We may make companies more energy efficient, we may persuade them to recycle more, we may persuade them to adopt more environmentally friendly practices . . . but guess what we won't persuade them to do: produce less, to market less actively, to buy less, to travel less, to have less of an impact in total terms on the world . . . As Rudolf Bahro says, even the greenest business person is really doing little more than cleaning the teeth of the dragon.[24]

I conclude that the emergent pattern needs to comprise a spectrum of enterprises ranging from those entirely in private ownership (perhaps confined to the micro-market comprising the second tier) to hybrids marked by increasing degrees of social ownership and control by their stakeholders. The latter, and especially those in the first tier of the economy, would operate in a highly regulated pseudo-market, designed to leave sufficient 'economic rationality' to give an adequate profit margin but otherwise shaped to eco-social need.

Beyond the market there would, arguably, need to be a small public sector where ecological and social needs were the sole criteria. Far from the communists' command economy or Morrisonian nationalisation, ownership and management in the public sector must be related as closely as possible to the needs it is intended to serve. This means that it must be vested so far as possible in representative regional and community organisations, and networked as necessary through the confederal structure. And if any other group or individual can deliver a better product or service within the same ecological and social constraints then they should be given the opportunity to do so.

There can be no future in an economy of capitalists versus eco-social controllers; of business people with their feet on the accelerator and bureaucrats with their feet on the brakes; of entrepreneurial greyhounds straining always at the leash of a muzzled market, threatening to topple the whole steady state project, and undo the work of an army of officials striving to keep the lid on, to block off all the holes, and to ensure, for a start, that every product was durable, repairable, and recyclable. What we must evolve is an holistic economic climate and mentality wherein ecological and social commitment is fused with a resourceful entrepreneurial spirit, so that an enterprise can at least break even and meet that commitment, or, better still, make a profit which can be used to support other enterprises where the satisfaction of need leaves no such margin. The market must be rigged to serve people and planet, and yet at the same time positively kept afloat so that it *is* able to serve people and planet. Where this is not possible there should be no hesitation in resorting to the potentially wide range of public sector options.

Finally there is the third tier of a green economy, whose growth could considerably diminish the problems we have been discussing. The formal economy within the community shades off into the informal economy of neighbourhoods and households, of shared as well as personal land, workshops and other production and servicing facilities. This is the economy of minimarkets selling local products and services originated within cycling distance by one's neighbours; of local currencies and neighbourly exchange; and of neighbourhood healthcare, education, libraries, welfare services and so on. Consumerism here dissolves into mutuality.

This informal and domestic economy figures prominently in visionary ecotopias. It is associated with new conceptions of work, employment, livelihood and citizenship, vividly illustrated by Ted Trainer as follows, the stuff of green soap opera:

> All people will have to spend most of their time as active producers, initiators and critical thinkers. They will be forced by their non-

affluent circumstances to go about saying to themselves things like 'How can the system (solar panel, nursery, roster, committee) be improved?' 'What will I read up next?' 'What ideas can I offer at the next meeting of the library committee?' 'What project should our neighbourhood working bee tackle next month?'[25]

The support of a guaranteed basic income for all would encourage a greatly enlarged voluntary sector of care and conviviality, together with an increased economic importance for individual households and their variously extended families and mini-communities.

Nurtured by new ecological and social imperatives, this whole informal sector would put heart into a community renaissance and satisfy many deeply felt needs presently starved by our restless, anxious individualism. Although Trainer confesses that 'villages and other very cohesive communities can be abominable places to live in', it is no less true that 'the things that make for community are non-material and they cannot be bought and sold: they are feelings of concern, respect, gratitude, obligation, togetherness, and identity that come from interacting with friends in a convivial environment and in important common activities'.[26]

Such visions of the neighbourly, economically self-reliant community are, however, much more likely to be realised in social cultures which have been traditionally filiative and given to mutual help, or where ecological and social breakdown has proceeded so far that formal economic and administrative structures have begun to disintegrate and there is reversion to semi-autarchy. Even without such a disaster, Trainer optimistically estimates that the informal community economy could expand to a point at which it reduced commercial production by some eighty per cent, putting four-fifths of the present commercial undertakings out of business. He does not question, however, why there should be a widespread willingness to abandon the relatively high standard of living made possible by a sophisticated but ecologically sustainable formal economy, and this alone would in my view be sufficient to limit the scope of his buzzing, communitarian informal sector.

Stability, community, civil society and bureaucracy

The discussion so far in this chapter has been very much in terms of structure, conflict, balance and complexity, both in the relationship between upper and lower levels of confederation, and in the relationship between the market and the eco-social demands that must be made upon it. However, as two other writers grappling with similar problems have observed:

The lesson of recent history is that non-structural factors are often just as important—the culture of political life, the motivation and ethos of those working in the state and voluntary agencies. The key for policy makers of the future, and for those concerned to bring the state and economy back under human control, is to accept that control can never be placed at one sole position in the system. True democracy takes multiple forms: in work, in the locality, in civil society, even while it recognises that an excess of democratic structure overloads the citizen by demanding too much participation.[27]

Psycho-spiritual development and the reclamation of community have already been introduced as potentially integrative and stabilising factors in the radical green social revolution, and particularly in strengthening eco-social responsibility. Some further developments to do with stability, community, civil society and bureaucracy are considered below.

The Green Party hopes and believes that 'within a tolerant community it will be possible for there to be a high level of individual self-determination, such as can hardly be envisaged in our experience of centralised society'.[28] On the contrary, even the volatile, brittle individualism typical of our present superindustrial culture would be a threat to ecological harmony and the steady-state economy, together with the social justice and egalitarianism needed to sustain them. A culture of sufficiency and simplicity can, however, be stabilised and enriched by a strengthening of community (as was proposed in Chapter 17). In contrast to the affluent individualism of the laisser-faire past, this would imply less freedom of choice in many areas of life, arising in particular from the localisation of almost everything (often in relatively small, dispersed communities) and the lack of some conveniences. There would be a shift from the cornucopian culture of adjusting reality to suit our every fancy to the older culture of adjusting our hearts and heads instead. There is a great deal of evidence that such a culture of well matured acceptance can in fact yield a great sense of well-being and inner freedom.

At several points I have maintained that personal empowerment needs to be achieved through community living in which responsibilities are no less important than rights, and which can provide a personal and group security, as well as being resistant alike to populist authoritarianism or addictive power-and-wealth achievement. Indeed, for most people personal growth flourishes best where there is the support of familiar structures and roles, and stable, shared and well worn meanings.

There have been plenty of reminders in this book about the dark side of traditional community life. Fortunately there is probably no way, short of cataclysmic ecological reversion, by which the norms of *traditional* community can be brought back to life. To the extent to which we do achieve an authentic revival of community values it will be at a higher level of the cultural spiral than traditional community culture, embodying a more mature and integrated individualism than the present destructive kind.

One contribution to such an evolution of community would be the development of a genuine *civil society*, as a countervailing power against the present dominance of both state and market in public life. At its minimal political level such a civil society would be supported by a written constitution centred on an environmentally updated bill of rights, including guarantees of freedom of information and backed by a code of administrative law and a constitutional court.

For the United Kingdom this would be no more than the kind of constitutional 'republican' government that is taken for granted in the United States and in the European Community. Increasing integration of the UK into the latter will build up pressure for reform of archaic British institutions and complete the historic movement towards a more truly representative democracy, inspiring Neil Ascherson's splendid annunciation:

> As that demolition happens, the worm-holed casket of authority will burst open at last. Power will escape, flying upwards to the Community—but also downwards to subjects who become citizens, to cities which grow proud and free, to nations like Scotland or Wales which acquire parliaments of their own.[29]

So much for the structures of civil society. What of the style? We need what Richard Sennett has defined as a culture of *civility*, which is:

> The activity which protects people from each other and yet allows them to enjoy one another's company. Wearing a mask is the essence of civility. Masks permit pure sociability, detached from circumstances of power, malaise and private feeling of those who wear them. Civility has as its aim the shielding of others from being burdened by oneself.[30]

It is not that we should eschew intimacy and authenticity. It is just that if our need for them is so desperate that we have to carry them into formal and public life, and wield them there, then we add our own potentially destructive overlay to ecological and social problems which are themselves difficult enough. Other times, people, and places could be more helpful and appropriate for working through our own stuff, and space needs to be made within community for that.

The prevailing cult of pseudo-community making owes much to the fear of depersonalisation, and its confusion with impersonality. Community is taken to mean intimacy, and yet historic communities depend on impersonality, role, structure, and ritual, which are 'given'. This creates a supportive, ongoing framework which enables warmth and intimacy to flourish without insatiable need, anxiety and alienation. In such an environment what is subtle, oblique and underspoken may carry the most value.

Ours is the first culture in which many see formal behaviour as somehow inauthentic, and which permits us so little *formal* space in which we can play safely and spontaneously. (It has been left to media personalities to do our playing for us). Again, Sennett's argument is worth close reflection: 'To lose the ability to play is to lose the sense that worldly conditions are plastic. The ability to play with social life depends on the existence of a dimension of society which stands apart, at a distance from, intimate desire, need and identity'.[31] When we are imbued with a sense of playfulness we do not take our public selves too seriously, and do not get in our own way in dealing with the problems that confront us. Playfulness, and the loss of it, are therefore serious matters. The Council of All Beings, introduced in Chapter 15, is an illuminating example of how role, ritual and social bonding can provide a strong support for despair and empowerment work which lacks nothing in authenticity and intimacy.

As well as steady-state people, a steady-state society needs steady-state institutions, which have something of the predictable cyclical routines of the seasons, pacing nature's slow phases of growth, decay and renewal. One aim of radical green politics should be partly to eliminate itself by helping to reach a situation of stable and durable institutions which can be adapted, reconditioned and eventually recycled. Just as, economically, there is a place for the automated production of cheap utility goods (as André Gorz has argued), so there is an argument for mechanising as much of the political process as possible, so that it is reduced to traditional Weberian bureaucratic administration—stable, predictable, impartial, but with computers to do the high speed drudgery, and with everyone free to tap into the information banks.

Let us have space for more worthwhile personal development than making our mark or making our pile, or even the restless communitarian busyness that cannot leave well alone and allows too little space for people and circumstances to evolve in their own time. When our energies have shifted from *having* to just *doing*, then we shall also begin to make space for just *being* . . .

Grounding the theory

It will next be necessary to bring theory about the shaping of a green society further down to earth, in terms of the very variable and often unpromising realities of the world in which we live.

For ideology there is only one Vision Splendid, and the real-life cultural variability—social, political and economic—of different countries is not allowed to intrude. So it is with green ideology, which is given to prescribing political and economic systems as universal bolt-on abstractions out of space and time, no less applicable, presumably, to Angola than to Argentina or Algeria or Austria. In this book, also, I have been playing with designer ecotopias, but it is time to emphasise that this can be no more than a useful preliminary exercise. Moreover, what I have had most specifically in mind here is feasibility within the Island of Britain.

A wide range of conditions, from gross ecological and economic facts to subtle national psychologies, will substantially determine how effectively, and in what ways, different countries will adapt (if at all) to the need for ecological stability. As to national psychologies or, rather, personalities, the research of the Dutch organisation theorist, Geert Hofstede, has shown that Britain, the US, the Netherlands and Scandinavia all score highly on 'individualism', with a preference for informally structured organisational and social life. But whereas Britons and Americans also display the 'masculine' traits of high assertiveness, Netherlanders and Scandinavians are motivated more by team work than the prospect of individual achievement. Again, in South-East Asia Hofstede found that the most favoured kind of social and organisational culture is easy-going, paternalistic, 'one big family' bureaucracy.[32] Traditional cultures appear to have greater potential for stability and cohesion (valuable attributes for maintaining ecological harmony), but less innovative dynamism (for getting there). The proportion of British who highly rated their attachment to social solidarity and cohesion, in a survey of six European countries, was only 32 per cent as compared with the next lowest, Denmark, at 61 per cent.[33] Such depictions of national cultures in terms of a few specific variables are, however, of questionable predictive value when it comes to casting ecotopian horoscopes. They are a useful reminder, nevertheless, of the extent of cultural variability and of the danger of universalising from out of one's own specific culture. Green ideology, for example, is very much a Euro-American phenomenon originating in the eighteenth-century Enlightenment movement, and is in danger of misleading peoples of other cultures as well as its own adherents.

An illuminating example is the idealisation and universalisation by minisculists of the Swiss Confederation. (It is said that one eminent minisculist carries copies of its constitution in his baggage, to distribute to bemused Azerbaijanis and Bulgarians with all the zeal of a bible puncher.) The Swiss cantonal system has evolved over several centuries (and more haphazardly than the national ideology would suggest) through the interaction of a wide range of social variables adding up to a unique mix. To assume that the formal attributes of this system can be abstracted and bolted together in Britain or Brazil is a bizarre example of the social engineering mentality. That being said, there *is* much in Swiss society that eerily echoes our earlier discussion of green confederalism. Switzerland's capitalist economy is the most tightly regulated in the world but it manages to be so productive that the country has the world's largest trade surplus in manufactured goods. The Swiss are immensely public spirited, community orientated, and socially integrated: government is by processes of incremental negotiation of labyrinthine complexity, bristling with checks, balances and safeguards. This has produced great social stability, but also government of unchanging complexion, a heavy-handed conservatism and a large and inert bureaucracy. In short, if you are not a Swiss, there are several good reasons for rejoicing that the much idealised Helvetic version of 'small is beautiful' is probably the least exportable social system on earth.

Radical green theory also needs to be tempered by a reminder of the combination of conditions under which most of the world's peoples have to live:

1 A ruling elite which is normally oppressive and exploitative and not uncommonly tyrannical and rapacious. The burdens it imposes may be increased by the demands made by institutions of the Overdeveloped World. And in a number of cases interminable civil war or the veritable collapse of the state and the economy may have created conditions of chronic insecurity.

2 A more or less ramshackle bureaucracy, where office is viewed primarily as an opportunity to exploit the powerless.

3 Arbitrary police and military power, with routine violation of human rights.

4 Exploding population levels which wipe out what little may have been achieved in raising living standards.

5 Undermining of the future and ruin of the present through the degradation of the environment by the rich (in emulation of the Overdeveloped World) and by the poor (to stay alive).

6 Cultural traditions and customs which may breed inertia, fatalism, conflict and division by religion, race, and caste (but see also below).

7 Poverty, disease and malnutrition for the mass of the population.

I think of the State of Bihar, in India, the world's largest federal democracy. Rich in natural resources, the great majority of its people are landless or marginal farmers (many of them cowed and disenfranchised untouchables), in thrall to landlords and moneylenders backed by the police and officialdom. Corruption is a way of life for all who are in a position to exercise it, right to the top. 'Hell on earth' was how the outspoken editor of the only independent newspaper described Bihar—and he was beaten senseless at the local police station shortly after he had gone to press. Recalling Bihar and the many other hells-on-earth does concentrate the mind mightily when musing about green political theory . . .

In many countries a combination of adverse circumstances severely discourages countervailing movements of grassroots empowerment. Or else these are hijacked or disrupted by 'shining path' ideologues, or the rage is destructively channelled by ethnic cleansers and religious fundamentalists.

Nevertheless, even in the most discouraging situations the struggle goes on, for dignity and integrity, for livelihood and land, usually ecologically informed and drawing strength from community and from all that is positive in traditional cultures and values. There is no honourable alternative. Neither is there an honourable alternative for comfortably off dwellers in the Overdeveloped World, though so overwhelmed are we by alternatives that this is not so starkly evident.

Those are the realities of social geography in which our perspectives of ecological and social justice have to be grounded.

The future setting for our work

A start was made in Chapter 12 where I speculated on the possible consequences if continued high growth rates turned out not to be ecologically sustainable. The enormously complex and unpredictable pressures of a deepening ecological crisis must be viewed, however, in the light of a variety of economic developments.

In the first place, the rising costs of an increasingly sophisticated but needful anti-pollution technology could push up prices faster than real wages, thereby reducing purchasing power and sending business into recession. Furthermore the present scope for increasing resource and energy efficiency will also progressively narrow, with costs rising against diminishing returns.

Third, we have already noted (Chapter 4) how continued automation, if not accompanied by a substantial compensatory overall growth rate, tends to create a large underclass of the permanently unemployed and economically marginalised, which depresses the market further.

Fourth, a stagnation scenario is supported by the alleged 'entropic effect'.[34] This refers to an upper limit to the maximisation of material production per worker beyond which the production process begins to choke on its own scale and complexity. Information, marketing, management and other production-enabling costs, as well as environmental, materials and energy costs, begin to offset the benefits of higher labour productivity. Attempts to stoke up capital investment and technological innovation beyond the 'thermodynamic' limitations of the system are, it is argued, doomed to failure. And since the golden age of superindustrialism, from 1950 to 1975, growth rates have indeed suffered a striking decline in the main industrial economies.

It seems increasingly unlikely that the superindustrial juggernaut will accelerate dramatically into the ecological buffers. We have as yet not even reached a stage where the imposition of environmental restraints has been sufficiently significant to have any dysfunctional effect on the world economy. Stagnation and even slow decline seem the most likely future scenarios. However, since the global techno-economic system is already operating at a level incompatible with the carrying capacity of the ecosystem, even stagnation at present levels would continue to precipitate ecological crisis. As to the response, it is likely to be one of increasingly desperate muddling through or, from another viewpoint, of skilful pragmatic adaptation to new challenges. Visionaries, social architects and catastrophists alike tend to underestimate the well-proven adaptability, resilience and creativity of social formations of all kinds (though often at the expense of the powerless within them).

At all events, as the free market economy became economically and socially dysfunctional, with accompanying political destabilisation, pressure would build up for stronger government. We may imagine in the industrialised democracies a move towards a wartime footing, with citizens enjoined to tighten their belts and pull together under the leadership of a government of national unity. Emergency powers might be introduced and democratic rights and civil liberties curtailed, possibly with harsh environmental curbs and controls imposed on business. All this might well be facilitated by a patriotic green populist atmosphere, celebrating a new, fashionable frugality, allotment holding, a revived public transport system, and other policies long advocated by radical greens, but in a very different political context.

The sense of unity of Fortress Europe and other wealthy industrialised enclaves would be reinforced by policing operations and resource wars to enforce 'internationally agreed' economic and financial sanctions against Third World countries behaving 'with insufficient global environmental responsibility'. For most Third World countries the weight of environmental and demographic disaster, combined with economic, political and military crises and the effects of the self-serving policies of the industrialised countries, could have catastrophic effects.

Nevertheless, a few countries might well become stable green enclaves which reflected something of the present ecotopian vision. Such might be the case with a few Third World countries still blessed with adequate natural resources, sustained by traditional, community-based economic and social cultures and not overburdened with more people than they could carry. But even these would need to free themselves of parasitic local elites, aid and debt burdens, destabilising pressures from the Overdeveloped World and the international institutions it controls, and military forays by desperate neighbours. And in Europe, too, several small geographically and culturally favoured nations might be able to shift to a democratic conserver society.

Elsewhere, in a broken backed industrial culture, centralised authoritarian regimes would prove to be increasingly inflexible in responding to the destabilising pressures of multiple and escalating crises. In such breakdown conditions the historic response has been economic and political decentralisation. This might range from democratic grassroots versions to the more conservative scenarios introduced earlier in this book.

As with all ecological crises, decline is likely to gather momentum and eventually to bottom out only when the demands which our species makes on the ecosphere are sufficiently reduced to permit the continued survival of what remains of human culture, so that, in William Ophuls' words, 'the entire Industrial Revolution will appear as a brief and anomalous spike in humanity's otherwise flat ecological trace, a transitory epoch of a few centuries' duration in which it seemed momentarily possible to abolish scarcity'.[35]

These are the probabilities towards which we appear at present to be on course. The next chapter will be about how we might work to change direction. But certainly the foregoing reinforces the need for a despair-and-empowerment kind of spirituality if we are to live and labour in good heart, freed of the consolations and confusions of ideology.

19 Eco-social liberation (the outer work)

Getting our bearings

In Part IV I reviewed the many different movements relevant to the transition to a green society or 'new age'. Each is preoccupied with making its own future, and yet each has an important contribution to make to the overall work of shaping a new society. A willingness to undertake positive dialogue and multilateral ideological disarmament would be welcome, and the creation of a common forum would encourage this.

The most explicit—and narrow—perspective on liberation from our ecological and social problems is the formal political one. This appeals strongly to those who can think of purposive social and economic change only in political terms. And of such political assumptions the narrowest is that the ballot box is the key to the transition to ecotopia. It is hoped that a rising tide of public opinion will eventually precipitate a green electoral landslide, voting into power a party or coalition which will begin to legislate the foundations of a radically green society. *Blueprint for survival*, back in 1972, was based on this assumption. And nearly twenty years later the Green Party resolved 'to secure a parliamentary mandate for green politics by the end of the first decade of the twenty-first century'.

Precedents range from the 1832 Reform Act to the 1945 Labour landslide which ushered in the welfare state, or the legislative decade which is assumed to have created Thatcherite Britain. If at some future time the huge and influential environmentalist movement were to come to believe that present rates of economic growth were unsustainable and leading to disaster, then the demand for more radical social and economic change would be unstoppable. But this would imply a much more profound upheaval than the previously quoted political and parliamentary examples. The analogy is rather with historic transformations like the Industrial Revolution, the Renaissance or the Reformation, involving altogether new mentalities and ways of life. The present becomes intolerable and the future essential. Indeed, the transition to a steady-state conserver society would be second in historic significance only to the agricultural transition (or neolithic revolution) which took place between 6000 BC and 2000 BC, but compressed into decades instead of millennia. There is something incongruous about even thinking of such an undertaking in terms of a parliamentary majority, unless what is really in mind is no more than a bigger environmental clean-up.

At this point in the argument it is important to distinguish between transition to a steady-state or minimal growth economy where power is still very much centralised and top-down (perhaps with the kind of populist, emergency-powers government referred to earlier), and a transition characterised by decentralised grassroots empowerment in the libertarian, small-is-beautiful tradition. I believe there is some truth in the radical green contention that a conserver, steady-state economy is best socially sustained by decentralising and balancing political and economic power in confederations of communities and regions empowered by direct democracy. But I do not believe that it can be conclusively argued that the latter social order is a *necessary* condition for a steady-state economy. History is never so tidy and predictable. What is indisputable, however, is that such a politically regulated, minimal growth economy would pose socially divisive questions about the distribution of wealth that had suddenly become finite. In short, transition to a steady state may be possible without socially equitable redistribution, but the necessarily authoritarian regime would have an unstable and uncertain future.

Even without taking on board the full libertarian agenda in the Green Party's *Manifesto for a sustainable society*, an incoming green government which seriously tampered with the prospects for continued rates of growth could be blocked and destabilised by the political/business/administrative/military establishment if its majority were backed by no more than a rootless and purely 'political' movement. It could only implement its policies if something of a pluralistic green social culture were already well established, colonising and neutralising established institutions, and working through new, alternative ones where necessary. A *radical* green electoral mandate could only be effective if such a transition were *already under way*. And of course radically decentralist legislation would be a dead letter unless a decentralist political and economic culture had already had time to establish itself in the country. As to the support of ideologically fixated, self-serving mass movements of the traditional revolutionary kind, history has by now pronounced sufficiently often as to rob them of credibility. In brief, the above train of argument suggests that it is nonsensical to conceive of a radical green transition primarily in electoral terms.

The green transition which I shall be exploring in the following pages is about how we might realistically set about shaping a pluralistic green social and economic culture as from now. Bear in mind that history will certainly serve up other ways, for better or worse, of negotiating the ecological crisis, depending on different national cultures and other circumstances. The libertarian way may be logical, morally compelling, and strongly motivating, but it is also the most ambitious and presently improbable form of transition. But it is possible. Before we get down to our grassroots business, however, some attention must be given to the important and controversial question of whether the transition is to be seen predominantly in terms of consensus or of conflict.

For some green radicals, and especially red-greens, the transition would be very much about the struggle to overthrow obstructive economic and political power centres. It would necessarily be a confrontational transition on the model of class-based social revolutions.

Contrariwise, the consensualists appear to live in a different world (and may indeed do so). Their vision is of 'aquarian conspirators' found across the wide spectrum of 'the rising culture', from politics to healthcare, from the arts to business, doing the work of peaceful, silent revolution as they shift the paradigm by means of dialogue and example, refashioning existing institutions and where necessary creating alternatives which by-pass them. Eventually the whole of our social culture will be permeated by the new values and what is left of the old order will simply decay into irrelevance. David Pepper, exploding in comic incredulity, explains how this looks to a green working class socialist:

> In the elitist and idealist view, [the transition] can be done by a group of intellectuals and well-meaning, socially minded people who, by dint largely of thinking about it, will be the vanguard of revolutionary change of mass consciousness. They will bring us to some post-industrial future of unimaginable leisure and greater wealth equality where, in place of the high material standards which many regard as a right today, all will experience relative poverty, but without 'misery', revelling instead in a nebulous concept of 'quality of life' (itself highly reflective of White Anglo-Saxon Protestant values).[36]

Systematic strategies for a predominantly consensual transition have been proposed by several writers associated with the new economics movement, and are nicely exemplified in James Robertson's book *Future wealth*.[37] There is great faith in 'reconceptualisation' as a means of changing reality. We have already referred to the belief that if only a new kind of economics can be elaborated then it will somehow lead us directly to a new economic order, notably through the power of reasoned argument to change the minds of top—but presumably reasonable—people. Robertson's book is full of brisk, global optimism and annual economic summits, and lots of legislative and administrative nuts and bolts, like the ten ways in which to develop the household economy.

Much of this new economics writing on the radical green transition has a curious unreality about it, far from the world of acquisitiveness, exploitation and abuse of power highlighted daily in the media. Thus, in Robertson's ecotopia 'oil companies will aim to help their customers to buy less oil, by reducing their dependence on it, [and] pharmaceutical and food manufacturing firms . . . will help to reduce their customers' dependence on drugs and convenience food'.[38]

In fairness, Robertson (and many others like him) when it comes down to it are not lacking in radical intent and resolution. Robertson does not deny the possibility of open conflict and would presumably be willing to resort to nonviolent sanctions if needs be. The following (admittedly rare) caveat suggests more common ground with David Pepper than might have first appeared likely:

> People with more power and wealth than others do not willingly give them up, and people who enjoy security and order do not willingly see them threatened. It would be foolish to underestimate potential resistance to the necessary economic transformation we are trying to bring about. It could be disastrous to underestimate the ruthlessness with which this transformation might be suppressed even in law-abiding countries like Britain, if ever it came to be seen as a vehicle for disruptive social and political forces.[39]

Green consensualism has several possible origins. There is the assumption that in our so-called post-industrial, more consensual world all sections of society will feel equally threatened by environmental crisis and equally willing to accept substantial changes and sacrifices. In the second place, there is the 'spiritual', holistic notion that conflict is somehow unwholesome and denies our underlying interconnectedness, forgetting that conflict and consensus are, like oneness and separateness, no more than mutually defining aspects of a single reality. And then there is the consensual 'everybody wins!' optimism of the egalitarian American frontier tradition. This has been absorbed into the international alternative value system, but it does not travel well . . . Finally, greens are predominantly white, middle class intellectuals, working in consensual professional environments, rather than the hierarchical and authoritarian organisations still typical of our society. They commonly have little personal experience of exploitation and disempowerment.[40]

It is easy to become attached, through personality or circumstance, to either a conflict or consensus mentality. But, as Ralf Dahrendorf has pointed out, every social element is co-operative yet conflictful, consensual yet beset by sectional interests, integrated yet marked by contradictions, bound by legitimated authority and yet involving power relations.[41] An example is the positive yet critical stance which I believe is required of greens in respect of private business and the market system. As we have seen earlier, these do tend to be ecologically dysfunctional (conflict), and yet at the same time they do arguably have an important function in making a green economy work (consensus).

What does all this amount to in terms of strategies for shaping a green society? In the first place, the capacity for consensual transformation in any specific situation needs to be pushed until we come up against its limits. Consensual, negotiated change can become practicable as a consequence of radical changes in underlying values and assumptions, which may undermine the credibility of certain policies and the received authority of those identified with them. There have been numerous examples in recent history (notably in some of the communist countries and in South Africa) where power which seemed impregnable has lost its authority overnight, after years of undermining by a variety of different forces and circumstances which have gradually transformed the social and economic foundations. In such cases established authority either resigns and departs, or is obliged to accept a shift in consensus and a new balance of power. When it does come this kind of change, if well prepared. tends to be deep-rooted and enduring.

If consensualists need to know when it is best to stand and fight, fundamentalist greens inclined to a conflict mentality need to appreciate the potential for consensual transformation. Inappropriate and unnecessary confrontation, whether successful or not, can create a 'no win' situation where there is prolonged bitterness and polarisation, and a potentially valuable consensual climate becomes difficult to create.

Building a green social culture

The remainder of this chapter makes proposals about how we might begin to build a pluralistic green social culture as a future society in the making. 'Pluralistic' is used here to mean three things:

a) The radical green project will need to attract commitment from all sections of society, from suburban conservatives to the long-term unemployed;

b) It aims at transformatory work across the widest possible range of concerns, from local government to art and literature, from the position of children and the old in society to the roles of the professions;

c) It is hospitable to a plurality of strategies for change, from mass opposition to personal example, and from the refashioning of what we have now to the creation of new alternatives.

As a preliminary, it will be helpful to recall the leading ideas.

1 To bring social activity back into harmony with the rest of the ecosphere. This means progressively reducing environmental damage and seriously addressing the problems of living without significant economic growth. In particular it means focusing on future livelihood and what we mean by the quality of people's lives. This is the radical green crunch. Is it problem or is it opportunity?

2 To work to reshape society, globally as well as locally, so that the whole range of basic human needs are satisfied as a moral right, even at the expense of some limitation on the satisfaction of the wants of others. Two intense moral obligations must be met: to the peoples of the Third World, and to enable our own so-called 'underclass' to free themselves from poverty and powerlessness.

3 To begin to shift power from the top and the centre to the bottom and the periphery, as a movement towards empowerment with responsibility. Populist authoritarianism will not have the power to co-opt and seduce those who feel themselves to be empowered members of a credible democratic alternative movement operating throughout society. This personally experienced empowerment will be the more assured if it is rooted not only in the supportive culture of many small groups and networks, but also in a culture of local and regional communities. This will need to be rediscovered and recreated in a new-found sense of identity.

The green transition will be considered under seven (interactive) strategies for change. These I have adapted from James Robertson's excellent little book *The sane alternative*.[42] They are: (A) drafting strategies for change; (B) empowerment with responsibility; (C) the enabling state; (D) opposition; (E) reclaiming and reshaping existing institutions; (F) creating alternatives; and (G) changes in lifestyle.

Robertson identifies thirty different concerns or activity areas in each of which the above range of strategies might be applied. There are other possible classifications, but the list is usefully suggestive: families, households, and local communities; roles of the sexes; roles of children, adults and the elderly; land use and land tenure; agriculture and food; conservation of minerals and materials; manufacture, repair and maintenance of things; provision of services and care to people; politics and government; economic organisation; energy; transport; cities, towns and rural resettlement; housing; roles of professions; science and technology; health; education; money and finance; work and employment; religion and philosophy; arts and culture; leisure, entertainment and sport; information and communications media; crime, prisons, police, law, etc.; animal welfare, wildlife, etc.; Third World; international relations; disarmament, peace and security.

(A) Drafting strategies for change

Written strategies, discussion papers, guidelines and visions would be needed both for specific fields of activity like those above and for specific towns, regions and other geographical communities.

Such strategies would not primarily be policies to be pressed upon government through lobbying and electioneering, but rather programmes and perspectives promoting many different kinds of initiative, and involving a wide range of people. Strategy papers would be concerned with all or most of the remaining six strategies in this chapter. They would not only provide guidelines for action and a means of co-ordinating many different activities, but also a focus for discussion, for learning together and building up networks of common concern.

Strategy documents should be seen as no more than temporary scaffolding, continually modified by experience. Indeed, several different strategies might be elaborated by different groups of people in the same area of concern. There is often more than one way of evolving in a particular direction, and the merits of one or another may only become apparent over time. Breadth, openness and flexibility are more likely to succeed than calculative search for 'the one right way', and will certainly attract more support. For all of the above reasons, working together on a strategy paper can be a first step towards collective empowerment.

(B) Empowerment with responsibility

The empowerment of the presently disempowered, ranging from women to the peoples of the periphery, and from the old to employees, is as essential to the radical green project as is the disempowerment of all those large and dominant social formations whose acquisitive power has been so largely responsible for the ecological crisis. It is important also, however, to consider how each instance of popular empowerment can also be fully responsible, to other sections of society, to the planet and its life, and to future generations.

In some societies power is quite markedly exercised by the few over the many. Elsewhere it is shared more broadly and works more subtly. But even in the latter a sense of relative powerlessness is quite widely experienced, though it may only make itself acutely felt at times of personal or group crisis, such as redundancy and unemployment, or in the frustration and helplessness experienced by the long-term homeless, or when faced with the we-know-best condescension of the professional over his client, or the take-it-or-leave-it finality of an official, or the failure to find justice and redress when confronted by some faceless organisation. At such times, if are not already habituated to a sense of powerlessness, it can come as a shock to realise just how powerless ordinary citizens really are when they fall foul of authority.

The term 'enablement' usefully draws attention to whatever needs to be done to enable empowerment to develop. The first enabling step in personal and collective empowerment is to bring a sense of disempowerment and dependency into full awareness. Disempowerment, whether by gender, class, race, upbringing or education, may be so historically embedded or so personally ingrained as to seem part of the natural order of things. Similarly, those who are, arguably, insufficiently informed about the ecological crisis, or are led to believe that the powers-that-be have matters well in hand, will not *feel* themselves to be powerless, even though green campaigners may try to tell them that they are.

Moreover, even where powerlessness is strongly felt, work may need to be done to enable the powerless fully to experience its reality, so that reclaiming power begins to appear both as a realistic possibility and a moral necessity. 'Consciousness raising' is a well known example from the women's movement. Work in small groups can build up trust and give psychological space and encouragement for people who aren't white middle class professional males, not only to have their say but also to work through deep feelings and conditioning associated with their sense of powerlessness. Those who belong socially and educationally to the dominant class in society, even if themselves working to end that dominance, easily take for granted their own sense of confidence, competence, and power to initiate, plan and project. They may fail to appreciate the habitual sense of inadequacy and self-blame of the powerless at being unable to change their situation; their habit of responding by adapting, coping, evasion and silence; their withholding of feelings in the face of members of the dominant group; their resort to black humour, self-mockery, and the supportive subculture of their peer group when faced with injustice and hypocrisy.[43]

The structures of disempowerment in our society conceal a huge and wasted human potential existing just below the surface. Jeremy Seabrook, writing of British working class communities, has remarked on 'the immeasurable quantity of unfulfilled talent, locked up resources, unwanted energy and power, that are only waiting for a moment of release, some energizing agent, to express themselves. I am struck again and again by the intelligence for which society has no use, the abilities that remain undeveloped, the talents that are not required by the market place'.[44] Similarly, Guy Dauncey writes out of his rich experience of self-help community initiative: 'I have seen inspiration grow in the hearts of local people when they have begun to understand that they can take matters into their own hands and begin to have a significant impact on their own local affairs . . . They begin to get excited, in the same way that a person with a paralysed arm does when she suddenly discovers she can use two fingers'.[45]

(C) The enabling state

Government, in the ideal model for transition to a green society, would be no more than a facilitator responding legislatively and fiscally to the pressure generated by deeper social changes that were already under way. This accords with the notion of the 'enabling state' as opposed to the state as an increasingly huge and complex direct universal provider. From a left-wing viewpoint the principles of the enabling state have been defined as follows:

> First, that the state remains the indispensable source of social solutions and meeter of social needs; secondly, that the state can rarely define needs well on its own, but that this must always be an active and reciprocal process with those who have needs; and, thirdly, that the state is better as an enabler than as an operator or provider in its own right, so that wherever possible the means of delivery too should be organised in as reciprocal, responsible and open manner as possible.[46]

In its co-optive role the enabling state brings consumer, women's, community-based, and other social and economic interests into its orbit through committee co-option, conditional funding, and using voluntary organisations as means of service delivery (as with tenant management of social housing). Examples are the Greater London Council (1981-86), and the regional governments of Euskadi (the Basque region of Spain) and Emilio-Romagna (Italy). The latter, instead of actively planning the regional economy, assist large numbers of small private firms and co-operatives to work together through joint marketing organisations, collaborative research and development and so forth.

The right of the political spectrum is also attracted to the idea of the enabling state, but as the 'minimal state' which interferes least with the market and established centres of wealth and power. Thus, in place of *collective* empowerments it is the *individual* empowerment of the 'entrepreneurial culture' that is favoured, together with such devices as 'school-choice' vouchers.

In the US in the 1980s many of the so-called New Paradigm Republicans found consensus with like-minded Democrats such as George Latimer, mayor of St Paul, Minnesota. Latimer has been hailed as 'the architect of entrepreneurial local government, using the power of city hall to mobilise private sector funds and energies, and empowering local people to solve their own problems. He set up non-profit voluntary groups to adopt individual parks and streets, to run energy audits of public buildings and recycling programmes for the city's trash. He brought in charitable foundations which wanted to test reform projects, and set up non-profit partnerships with local businesses to redevelop declining downtown areas. Similar partnerships redesigned the civic power system to use waste heat in the hot-water system and to invest in low-cost housing'.[47]

In examining such strategies it will be evident that, in the over-developed countries, the political and economic establishment does have some interest in promoting at least limited forms of grassroots empowerment, just as it has an interest in limited forms of environmental protection. Where there is such consensual latitude there may be useful opportunities to take up 'slack rope' (in terms of power and funding) until resistance is felt and the question of who is co-opting whom is resolved. By all means let us avoid fruitless and counter-productive confrontations; but let us remember also that there are fundamental questions at stake in the transition which cannot be compromised. 'The question is,' said Alice, 'whether you can make words mean so many different things.' 'The question is,' said Humpty Dumpty, 'which is to be master—that's all'.[48]

(D) Opposition

There are certain ecological and social abuses, together with the institutions responsible for them, which require outright opposition as an integral part of the work of transition. Opposition will be the more effective if the following criteria are met.

i Are constructive alternatives offered, both long and short term?

ii Is the campaign conducted as an educational, eye opening experience which enables people to see the larger picture of which the abuse is a part and to appreciate its underlying causes? In particular, is it possible to demonstrate the interconnectedness between action to protect the environment and issues of social justice and world peace?

iii Does the campaign pay attention to the sincerity of the opposing standpoint and to adversaries' concerns for what they see as a threat to their vital interests? Does it attempt to respond to their needs as far as may be possible without compromising fundamental principles?

iv Does the campaign mobilise the widest possible opposition coalition?

v Is it conducted in ways which help to strengthen participants' personal and collective sense of empowerment in the face of seemingly impregnable institutions?

A good example is the campaign against nuclear power. Credible proposals for alternative sources of energy generation are needed (i). The critique of nuclear power can be instructively revealing in many different directions. It can throw light, for example, on the power and secretiveness of vested interests, and the connections between the industrial, political, scientific and military establishments (ii). There needs to be constructive concern for workers threatened with loss of livelihood if nuclear plants are shut down (iii). To mobilise the widest opposition it is important, for example, to ensure that anxiety about global warming as a result of fossil fuel power generation should not lead to a mistaken enthusiasm for 'environmentally friendly' nuclear power (iv). Finally, tactics like (in Britain) withholding the eleven per cent 'nuclear tax' when paying electricity bills can give a strong sense of personal, committed empowerment (v).

(E) Reclaiming and reshaping existing institutions

The term 'institutions' here covers a very wide range of entities, from trade unions to churches, from professions to whole social sectors like sport and entertainment, and could be extended to include bodies of knowledge like theology and economics. What is required is to move beyond the environmental audit level and to consider the specific contribution each individual entity could make to the transition, and what its place would be in a politically and economically decentralised steady-state conserver society. This requires an imaginative understanding of the relevance of the whole radical green project to particular situations and cases, and we clearly still have a long way to go before even thinking in these terms becomes at all widespread.

The situation is confused in that some existing power centres have already not only initiated environmental policies but also co-opted power sharing as a means of improving their image and their effectiveness without any significant loss of the power that really matters. For example, it has long been the practice to empower employees to take responsibility for a wider range of job decisions, thereby both increasing job satisfaction and improving the efficiency and flexibility of the organisation's operations. A token shareholding and representation on the board may further enhance the sense of empowerment and help to make 'labour problems' a thing of the past. Organisation professionals, in particular, have been likened to privileged eunuchs of the harem, in that they were free to do anything as long as it did not interfere with the main purpose of the organisation.

The present position regarding a radical green 'reclaiming and reshaping' is that we are still trying to reach the level of effective environmental audit of our institutions and organisations, with darker green political and economic perspectives lying far beyond. Sometimes it seems as if, on the contrary, green ideas themselves were being 'reclaimed and reshaped'!

(F) Creating alternatives

There is a belief that the creation of alternative institutions and social structures would itself be sufficient empowerment as to render the established order redundant. So long as nobody needs any longer to work for it, pay its taxes, buy its products or seek its professional advice, it will just fall without being pushed. And this strategy also removes the danger of being co-opted by bodies which we are supposed to be reclaiming and reshaping.

The contrary view is that the economic and political establishment will only tolerate alternative initiatives on the margins of society. There they may even help to alleviate local economic problems, provide supplements or substitutes for public provision which government wishes to cut back or abandon, and generally direct people's energies away from criticism of the establishment.

The new economics movement attaches much importance to the development of local, self-reliant green economies as part of the general strategy of enablement which it hopes will bring the new economy into being.

Books like Guy Dauncey's *After the crash*[49] make inspiring and exciting reading in reporting a promising variety of community self-help initiatives. But although they are demonstrations of what could be achieved, only marginally do they amount to the beginnings of a green grassroots empowerment movement. Nevertheless, of the seven strategies for change other than oppositional campaigning, it is presently only in the area of alternatives (including personal lifestyles) that, even if only in small and still marginal ways, a future green society *is* being prefigured. Organic farming, renewable energy technologies, complementary medicine, the small school movement, eco-socially positive investment opportunities, and recycling schemes are among the miscellany of such growth points.

It is to the Third World that we must particularly look for a growing number of autonomous, community-based and ecologically orientated development projects. Bernard Ledea Ouedraogo, founder in Burkina Faso of one such movement, identifies four reasons for their success: 'Dynamic local leadership and activity; maintenance of traditional values; proscription of any social, ethnic, political or religious discrimination; training and motivation coming from within the group based on the principle: act on the basis of what people *are*, what they *know*, how they *live*, what they *do*, what they *know how to do*, and what they *want*'.[50]

Thousands of such groups are now undertaking a wide range of village projects in food production and conservation, reforestation, irrigation, setting up credit and savings schemes, healthcare and family planning, literacy, human-scale technology enterprises, and traditional medicine. And it is the women, the major food producers in most Third World countries, who are in the forefront of many of these projects, such as the Kenya Green Belt movement, a women's network which has planted over ten million trees.

For an example of urban and more confrontational types of movement, consider the following from Mexico:

> Over 600,000 squatter families are organised nationwide in Mexico's 'urban people's movement', which has grown from a collection of local struggles to become a force capable of challenging the regime. While resisting co-optation by the ruling party, and insisting on autonomy from the opposition, the movement has shown that democratic community participation not only can solve some of the drastic problems facing the poor majority; it can be a vehicle for revolutionary change.[51]

By the late 1980s, out of some two billion rural poor, a hundred million

worldwide were benefiting from grassroots development initiatives.[52]
However, it has to be said that, in the words of Paul Ekins, these initiatives
are 'still fragile' and that 'most of the major global trends are still going in
the wrong direction, some at an accelerating rate'.[50]

(G) Changes in lifestyle

The necessarily limited significance of changes in lifestyle has already been
noted in the earlier discussion of green consumerism. But presumably a
radical green lifestyle entails much more than becoming a vegetarian cyclist
who uses ecologically friendly washing up liquid, and more, even, than
adopting a lifestyle of simplicity, consuming less and making possessions
last longer.

It would surely imply self-empowerment through commitment of time
and energy to the work of building a green transitional social culture in
whatever areas of life one can best contribute to.

It would imply a choice of livelihood of positive value to people, creatures and planet, or at least one which was not actually destructive.

It would require a commitment to trying to live one's life in ways which
affirm interdependence and mutuality, particularly in relation to other
people. This, in my view, would imply some commitment to the kind of
inner work introduced at the end of this book.

Pointers from West Wales

The following notes from my own experience will give some heart and
substance to the general argument. Earlier, in Chapter 17, I referred to a
sensational parliamentary election victory in 1992 by a green Welsh
nationalist, Cynog Dafis. Dafis was returned as a Plaid Cymru (Welsh
nationalist party) member, but the campaign was fought on a 'Plaid
Cymru/Green' ticket based on a strong ongoing alliance with Ceredigion
Green Party and an uncompromisingly radical green programme.[53] The
victory was seen by the allies as a mandate to make at least a modest start
with building the promised 'green Welsh future'—a truly amazing,
humbling and unique experience for radicals anywhere in Britain in that
year. Although there are special circumstances in West Wales, nevertheless
some of the lessons we have learnt are transferable elsewhere.

Policy is a close weave of ecological, social, economic, community and
national aspirations. With some 66,000 electors, this is a rural
constituency of small farms and businesses, economically marginalised and
suffering from chronic low pay and high unemployment. Although its
Welsh character has been diluted by waves of English incomers, many of

the latter now identify with the region and its culture. The Plaid Cymru/Green Party constituency campaign has been concerned to nurture a local, individual *and collective*, entrepreneurial response to the region's problems, to be backed by a strong, resurgent local government and an adequate public service infrastructure. The exceptionally rich potential of West Wales in renewable energy, sustainable forestry, and 'soft' community and environmentally friendly tourism is emphasised. A thriving local economy of small private, co-operative and community businesses could add value to farm and forest outputs and help to develop a regional market. Regional economic self-reliance and community empowerment are presented as the means of 'improving the quality of life of all our people in the context of our global responsibilities', not only in terms of livelihood, but also in defence of the strongly felt identity and distinctiveness of place, language and lifestyle.

During the election campaign policy discussion papers on small business, farming, renewable energy, forestry and coastal pollution aroused considerable interest.[53] Subsequently project groups were established for these topics, plus transport, healthcare and language and identity. These groups are linked by a joint campaign committee of the two parties. Some have developed into tough campaigning groups, others are stimulating public policy discussion, and others again are trying to get specific projects off the ground. Membership is drawn not only from the two parties but also from environmental groups and 'non-political' specialists. People are welcomed to join from 'across and beyond party-political divisions'. Working together in this way has proved extremely stimulating, with different strengths complementing one another whether in terms of perspective, background, expertise, or style of work. The whole has turned out to be more than the sum of the parts, and the limitations of conventional one party politics have been brought home to us.

A unique alliance across cultural and linguistic divisions, supporting a broad but integrated policy, and expressed in a down-to-earth and open-minded kind of idealism, have combined to create an excitingly *inclusive politics*. This became more evident as the election receded, and opponents who continued to play silly party-political games found it difficult to get a toehold in the new situation.

Community and regional politics is not an *alternative* to national and global politics. It is an arguably more effective and less corruptible way of doing politics.

In the first place, there are numerous global connections to be made. Farm forestry policy, for example, is about helping to restore the global climatic balance as well as the bank balances of Welsh upland farmers.

Renewable energy policies are as much about the start already made in exporting intermediate, human scale technologies to the Third World (like the solar-powered hospital which local engineering consultants have facilitated in Eritrea) as about ending the reluctant migration of young people from Ceredigion.

In the second place, regional initiatives do, of course, soon come up against the rules of the present political and economic game which are rigged against them. Renewable energy schemes—and particularly small-scale, local ones—are hampered by current legislation. Similarly, local production would benefit from taxing long-distance road haulage, thus emphasising its true environmental costs, and particularly if the tax were used to boost a more self-reliant regional economy. The people of Wales as a whole are being systematically disempowered, politically and economically, by the top-down policies of the Secretary of State for Wales. This government minister rules through the proliferating bureaucracy of the Welsh Office, advised by a growing network of committees made up of politically reliable appointees usurping the powers of democratically accountable bodies.[54]

The keystone of Plaid Cymru/Green Party policy in Ceredigion is therefore the demand for a legislative parliament ultimately heading a Welsh Confederation which would draw strength from a Europe of the Regions. It is in confident and united communities and regions that a head of countervailing power can most effectively be built up which, whatever the frustrations along the way, could eventually make the old order no longer tenable.

The final learning is a reminder of the power of fresh, live and locally grown political idealism. In the Thatcher years the taste of the real organic stuff was almost forgotten. All who managed to get into the opening campaign rally addressed by Jonathon Porritt and Cynog Dafis felt its empowering current—a novelty for the youngsters and sixties nostalgia for the oldsters. Nothing succeeds like success. Empowerment begins as a state of mind. This credibility empowers achievement on the ground. This empowers a new state of mind, and so on . . . But such aspirations need to be carried lightly and realistically, lest visionaries yet again become the prisoners of dreams gone sour. For ours is really quite a fragile little enterprise. But, come what may, it has reminded us of how public life *can* be lived and of the possibilities to be found even in our unpromising times.

In addition there are in England several local Green Parties which also testify to the potential for a radical green politics which is community based. And, like Ceredigion, they remain largely unaffected by the ills of the parent party. Particularly noteworthy is the the Oxford local party, with a membership of over one hundred, an annual turnover of between £4,000 and £5,000 and a successful electoral track record. Today in Britain a radical green politics is relevant and practicable. It is the Green Party that is its own problem, like so many other radical formations before it.

PENTRE GWYRDD A.D. 2050
VISITING A COMMUNITY IN GREEN WALES
[The following little ecotopian indulgence completes the picture and illustrates another way of getting the message across].

Viewed from the TrawsCambria rapid transit railbus, the threeblade wind turbines resembled dancing dervishes in the morning sunshine. They were a reminder of how rich the Welsh Confederation is in clean and renewable energy. First it was coal we exported to England; now it is cheap wind-and-wood-and-water electricity. Coming over the hills is the morning Cardiff to Dublin airship. Droning quietly towards the Aberystwyth mooring mast, it can't be making more than 90 mph against the headwind. Since its lift comes mainly from the helium, the bio-diesel consumption is modest compared with a heavier-than-air machine. And there's probably no safer form of transport today.

Aberystwyth was a nice surprise. It had largely escaped that last surge of 'development' in what the history books call The Final Madness at the turn of the century. Mair Smith, chairperson of Pentre Gwyrdd (Greenham) community council, was so pleased to meet me that she almost forgot to unplug her little *modur gwlad* (country car) from the public battery charging point. It was a simple, durable, utility runabout, easily maintained and repaired, which had been designed to enable country people to get to the nearest public transport pick-up points in this region of scattered homesteads.

I was surprised at the size of the village—evidence of the rural repopulation by young people from the towns. There were old people who could still recall it as a ghost of a place, with prettified cottages empty most of the year, and surrounded by nothing but sheep walks and conifer plantations. It is now a busy, thriving centre, with new dwellings spreading out into clearings in the beautiful varied woodlands.

Mair explained that much of the woodland is communally owned, just like the traditional common grazings which it shelters and fertilises. There are also numerous private landholdings, but their size is limited by law. Agro-forestry is a family way of life, not an agribusiness for growing rich.

Just looking at the varied pattern of the community's landscape showed

A forest-croft township in the Second Great Wood of Caledon

how livestock, forestry, organic arable, and the several small timber and food processing businesses all supported each other. 'What we take from nature we put back,' Mair explained. 'Everything is recycled. We believe in keeping our wealth in the community. It's difficult to imagine those crazy times when human manure was mixed with toxic industrial and agricultural wastes and, at considerable expense, was pumped into a polluted Cardigan Bay!'

From Mair's garden we could see the biggest group of buildings in the village—the community timber yard. The village retains most of its timber, for household and community fuel and for the several little businesses that make everything from timber framed houses to domestic utensils.

Looking around the kitchen garden was a reminder of how much the global warm-up had encouraged people to grow their own, though a lot was sold or bartered at the weekly market or through the village shop. Now that heavy energy taxes make it so expensive to bring in long-haul foodstuffs there's a big incentive towards local and regional self-reliance—*and the control that goes with it.*

Mair's house was lined with pine, real wood instead of laminated chipboard, and warm, insulating and beautiful. As is now the fashion, the household goods were few and simple, cheap, long-lasting utility goods mingled with attractive hand-crafted things. Since the house is near the centre of the village it benefits from the community-owned combined heat and power system, based on a wood fuel generator behind the timber yard. Outlying houses have their own high-tech wood burners, supplemented by cheap electricity from the community generator (which also sells into the grid). I was reminded that by now twenty per cent of Welsh energy needs are met from willow, poplar and other energy plantations.

Mair introduced me to the facilitators of the different management groups through which the community council runs much of the local economy, as well as the social services. Just about everyone is in on the act somewhere! This proud little community tries to live up to the three watchwords on the official notepaper: CYDWEITHREDIAD; ANTUR; DIGONOLDEB (co-operation; enterprise; sufficiency).

Of course, Ceredigion, like other Welsh county councils, is very much a power in the land. But it uses this to empower and enable willing community councils to manage and even create their own services. Typical is Pentre Gwyrdd senior citizen committee (with a majority of oldsters on it), which provides comprehensive care and support for the elderly, receiving specialist advice and assistance from the county council—not that most people ever really 'retire' in a place like Pentre Gwyrdd! Here as elsewhere, however, there *are* a number of older, chronically sick people to care for. You see, it wasn't the global warm-up that eventually forced The Great U-Turn. It was the profound alarm created by a sudden awareness of the 'eco-epidemic' of cancers and nervous and degenerative disorders.

Of the community leaders in the room most were women and all were bilingual. The first reminded me of how limiting it must have been in the old days to be without all the especially *female* talents we have now. After all, it was the women who really pushed through the Great Transition. As to the Welsh language, it's not only that everyone was schooled in it. There's so much going on in the community you feel you really have to be bilingual. It is amazing that we used to make so much heavy weather of the so-called language problem. Nowadays, every educated Welsh person is bilingual or trilingual, like every Belgian, Basque or Swiss. In many districts of the Welsh Confederation English is in fact recognised as the 'first' official language, though both Welsh and English have equal status in law.

The village school is quite small, and a reminder of how unfashionable it has become to have more than one or two children. It is the childless couples who are now well regarded, as having made 'future space' for others' children. I think our biggest achievement is to have guaranteed our children a healthy future.

The teenagers are so involved in community life that some have so far not even used their first overseas air travel coupon. Public transport is cheap and easy, and it's not only in the towns that there is much going on. And anyway computer networking is all the rage at present.

It all sounds utopian, but I learned that here as elsewhere there is plenty of disagreement and conflicts certainly do arise. Even round here you can still find selfish people who, despite the hundred per cent wealth and income tax ceiling, are still running round like headless chickens, trying to make their pile, and set off the old growthmania all over again. However, acquisitive and competitive behaviour are nowadays seen as antisocial hangups, much like heavy drinking. Co-operation, mediation and conflict resolution are the skills most in demand.

Mair felt that one development which now makes it easier for people to get on well together is the revival of a meditative Celtic spirituality in the Confederation. The longstanding scatter of Buddhist and similar groups in rural Wales has contributed in the same direction. And whether you are church or chapel or neither, it is very much the thing to 'do your own work', both alone and in your little group. This spiritual revival and the profound change in lifestyle help to explain why people are more relaxed and contented than they were in the old days. The old people say that our generation is somehow more playful, and has more time.

How did it all happen? Eventually enough people realised that things just had to change if there was to be any tolerable future, and that we could not wait for the politicians to do it all for us. And a different kind of person started to go into politics.

20 Psycho-spiritual liberation (the inner work)

The need for inner work

So far in Part V I have considered various ways, social, political and economic, in which the green libertarian vision might be made a more realistic proposition. Even so, to actualise it will depend also upon intertwining a vigorous inner work movement. Individually and collectively we shall need to work upon ourselves as well as upon society, in order to create some shift in the kind of people we are and in the characteristic ways we relate to each other and to nature.

Like so many revolutionary idealists before them, not even the radical greens themselves have proved able to live out their professed values in their organisational behaviour. Green parties have been marked by vehement strife, with little attempt at conciliation and conflict resolution. Similar experiences have been commonplace in the peace, women's and other overlapping movements of the 'rainbow alliance'. Commenting on an episode of 'childish and destructive squabbling' among the editorial group of *Peace news*, one observer confessed that he had 'always found peace meetings and peace groups to be the most unpeaceful environments I have ever worked in, compared to which a meeting of NATO generals must be a truly soothing experience. The true significance of all this is spelt out by Caroline Harwood: "Brave phrases about achieving a nonviolent, peaceful world lose much of their persuasion when the means used to achieve those ideals imitate the methods of power seeking, patriarchy and control we claim to be struggling against. Are we the ones who think we know better than scrapping and squabbling politicians about how the world should be run?"'[55]

Many radical activists invest their selves—their time, energy and idealism—with a wholehearted commitment. And so stress, frustration and obstruction can ignite explosions out of all proportion to the issues at stake. The history of the US greens, for example, has been described by

one activist as being marked by 'chronically simmering ideological, person-
alist and value differences'.[56] And Rudolf Bahro observed of the German
Green Party: 'There are a lot of unfulfilled needs for self-realisation, so the
very kind of competition we want to abolish thrives within the Party'.[57]

Reflecting on a lifetime's experience as an international mediator, the
Buddhist Quaker Adam Curle came to see that 'the way we perceive
human nature, *especially our own*, is of overarching importance. It is indeed
an absurd illusion to consider that we can work for peace . . . if we are
inwardly turbulent and ill at ease; or to help people change their lives for
the better if our own existence is disordered and impoverished'.[58] And
from the same roots there springs an ultimately futile and even destructive
hyperactivism, of which Thomas Merton has written:

> There is a perverse form of contemporary violence to which the
> idealist fighting for peace by non-violent methods most easily
> succumbs: activism and overwork. The rush and pressure of modern
> life are a form, perhaps the most common form, of its innate
> violence. To allow oneself to be carried away by a multitude of
> conflicting concerns, to surrender to too many demands, to commit
> oneself to too many projects, to want to help everyone in everything,
> is to succumb to violence. The frenzy of the activist neutralises work
> for peace. It destroys the fruitfulness of work, because it kills the root
> of inner wisdom which makes work fruitful.

It is for these reasons that a few prominent radical greens have consis-
tently maintained that (in the words of Petra Kelly) 'the greens must
become a spiritual movement, not in any fixed religious sense, but in the
sense of transforming certain values and conserving others, such as solidarity and tenderness. We must be able to communicate this. [At present]
we are all caught up in a terrible and painful process of finding ourselves'.[59]

The problem is that simply to embrace new beliefs and values and make
good resolutions is clearly insufficient to change deeply rooted patterns of
behaviour. In Part II I tried to answer the question Why has it all come to
this? by showing that the roots of ecological and social crisis must be
sought ultimately in the human condition itself. It is the hunger for
meaning and identity in the face of existential fear and insecurity that has
powered human history. The ever-failing struggle to satisfy this need
through aggressiveness, acquisitiveness and often fanatical forms of belongingness has created social structures and processes which have in turn
amplified and inflamed them. We have, in Gary Snyder's words, become
'economically dependent on a fantastic system of stimulation of greed
which cannot be fulfilled, sexual desire which cannot be satiated and

hatred which has no outlet except against oneself, the persons one is supposed to love, or the revolutionary aspirations of pitiful, poverty-stricken, marginal societies'.[60]

A large part of our inability to deal effectively with the eco-social crisis we have created lies in our persistent refusal to recognise that our political and economic remedies must be grounded in transformative strategies that go to the heart of the human condition. Such was the unavailing warning delivered to the 1985 International Green Congress at Dover by Peter Ball, the local bishop: 'I must say this to you: you haven't got a hope in a million years of changing anything by political methods unless you concentrate on changing attitudes, changing thought forms deep, deep down in society, or at least understanding the need to do this. [Otherwise] a political party is just a wonderful sort of spanner that fits no bolt'. All the world's spiritual traditions bear witness to our potential to transcend our fear-driven self-destructiveness. Findings in psychology and anthropology point in the same direction. And with even a modest experience of meditation one can begin to confirm this for oneself. Repressive societies and violent person-alities are not inevitable. On the contrary, in the light of perennial spirituality they are remediable deviations from our quintessential nature, our original blessing.

Finally, it must be emphasised that this is necessarily an upside down kind of book. For psycho-spiritual work is not only necessary for the creation of ecological and social harmony. On the contrary, it is the fundamental lifetime task which is set for each of us by the simple fact of being human. Furthermore, the very work of shaping such a society can itself be part of that inner work. And, beyond that, the ultimate purpose of that society should itself be to provide optimum conditions for its members to undertake the psycho-spiritual work which can free them from existential fear and anxiety. Finally, in the course of this endeavour we can discover that the work of personal and eco-social liberation are one and the same project. To the extent that we are freed of self-need, we *become* our response to others' needs.

What is required of the inner work?

One of the less quoted passages in Schumacher's *Small is beautiful* is his conclusion:

> Everywhere people ask 'What can I actually *do*?' The answer is as simple as it is disconcerting: we can, each of us, work to put our own inner house in order. The guidance we need for this work cannot be found in science or technology, the value of which utterly depends

on the ends which they serve; but it can still be found in the traditional wisdom of mankind.[61]

But although I emphasise the kind of spiritual insight Schumacher had
in mind, it would be misleading to set up some kind of hierarchy of the
different kinds of inner work. One person may embark on some advanced
spiritual practice and become progressively more rigid and closed off,
whilst some quite modest psychotherapy might release another into a
flowing and joyful openness. It is important, therefore, to keep an open
and inclusive mind in considering the relevance to our radical green
project of the many different kinds of inner work, ranging from small-
group dynamics to tantric meditation, from playing with clay to
nonviolence training, from bioenergetic therapy to consciousness raising
skills with the disempowered and dependent.

The ultimate criterion for the many different kinds of inner work now
available from the world-historical supermarket is surely the change in
personality and behaviour which typically results from it. 'By their fruits ye
shall know them'. A proselytising religious tradition, claiming a monopoly
of truth, is unlikely to offer an inner work experience which nurtures
open-minded and receptive relations with others. Neither will a cult
which creates neurotic dependency on a guru, the brilliance of whose
insights is matched only by a spiritual egotism often combined with sexual
exploitation and other tawdry addictions. The contrast is with what Paul
Tillich described as 'the strength of people who have deep convictions
without being fanatical, who are loving without being sentimental, imaginative without being unrealistic, disciplined without being submissive'.
So, from the way they talk and act, what kind of reality has this person or
that group made for themselves? How well are they able to take care of the
fear and rage we all keep hidden away in some pocket or other? When
faced with contentious and divisive problems do they have to make them
even more so by supercharging them with intrusive personality needs and
addictive ideologies?

The cultivation of some kind of self-awareness is surely the most important single requirement of inner work, since so many other needful
qualities are associated with it. Greater awareness of the kind of personal
reality we create and why we create it does of itself modify our perceptions
and behaviour. Self-awareness makes us more conscious of the deep well of
fear that separates us from other people, as also from our bodies and
rejected parts of our personalities. Self-awareness opens the way to accepting and befriending this 'negativity' and becoming more at one with all
that has been denied in a spontaneous empathy, and in a willingness to

accept, value and trust others. Where there is division and conflict, it implies a compassionate concern to share common humanity and to find a creative way forward which enhances the dignity and autonomy of both parties.

Inner work can also develop in us a certain strength and stability of character, an inner-directed independence. This rests upon a sense of identity which is simply an *awareness identity* (as Adam Curle calls it), rather than an identity buttressed by belongingness, whether to an ideology or a movement, or by power and possession. When comfortably at home in ourselves, we can be assertive if needs be, without being aggressive (or submissive). We can be generous without reservation. We can be decisive without being afraid of making the wrong decision. And we shall be less attached to, and less dependent on, our likes—and dislikes—and hence less vulnerable to disappointment, failure and burn-out.

To respond effectively and realistically to demanding problem situations means to confront them in full awareness, without the (largely unconscious) need protectively to filter out whatever too much discomfits us (a major function of ideology). This implies wholehearted acceptance of complexities and contradictions which disconcert our accustomed ways of thinking, a willingness to suspend judgement, and to make creative use of unknowing. It implies contextual decision making and situational morality rather than the security of always knowing what's right and what's wrong. It implies a willingness to trust feelings and the courage to accept one's mistakes and inadequacies.

This ensemble of virtues (which, incidentally, implies a nice balance of the masculine and the feminine) may recall one of those extravagant and intimidating job descriptions for some apparently quite ordinary employment. But at least these are qualities which commonly are found together. A few of us are fortunate enough to have been born with them; most have to learn the hard way. Although inner work requires will power in order to keep at it, these virtues cannot themselves be willed into being. If we attempt to do so we are likely to find ourselves saddled with their opposites. Strength of character, for instance, becomes rigidity and hardness of character. Where they are truly natural and spontaneous there is a lightness and transparency about them; they do not have to bear the anxious weight of inner need. And there is commonly an underlying sense of humour, an awareness of the black comedy of our often dangerous antics to be something other than we are, instead of just enjoying being our true selves. For that is what 'spirituality' is really about. So simple; so hard.

The nature and relevance of spiritual practice and experience

The need for secular-spiritual dialogue

Each of the different radical movements introduced in Part IV is concerned primarily with extending its own influence. If we are ever to evolve a green social culture it is essential that they begin to put more of that energy into dialogue with one another, and into ways in which they might make common cause. This particularly applies to popularising some kind of inner work movement integral to radical ecological and social transformation.

My particular concern here is to offer an engaged spirituality readily accessible to secular minded people, rationalists and humanists who are deeply committed to planetary survival and social justice. Many are distrustful or even hostile to what they understand as spirituality. My motive is not conversion, but a better understanding as a basis for working together. In addition, there are many who are drawn to spirituality and yet cannot see how it might be practically and fruitfully integrated with their work for people and planet.

The following telling passage will give some idea of the tangle of misunderstanding and half truths which need to be addressed. It appears, in a startling change of style, in an otherwise sober and well informed book by Boris Frankel, a greened Marxist:

> To construct a new democratic public sphere will not be possible if a majority of people find greater psychic security in privatised arrangements, irrationalist traditions and occult practices . . . Those spiritualist [sic] and occult beliefs which de-emphasize the need for democratic public institutions, by cultivating an over-emphasis on emotional feelings, gurus, hyper-anti-rationalism, and exaggerated introspection, only weaken the development of a democratic socialist citizenry . . . Nor do I believe that to over compensate for the anti-humanism and anti-rationalism of technical rationality, by a turn to Eastern religions and spiritualism, will help to bring about a democratic and ecosocialist future. What is needed is a new rationalism—the promotion of a cultural diversity and naturalism which rejects the exploitative and censorious elements of puritanism, racism, sexism, homophobia, and the domination of nature—whilst not succumbing to an aimless, hedonistic and drug addicted pseudo-democracy.[62]

This is the only place in the book where any strong feelings disrupt the author's desiccated Marxian prose. More encouragingly, there are enough typical half-truths here at least to provide a foothold for dialogue.

In the first place, secular minded progressives commonly equate spirituality with religion, which they see as altogether retrogressive. Many religious people would doubtless agree at least in part, but would refer also to the many influential movements which contradict this view. They would add that there are, moreover, many other and no less significant things to be said about the phenomenon of religion. Moreover, humanist criticism of theistic religion is invariably about the (admittedly predominant) *dualistic* kind, where the punitive and judgemental Lord God of Hosts makes an easy target.

In the second place, there are those like ecologist John Horsfall who 'fear for the association between the irrationality of religion and the plain speaking, empirical approach to environmental problems that is going to be needed'.[63] A spiritual renaissance is seen as a threat to the whole hard won humanistic and scientific tradition, wherein our only salvation is presumed to lie. Horsfall evidently has in mind some of the more extravagant new age versions of spirituality, with their cavalier dismissal of the scientific tradition as fundamentally flawed.

In fact, the perennial spiritual tradition invites the enquirer to undertake experiential investigation of certain hypotheses, employing well proven techniques. Such exploration is traditionally conducted with safeguards against deception and a pragmatic rigour reminiscent of scientific enquiry. Mutual antagonism is only possible between pseudo-science (scientism) and pseudo-spirituality (fundamentalism), each laying absolute claim to the other's realm. Science and spirituality are not conflicting ways of knowing but different *kinds* of knowing, operating at different levels of consciousness, notwithstanding the convergent views of reality displayed by mysticism and subatomic physics.[64] My concern here is not to gloss over differences, but to point to misunderstandings and habitual polarisation which impede people with scientific and spiritual backgrounds from working together to some good purpose.

In the third place, as Frankel's charges bear witness, it is the 'opium of the people' argument which weighs heaviest. Sandy Irvine, a green activist, echoes Frankel when he complains of 'more and more people turning their backs on the problems of society and the environment, preferring the solitary contemplation of their own minds and bodies to the exclusion of all other concerns—which is exactly the kind of citizenry which superindustrialism will require'.[65] There is, again, a lot of truth in this charge. The preoccupation of other-worldly sectarians with their personal salvation (or the transmission of good vibes to those who cry out for bread) is no less a matter of concern to those of us who are trying to promote an eco-socially engaged spirituality.

On the other hand, there is the assumption here that the exploration of how we experience reality somehow cuts us off from what we evidently perceive as an unproblematic, matter-of-fact reality 'out there', and disables us from making effective response to what it requires of us. On the contrary, as Schumacher warned:

> It is a grave error to accuse a man who pursues self-knowledge of 'turning his back on society'. The opposite would be more nearly true: that a man who fails to pursue self-knowledge is and remains a danger to society, for he will tend to misunderstand everything that other people say or do, and remain blissfully unaware of many of the things he does himself.[66]

In brief, it is the failure to undertake the inner work of exploring our self-created reality that is politically disabling, and this is the fundamental contention which the secular minded and the spiritually minded need to explore together. And, since it has so many facets and possibilities, it is potentially a fruitful and worthwhile project.

The nature of spiritual experience

The following consolidates earlier references to spiritual experience, notably in Chapters 8 and 15.

Spiritual experience cultivated within different traditions throughout human history has certain common and quite well defined characteristics. When the mind state has been stilled and ripened by various well established practices, fundamental insights occur as matters of fact, and not through conceptualisation or an exercise of will. These are insights into the nature of reality, including our normal, everyday state of consciousness, which they subsume. These insights may give access to a higher level of consciousness which has been described as unity consciousness. Here self and all phenomena exist only by mutual definition, and hence are separate and different and yet at the same time interdependent and one. (Paradox is the essence of spirituality, as Jung was fond of emphasising.) Phenomena are defined through their dynamic interrelationship. This is, incidentally, an ecological consciousness in the most total sense! Albert Einstein wrote of it:

> A human being is part of the whole, called by us 'Universe'; a part limited in time and space. He experiences himself, his thoughts and

feelings as something separated from the rest—a kind of optical delusion of his consciousness. This delusion is a kind of prison for us, restricting us to our personal desires and to affection for a few persons nearest to us. Our task must be to free ourselves from this prison.[67]

This unity consciousness, together with insights and experiences which point in its direction, is what I have in mind here when I refer to spiritual experience. There are, of course, many different kinds of altered states of consciousness, such as near death experiences, drug induced states, and states of consciousness heightened by grave illness, bereavement, isolation, aesthetic experience, creativity and other deeply moving situations. These may or may not give some insight into higher levels of consciousness. They may also give rise to dramatic visions and similar experiences which the beginner in the mainstream mystical traditions is urged to ignore. For what is important is profound and enduring change in the way in which we experience the world and relate to others.

The experience of insight will take on the forms of the particular spiritual culture of the experiencer. In this book I use nontheistic language both as a Buddhist and because it it will be more understandable and acceptable to many readers. However, whether you experience divine salvation or inconceivable liberation, the *nature* and *consequences* appear to have much in common (after making some cultural translation), as do also the *practices* which open you to God's 'grace'—or the way things are. It is to the monist, at-one-with-God Christianity to which this most evidently applies, as illustrated by the following explanation of unity consciousness from the gnostic gospel of St Thomas:

> They said to Him: Shall we then, being children, enter the Kingdom? Jesus said to them: When you make the two one, and when you make the inner as the outer and the outer as the inner, and the above as the below, and when you make the male and the female into a single one, then you shall enter the Kingdom.

The higher levels of consciousness reveal our fear driven struggle as simply unnecessary: the unwinnable lawsuit with reality which is characteristically what our life is about. We are no longer driven by the need to belong, achieve and acquire, whether in gross or subtle ways. We are neither exhausted and exhilarated by 'life's race', nor bored to death by it: there is nothing more to do than to allow our life to live us. For such insight is, as Thomas Merton observed, 'not our awareness, but Being's awareness of itself in us'. We are freed to love without possessiveness, to hold beliefs without clinging to them, to oppose them without bitterness, to respond to others' needs without feeding our own need to be useful, significant, virtuous or ideologically superior. Our own liberation from separateness, from alienation, is thus the condition for our unreserved contribution to the liberation of others—physically, emotionally, politically, economically, and spiritually. 'Nor', writes the Quaker Thomas Kelly, 'is the God-blinded soul given blissful oblivion, but, rather, excruciatingly sensitive eyesight toward the world of men. The sources of suffering for the tendered soul are infinitely multiplied, well nigh beyond endurance. Ponder this paradox in religious experience: "Nothing matters, everything matters"'.[68]

That is indeed the fundamental paradox empowering spiritually informed activism. F. Scott Fitzgerald put his finger on it in a passage in his novel *The crack up*, although for him it was 'the test of a first rate intelligence' to be able 'to hold two opposed ideas in the mind at the same time and still retain the ability to function. One should, for example, be able to see that things are hopeless yet be determined to make them otherwise'. How to go on working for a better world in the face heartrending discouragement? Hisamatsu Shin'ichi, a pioneer of socially aware Zen, posed the following *koan* or training riddle for inner-working activists: 'Right now, if nothing you do is of any avail, what will you do?' So, if other meditative practices do not appeal, why not try wrestling with this question until, way beyond intellectual exhaustion, you are driven to enough despair to allow space for the answer to appear?[69]

When we experience a reality from which we no longer struggle to protect ourselves for fear of falling apart, by solidifying it, structuring it and generally devitalising and desensitising it, then it appears brilliant, spacious and somehow infinitely manageable. Physical and emotional pain, heartless oppression, bloody-minded violence and planetary ruin all remain and are, out of a deep compassion, the more keenly felt. But, freed of ambivalence, anxiety and our tight grip, we are freed to respond as best we can. I express it thus:

> It is not reality
> that asks the questions and makes the demands;
> but *we*
> who ask the questions and make the demands.
> To see profoundly into this
> is to be freed of fear
> and freed for action.

The sense of release and gratitude when reality (or God) opens to us is typical of experience which is only 'mystical' when viewed from our customary unreality. At such times we do not know whether we are laughing at the comedy or weeping at the tragedy.

> He had a ground floor flat,
> but didn't believe it.
> So he never dared walk out
> into his life
> for fear
> of the drop
> concealed
> by the bright curtains
> of success.

Unfortunately, the subsequent work of embodying insights into unity consciousness is for many rarer than the insights themselves. This is the important work of slowly dissipating the momentum, the *karma*, of rooted and tangled desire and aversion deep in the personality. Otherwise awakening can go to the head, producing a spiritualised super-egotism of power abuse and exploitation. Virtue has to be cultivated by a deepening insight that is lived out daily; it is not granted overnight. A Zen master, Kuei-shan, has observed that great liberation is a pearl of rare price, but, nevertheless, when it first appears it is embedded in a pile of accumulated shit.

Insights into higher levels of consciousness are available to anyone who is sufficiently dedicated to well-tried spiritual training methods (and to some without even trying!). Short of a profound experience of unity consciousness, there are much more readily and widely experienced insights and personality shifts which can be nurtured by basic spiritual practices.. These *could* enable a 'critical mass' of us to fulfil ourselves through living together caringly and responsibly, with the market and the state as no more than conveniences. The following are among the benefits which a basic kind of awareness practice (as described later) might be expected to yield over the years.

We become more aware of our own particular ways of coming to terms with life and how, beneath layers of conditioning and concealment, we respond to the pressures of both who we feel we are and of 'out there'. We begin to sense how our eco-social activism is not only a response to objective problems but also to deep personal needs, ranging from making our mark to the belongingness attractions of membership of a movement. This is not a criticism of either motive; only a plea for awareness, which will of itself affect our perceptions and behaviours. Reality 'out there' is increasingly seen as being shaped and coloured by our attempts subjectively to come to terms with it. Threatening aspects may be magnified by our own fears to the extent of making life appear almost intolerable. 'Wipe your glasses!' warns John Hegley:

> You've got to clean your glasses
> if you want to keep them clean
> if you look across the valley
> and the grass is none too green,
> it might be something
> with your eyesight,
> or it maybe
> something wrong with the grass,
> or it could be that
> you've got a cowpat on your glasses.[70]

For example, the activist who complains about being pressured by time and commitments may discover that in fact she piles up the latter in a desperate attempt to make her life more, meaningful and significant. Up to then her commitments had been experienced as burying her alive and burning her out, yet somehow unavoidably *imposed* upon her. A sufficiently penetrating meditative awareness can free her to regain control of her life, seeing, like Thoreau, that time is no more than a river in which to go fishing, instead of being slow death by Filofax. There is a veritable liberation movement if we take the search back:

> Not the time,
> but the experience;
> not the experience,
> but the desire;
> not the desire,
> but the fear;
> not the fear,
> but the emptyness
> of fear, desire, experience and time.
> Enjoy it!

Such uncovering is, of course, familiar in depth therapy, and meditation has been described as the cheapest analysis in town. A notebook recording such revelations soon fills up, and most of it is bad news . . . Befriending oneself does not come easily. But desires and aversions do gradually begin to lose their formerly compulsive grip, and become gentled into more manageable *preferences*. We no longer need to try so hard, and life begins somehow to look after itself.

No longer so self-protecting, we become more open to the awesome interconnectedness of things. There is nothing more subversive than seeing through the distinction between you and me, mine and yours, animate and inanimate. Once it ceases to be the experience of an esoteric minority, such insight will prove the meditation cushion to be infinitely more revolutionary than the ballot box or the assault rifle.

Paradoxically, a sense of at oneness with others is accompanied also by a more profound sense of their uniqueness, as we begin to see them just as they are, without self-serving prejudice and distortion. The thirteenth-century Zen master Dogen expressed the inherent dignity in every living thing as follows:

No creature ever comes short of its own completeness;
Wherever it stands, it does not fail to cover the ground.

The struggles of our fellow human beings each to come to terms with life, whether in heroic folly, quiet desperation or deathdenying bloodlust, awaken deep compassion. At the crowded meeting, feelings are running high; 'issues' which 'are to be settled once and for all' are being passionately argued. Each person is once again running his or her stuff through the projector: all those autobiographical agendas! There is a sad but endearing incongruity about it all which cannot be revealed without accusations of 'not taking the issues seriously'. But who is it who is not taking the issues seriously?

A confirmatory summary of much of the foregoing is to be found in the conclusions of the Alister Hardy Research Centre, investigating experiences variously described as 'religious', 'mystical', 'transcendental' and so on:

People commonly claim that such experiences have profoundly affected their lives, usually involving some of the following changes: fewer feelings of alienation from others and from the environment, an increase in the sense that life is meaningful, increased ability to cope with and survive crises, improvement in psychological balance, reduced dependence on material goods as a source of security, and increased concern for the good of others. The research being done at the Centre is now showing that, far from vanishing off the seemingly arid urban-industrial landscape, the visionary aspect of human experience is alive and well. The research also shows that peak experiences are not restricted to any particular group of specially endowed people. On the contrary, to be in touch with one's visionary faculties is an essential part of the definition of an integrated, normal person.[71]

Opportunities for spiritual practice

Traditional spiritual practices, mainly meditative and contemplative in character, are currently enjoying a renaissance in the Judaeo-Christian tradition. As noted earlier, there is also a range of practices in women's, green and new age spiritualities, some taken over or developed from ancient biocentric traditions (like that of the native North Americans). Finally, ever since the 1960s Buddhism, Hinduism and Taoism have continued to attract a significant number of Westerners.

Buddhism in the West has, like much else, tended to be privatised as one product in the supermarket of 'personal' spiritual development systems. Yet the Buddha enjoined his followers to 'go forth on your journey, for the benefit of the many, out of compassion for the world, for the welfare, for the benefit and joy of humankind'.[72] So far this has been interpreted, for the most part, in an exclusively quietist sense. But times are changing. Sulak Sivaraksa, a leading Thai Buddhist activist, has no doubt that:

> The teaching of Buddha is not concerned with the private destiny of the individual, but with something much wider: the whole realm of sentient being, the whole consciousness. This inevitably entails a concern with social and political matters . . . To attempt to understand Buddhism apart from its social dimension is mistaken. Preoccupation with the individual places limits on love, and Buddhism is an attempt to deal with what it sees as the disease of individualism. Buddhism is primarily a method of overcoming the limits of the individual self; consequently it entails a concern with the political and social dimensions.[73]

Sulak is a founder of the International Network of Engaged Buddhists, which promotes a green, grassroots 'radical conservatism' highly relevant to the Third World. INEB has affiliates in several countries, including the UK, and the Buddhist Peace Fellowship in the US.[74]

For interested activists there are many accessible opportunities for spiritual practice, many of which are veritable training systems. Among the problems which will be encountered is finding the time and persistence to discover among the labyrinth of possibilities a practice which is personally helpful. Moreover, this may be clothed in what, on first acquaintance, appear as alienating religious forms whose significance may not be evident until later. Although even a little can go a long way, serious spiritual training requires determination and staying power, going against the grain of a predominantly secular society. Moreover, most of the practices and groups, whether Eastern or Western in origin, are not specifically concerned with unifying spiritual practice with activism and may be indifferent to the latter.

Systems of spiritual practice include meditation (contemplation, in Christian terminology), visualisation, ritual, chant, dance, graphic and plastic arts, and the use of myth. Many of the practices developed in one faith may readily be used in others or by people of no particular faith. Traditionally, the spiritual seeker has relied upon an authenticated guide (teacher, spiritual director, guru, roshi, staretz, shaykh). The guide will already be familiar with the levels of consciousness to which the trainee is opening up, is aware of the delusions, pitfalls and dead ends which can be encountered, and will be experienced in counselling and unblocking many different kinds of seeker. The nearest secular equivalent is an athletics coach.

Good spiritual guides are hard to come by, and this makes the second traditional support all the more important. This is the community or group of fellow practitioners. The foundation of an inner work movement would lie in networks of small, closely knit affinity groups of people engaged in similar spiritual (and/or therapeutic) practices and active, at the same time, in working for people and planet. Some diversity of practices and concerns in such a group could even be a source of strength.

Awareness practice

The following guide to awareness (or mindfulness) meditation may encourage the reader to try her hand, alone or with friends. It is a basic Buddhist meditation which can take you as far as your determination (though somewhere along the line what-you-are-in-fact-not-separated-from will begin to carry you along anyway). It has parallels in other religious traditions and can be used by people of any belief or none. For example, that classic of Christian mysticism, *The cloud of unknowing*,[75] contains detailed instructions for this 'contemplation with naked intent', and it was the regular spiritual practice favoured by Fritz Schumacher, about which he wrote in his *Guide for the perplexed*.[76]

The foundation of this practice is a daily period of sitting meditation, working up to an hour or more. Sit in an alert posture, preferably in such a way as will enable you to keep a straight and unsupported back without strain. With your eyes closed or just lidded, simply observe whatever comes to your attention, be it the passing of thoughts, bodily sensations, or some underlying emotion. What you will probably find is an insecurely tied parcel of thoughts and feelings, though still with a name, address and other identifiers to prevent it getting totally lost . . . It is natural for the mind to secrete thoughts, and neither these nor anything else that comes up should be suppressed. Just prevent thoughts from linking up in association, taking you over and carrying you off, by bringing back your attention to them. If you try too hard you will only give strength to what you are rejecting. This is one part of life where it is actually counter-productive to strive to achieve some specific result, to 'do well'. That particular urge is just something else to which to give your bare, unjudge-mental attention. Once you get the hang of it, this can be the one truly liberated zone in your daily life.

Concentration can be strengthened by focusing attention on, say, each outgoing breath, or even silently counting the breaths up to ten, returning to one when you get there or when you lose the count. When the mind becomes still, leave gaps in the counting, through which insights may appear. Or you may prefer to focus on a mantra or a short prayer, or to turn over again and again the *koan* mentioned earlier.

Sooner or later the agitated surface of the mind will still. More and more of previously submerged mental furniture will come into view, including the monsters that lurk in the lower depths, first rage, then fear, and, deepest of all, nothingness—a void. These experiences can be fright-ening, but if the strong container of 'just accepting' has had time to build up this will protect you, giving a grounded sense of stability. Bare attention will by itself gradually begin to gentle the monsters, which are no more than our vital energies. Rage, for example, can suddenly flip over into a release of joyful energy, as if an electric current had been switched on. 'If you bring forth what is within you, what you bring forth will save you', said Jesus in the gospel of St Thomas, but 'if you do not bring forth what is within you, what you do not bring forth will destroy you.'

These 'bare awareness' sessions will begin to carry over into the daily round. We then begin to realise how much of our lives is 'unlived' in an intermediate zone of fantasy, unaware, on the one hand, of what is going on in our minds (because of being carried along by it), and, on the other, not being fully alive to what we are doing. The aim of awareness practice is similar to that of gestalt therapy, as described by Fritz Perls: 'To lose more and more of your "mind" and come more to your *senses*. To be more and more in touch; to be in touch with yourself and in touch with the world'.

So, on the one hand we need to return our attention, over and over again, to what is happening out there (like really listening to something that is being said). And on the other, we need to give bare attention to the rising and falling of our emotions, whether volcanic (like anger) or oceanic (like bitterness). This takes much practice, since what we experience as negative emotions can be very threatening. Either we discharge them (like wallowing in self-pity) or we suppress them (by trying to forget them, deny them, rationalise them, or by blaming ourselves or others). It takes time to learn how to hold an emotion in attention, to feel its raw power, its smell, its colour, until it transmutes itself, becoming soft and manageable in an energy-releasing clarity. Thich Nhat Hanh, a Vietnamese Zen monk and activist, explains:

> Treat your anger [and all strong emotion] with the utmost respect and tenderness, because it is no other than yourself. Do not suppress it: simply be aware of it. Awareness is like the sun. When it shines on things they are transformed ... Mindfully dealing with anger is like taking the hand of a little brother.[77]

A well tuned awareness is particularly important for activists, subjected to a wide range of highs and lows, time hassles, burning obsessions, and bitter frustrations, which can pull us off centre and fog compassionate and skilful response. Awareness training is particularly necessary if we want to penetrate through years of subtle self-conditioning in order to undertake the work of ideological disarmament.

Practice like the foregoing will sooner or later ripen the healing *wholeness* splendidly expressed by Christina Feldman:

> The authentic mystic knows deeply and surely that, living within her body, she is sexual, and honours the expressions of love, joy and sensitivity that are made possible through her body. She is social and in each moment of her life she interacts with the world around her. She does not ignore a world that suffers and wars but responds wholeheartedly with her wisdom and love. She is political because she is aware and a conscious participant in life. She is committed to the end of estrangement which is the doctrine of too many of the structures and value systems that govern our lives. She is contemplative, rejoicing in the richness of her aloneness. She is alone and she is bonded with the world. Her abiding in her vision of connectedness dispels all seeming contradictions.[78]

Women's spirituality and the humility trap

Spiritual institutions and practice have for the most part been developed by men and for men. Even where (and still exceptionally) traditional patriarchal dominance has been formally dismantled, assumptions may survive which can prove very delusive and confusing for women.

Spiritual training nurtures patience, humility, acceptance and selflessness in a self which, particularly if it is a typical masculine self, is anxious to sustain a strong, self-aggrandising identity. Of this—and of its futility—we become profoundly aware through long hours of emotional and physical discomfiture (and boredom) on the meditation cushion. This ripens a spirit of acceptance and humility which, as we have seen, is an important step on the way to liberation to unity consciousness. But it may be that, through personality or social conditioning, people will actually seek security and self-confirmation and even gratefully accept compliant and subservient roles which they are required to fill. Those with a poor sense of self-identity and self-worth tend to respond in this way, whether inside or outside spiritual training. So also do whole subordinated social groups, whether it be nicely brought up young women, the 'good nigger' Uncle Tom, or 'the poor man at the gate' in the Victorian hymn who every Sunday learned anew the virtue of humility.

It is important, therefore, for those who have traditionally been put down (and perhaps become accustomed to putting themselves down) to be aware of this humility trap in conventional spiritual practice, and of the need to develop an integrity and self-worth mature enough to identify *authentic* selflessness and a humility which is not humiliation. Indeed, arguably there can only be profound spiritual realisation if there is initially a strong enough sense of a separate self to be dropped. Otherwise no significant change can take place. Instead, there is a parade of humility which is evidence not of inner spiritual strength but of grateful acceptance of a practice which, *for that personality*, actually rewards their self-evasion and blocks their growth.

A perceptive teacher will provide guidance and a practice which will enable the student to become aware of what is happening. Here, as elsewhere, there is a strong case for more women spiritual teachers and role models. However, I have the impression that over the years, the practice can develop a more yielding, gentle openness of spirit in men and a greater resolution and fortitude in women. In each sex the masculine and feminine qualities become more evenly balanced and matured, actualising the androgyny project referred to in Chapter 16.

Therapy as inner work

The other main kind of inner work comprises therapies based upon humanistic psychology, which acknowledges the 'client' as an autonomous, inner-directed person. These are associated with a 'human growth' movement for which therapy is primarily a means of personal development instead of, traditionally, a means of rectifying a person's 'maladjustment' to the demands of society. The summary treatment of the therapies here is no reflection on their merits as inner work relative to spiritual practice. It is simply that I believe them to be rather less open to misunderstanding than spiritual practice, and moreover it is in the latter area that my own experience mainly lies.

Humanistic therapy enables us to become more integrated personalities, more in touch with our feelings and our bodies, and with greater inner strength to take charge of our own lives without depending on authority or belongingness of one kind or another. It enables us to respect the autonomy of other people and to relate openly and caringly to them, and to encounter new experiences and challenges without rigid and defensive reactions. For the most part these ends are achieved by bringing into awareness buried emotions, traumas and 'unfinished business' relating, for example, to childhood griefs, sexual phobias or destructive relationships, and which distort and inhibit our perception and behaviour.

Therapy can clearly make an important contribution to developing the qualities proposed earlier as the necessary personal underpinning for the work of radical social transformation. Arguably, each of the many different therapies is appropriate to a different level of consciousness development. At the basic level there are simple forms of counselling to help a person get in touch with unexpressed feelings. At the middle level are therapies like gestalt work which, characteristic of our high egoic culture, liberate expressiveness and assertiveness. But they fall short of nurturing that sense of at-oneness with all that is other which is the concern of the more recently developed *transpersonal* psychology. With these higher level, psycho-spiritual therapies there is therefore a shift from self-development to self-transcendence.

The relationship between the two kinds of inner work, therapy and spiritual practice (or, more specifically, meditation), is complex and controversial and is further complicated by individual differences in personality and conditioning. At its lower levels meditation is itself commonly of mainly therapeutic significance. Skilful use can be made of both kinds of inner work. Therapy, for example, is of proven value in removing various specific blocks to spiritual unfolding.

A noteworthy contribution to the theme of this book is the 'human needs' perspective. This posits a hierarchy of 'basic human needs' upwards from physical needs through belongingness, esteem, autonomy and growth. The denial of satisfaction of these needs results in alienated compensatory behaviours damaging to ourselves and to others. The need to develop awareness of this process is emphasised, ultimately with a view to evolving a society which provides all with opportunities to achieve fulfilment of the whole range of vital needs, in place of the denial and distortion which widely prevail at present.

This is a useful amplification of the Buddhist perspective argued in these pages. But it does have some disquieting limitations. Because it does not trace the non-physical needs down to a root existential angst it is unable—short of a superficial circular argument—to explain why human beings have not in the first place evolved societies which satisfy their needs. And the idea that fulfilment lies in gratifying a succession of specific needs until reaching 'spirituality' at the top of the tree is at best a half truth. The human struggle with the problem of being human is much grander, more complex and disorderly. What of those, for example, whose humanity flowers and whose insight deepens out of the kind of response they are able to make to being *deprived* of esteem and autonomy, whether by oppressive social conditions or personal deprivation and pain which threaten to undermine their very humanity? There is an ultimately spiritual process at work here which transcends the gratification of this or that need.

This basic needs perspective bears witness to both the achievements and the limitations of its high egoic humanistic and libertarian origins, preoccupied as it is with emphasising freedom from repression and oppression. But in an ecologically and socially demanding future each basic need carries a basic responsibility, and ultimately the compassion to lose ourselves in the service of others. How are people to develop the wisdom to meet those responsibilities or do they first have to gratify their way up the whole needs hierarchy and come out spiritually on top?

I would not wish to *subtract* anything from this theory. But, like much else in humanistic psychology, I believe it needs to be spiritually and transpersonally deepened if it is to serve as a wholly adequate resource in the face of the threat of social and ecological breakdown.

As well as being better fed the ego can also, as an aid to social change, be beefed up with the 'power of intention' approach of 'I can and I will'. A variety of techniques is employed to build up personal and collective determination. What appears impossible is to be willed into possibility and achievement. This 'will to believe', as Henry James called it, is characteristic of certain therapies and flourishes most strongly in the—to Europeans—innocent open frontier culture of North America, where anything appears possible given enough push. In its concentration of energy upon rationality and volition it contrasts sharply with spiritually based approaches such as Joanna Macy's, where opening to anger, frustration and despair gives release into empowerment. The latter have a less instant appeal and do not promise such ready results, but are likely to be more profoundly transformative in the long run, and particularly in nurturing a sense of interconnectedness.

If the therapies are to contribute significantly to mass personal empowerment they will need to be made widely acceptable and accessible. This would exclude the expensive, long-term therapist-and-client relationship concerned with deep consciousness exploration. The emphasis will evidently need to be on group work with trained facilitators, and on approaches such as transactional analysis which lend themselves to do-it-yourself groups. There are, however, some therapies, like psychosynthesis, which are extremely flexible and adaptable. Much, however, can be achieved even by such relatively simple approaches as co-counselling. The UK Green Party's Emotional Needs Working Group, for example, has provided opportunities for counselling at Party conferences to enable delegates to 'express their feelings of anxiety and frustration'.

The first advertisements have appeared for workshops specifically designed to enable participants to 'bridge the gap between personal awareness and social action' (a London Gestalt Centre 'peace building' workshop); or presenting a 'psychopolitics integrating individual and social change' (a Reichian bioenergetics workshop), as well as the despair and empowerment incorporated in deep ecology workshops.[79] I am currently experimenting with weekend events for about a dozen participants, inexpensively home-based, and blending silence with conviviality, meditation with group discussion, and formality with fellowship. The results so far have been promising. However, enterprises like these will not be able to take off until the socially committed see this as truly empowering work of which everyone has need and can benefit, and which is no less important than traditional extrovert activism and not just a casualty clearing station for lame ducks and burnt-out cases.

Mention must also be made of a variety of publications (including workshop manuals) designed to help activists improve their effectiveness and well-being. These range from community development strategies[80] to individual and group empowerment work. Among the latter is a well-proven workshop manual by Joanna Macy which has a similar approach to this book.[81] An example of an overall guide which interweaves inner and outer work is Katrina Shield's *In the tiger's mouth*.[82] Social activism is clearly a many-sided trade which needs to learnt, if only we can take time off from 'being active'.

Instrumental inner work

Instrumental inner work refers to the many secondary, functional kinds of activity which can supplement, project and consolidate the psycho-spiritual work examined above.

First, there is the widespread and often seemingly insoluble problem of conflict, both between groups and individuals within an organisation, and also in the way the organisation manages its external, campaigning conflicts. Spiritually informed nonviolent campaigning in the Gandhi tradition becomes necessary when all efforts at conflict resolution have broken down, but always with the possibility of a resumption of such efforts consequent on the progress and achievements of the campaign. Whether inside or outside the movement there is always a paramount need, in Adam Curle's words, 'to work for harmony wherever we are, to bring together what is sundered by fear, ignorance, hatred, resentment, injustice or any other condition that divides us'. In such situations the human condition itself commonly emerges as the most transparent and intractable part of the problem: deep individual and collective resentment latches onto the situation the more strongly to define and assert polarised identities. The objective problem is thus inflamed and distorted by subjective need, and may indeed be little more than the right pretext at the right time for a violent manifestation of that need.

Mediation is a first step in conflict resolution. Adam Curle has defined it as 'a psychological effort to change perceptions both of the conflict and the enemy to the extent that both protagonists gain some hope of a reasonable resolution and are so prepared to *negotiate* seriously'. Curle emphasises that, beyond the formal skills and guidelines of mediation, what is above all important is an 'ability to relate less judgementally to others, and with warmth, empathy and trust, and truly to listen to them and open to them'. He adds that 'mediators need the same psychological equipment of impartial goodwill, perseverance, imperturbability and objectivity, the same flexibility, and preferably the same sense of humour whether they are dealing with a crisis in their home or neighbourhood, or place of work, or because somebody's marriage is on the rocks'.[83] Here again we find repeated much the same constellation of personal qualities as is developed by psycho-spiritual work.

A second instrumental area in which these qualities can ripen is that of small group work. The small group or team of some six to eight people is now widely recognised as a superb tool for problem solving and many other organisational and campaigning tasks, as well as having great potential value for the personal development of its members. Networks of such groups will be essential for the work of shaping and sustaining a green society.

Effective group work, however, has to be learnt. Otherwise it can be a frustrating and disillusioning experience as members mix their personality work-outs with the formal business, hammering facts and arguments at one another in a mad rationality, and largely unaware of the forces that are really powering the discussion and making it such a negative and stressful experience. In order to learn the dynamics, a group needs a skilled and experienced facilitator and much determined on-the-job practice. There are, however, many useful self-help manuals. The rewards in personal growth and satisfaction and in organisational and campaigning effectiveness can be very high. Here as elsewhere there is 'never enough time', even though so little time is given in radical movements to inner work of any description. A widespread realisation that the inner work must be allocated large chunks of relaxed time protected from overloaded agendas and crowded diaries would in itself be a wonderful and liberating breakthrough.

A third area of secondary inner work is the shaping of organisational structures, procedures and ways of working which are supportive of the inner work and enable it to bear fruit. They need, for example, to be mutualistic and inclusive (like aiming to make consensual decisions) rather than adversarial and exclusive (the way the classic rules of debate are set up). Here again *process* must be emphasised as being at least as important as *content*—how things are done as well as what things are done. The Green Party in its heyday did have an 'Other Ways of Working' group which was sufficiently influential at one time to change the ways in which conference business was conducted.

In conclusion, there is surely a need for a network linking inner work and outer work groups concerned with radical eco-social change, beginning perhaps on quite a modest scale. Its aims might be as follows:

1 To identify, describe, systematise and publicise the various resources for inner work that already exist. These would include not only workshops and retreats, but also ongoing assistance from consultants attached to organisations, to help develop new styles of public work, more participative decision making, conflict resolution, small group work and the like, as well as direct psycho-spiritual work among interested organisation members.

2 To monitor the above activity, identify gaps and shortcomings, and develop new resources as needs be.

3 To popularise the inner work so that it becomes a major and much valued activity across the rainbow coalition of organisations for eco-social change.

4 To promote the formation of inner work affinity groups in different parts of the country. These could bring together like-minded people from organisations which have a similar outlook, and provide support, guidance and inspiration.

Epilogue

THESE are times of profound economic crisis and hardship even in wide sections of the affluent societies, combined with extensive social dislocation, and eruptions of racism, militant fundamentalism and other forms of violence. In democratic societies the wealthy and powerful do and say things that would scarcely have been tolerated even a few years ago. Their responses to such rebuffs as they do receive for their more outrageous excesses (like Britain's infamous poll tax) turn out to be no more than tactical retreats. Those of us who spent our formative middle years in the 1950s, 60s and 70s find ourselves exiled by time in an alien country that is hardly recognisable as our own.

The collapse of socialism (and particularly its more ideologically permeated forms) has left a credibility vacuum, a void, empty of any radical critique or alternative perspective. And underlying this appears to be some alarming loss of nerve and a dull and bewildered acceptance varied by occasional outbursts of helpless rage (as from beleaguered trade unionists).

Recently even the 'environmental' crisis has been marginalised and reduced to a nagging ache which few associate with terminal illness. For all but a tiny minority the ecological crisis is in any case about no more than environmental clean-up and sustainable growth. The merits of putting time and energy into obtaining a local recycling scheme or reducing toxic emissions from a nearby chimney, rather than agitating for some never-never ecotopia, are wholly understandable.

However, whether it comes about through some dramatic and frightening lurch in the ecological crisis or some social convulsion marked by a recovery of radical confidence, sooner or later the libertarian response will again become an option. There seems, on the left, no credible alternative in view. And yet the writing of this book has deepened my awareness of the extravagance and improbability of the *goals* of libertarianism (green or otherwise) in the light of the human condition as repeatedly manifested in history. The utopian dream of high minded and impassioned ideologues has so often come to nothing. Or it has triumphed and then degenerated into new nightmares of oppression, poverty and sheer human waste, so that the proclamation of yet another New Age fills me with apprehension. If a libertarian option *were* likely, then that is the one for which, *as matters stand at present*, we would be on course, disabled by a romantic idealism which barely conceals its dogmatic righteousness. It is all too familiar. This book is an attempt to bear witness to the need to liberate ourselves from this kind of historic disablement which I have called ideology—the collective expression of our individual blindness about who and what we are.

These reflections make it all the more important not only to work to put the values of the radical green project into effect, but to cherish them and reflect on why they have in practice so often turned into their opposites.

If there is one underlying theme of this book it is our need to cultivate awareness through a self-awareness which can liberate us from distorted perceptions of the world and from behaviour alienated from our intrinsic humanity. Such awareness can enable us calmly to experience social (and other) realities and the possibilities that lie within them, freed of all the mind-forged ideas, beliefs, values and other overlays with which we so needfully confuse them. This at the same time frees helpful ideas for our light and skilful use. Christopher Titmuss, who is both a green parliamentary candidate and an international meditation teacher, gives the following example:

> Focusing too much on results brings nightmares—literally and metaphorically. There is a perversion of perception, and this is something which each of us must watch with the same kind of vigilance as if we had a cobra in a small room with us. The ego comes up in the form of 'I' or 'we' and says, 'We are too small. I am too small. We can't confront the huge circumstances and crises of life.' This has a paralyzing effect on emotional life. It deadens the spirit. And this wretched system we live under, day in and day out, is putting out that message.[84]

How to be a practical idealist is a baffling paradox of seemingly conflicting opposites to those who are hanging on to their mysticism or their militancy. A practical idealist is one who is accepting of her fear (and there is plenty to be afraid of) without being possessed by it. Living beyond optimism and pessimism, she is a patient and clear-sighted *possibilist*.

The new kinds of society which arrive and endure are those which have been well and slowly rooted. That is why I have emphasised the need to find ways of shaping the beginnings of some kind of green society now, within the interstices of the present one and challenging of it. To wait is too late. And the obvious growing points are the various movements introduced in this book. More specifically, we shall need to clarify the different kinds of work that need to be undertaken and to popularise them and pioneer examples. No less important is the need to join hands in a movement for inner work and ideological disarmament.

Even an embryo movement for the kind of social transformation argued in this book will have a practical appeal if it can demonstrate that radicalism does not need ideology, and that idealism need not trap us either in fundamentalism or in impractical dreams. Only then will it attract the passionate moderates, radical conservatives, reasonable revolutionaries and temperate extremists it so badly needs.

Men and women are everywhere born free. We have nothing to lose but those chains to which we cling unknowingly, and by which we are bound and bind others in so many different forms of grievous and oppressive bondage. This is the perennial wisdom in which lies our ultimate liberation of learning how to allow ourselves to be our true selves. Therein is the only final guarantee of liberation from ecological self-destruction, and from social misery and injustice.

Cwm Rheidol
New Year's Day, 1993

References

Introduction and Part 1: Understanding our situation

1 Jones, Ken H., *The social face of Buddhism*. Boston: Wisdom, 1989.

2 Ponting, Clive, *A green history of the world*. London: Sinclair Stevenson, 1991.

3 Wilber, Ken, *Up from Eden: a transpersonal view of human evolution*. London: Routledge & Kegan Paul, 1983. The subsequent quotations are from pp284 and 288. This awesome disjunction in human history is narrated in the world's first great literary work, *The epic of Gilgamesh*.

4 *The Guardian*, 29/30 September 1990.

5 Delatouche, Raymond, *La Chrétienté médiévale: un modèle de développement*. Paris: Tequi, 1989.

6 Berry, Adrian, *The next ten thousand years*. New York: Dutton, 1974.

7 Schumacher, E.F., *Small is beautiful*. London: Abacus Sphere, 1974, p28.

8 See, for example, Ehrlich, Anne and Paul, *Earth*. London: Thames & Hudson, 1987.

9 Simon, Julian L. and Kahn, Herman, *The resourceful Earth*. Oxford: Blackwell, 1984.

10 World Commission on the Environment and Development, *Our common future* [The Brundtland Report]. Oxford: Oxford University Press, 1987.

11 Leghorn, Lisa and Parker, Katherine, *Women's worth: sexual economics and the world of women*. London: Routledge & Kegan Paul, 1981, p96.

12 Quoted in Ehrlich, Anne and Paul, as above (ref. 8).

13 Lovelock, James, *Gaia: a new look at life on Earth*. Oxford: Oxford University Press, 1979.

14 Williams, Raymond, *What I came to say*. London: Hutchinson Radius, 1989, p169.

15 Williams, Raymond, *Towards 2000*. London: Chatto & Windus, 1983.

16 Galbraith, John Kenneth, *The culture of contentment*. London: Sinclair Stevenson, 1992.

17 Brown, Lester R. (ed.), *State of the world 1991*. London: Earthscan, 1991, p166.

18 Richard Seymour, in Gardner, Carl and Sheppard, Julie (eds.), *Consuming passion: the rise of retail culture*. London: Unwin Hyman, 1989.

19 Lasch, Christopher, *The minimal self: psychic survival in troubled times*. New York: W.W. Norton, 1984.

20 Thatcher, Margaret, in *Woman's own,* 1 November 1987.

21 Seabrook, Jeremy, *The myth of the market.* Hartland: Green Books, 1990, p157.

22 Morrissey, M. and Gaffikin, F., *Northern Ireland: the Thatcher years.* London: Zed Books, 1990, p65.

23 Stonier, Tom, *The wealth of information.* London: Methuen, 1982.

24 Handy, Charles, *The future of work.* Oxford: Blackwell, 1985.

25 Jordan, Bill, *Mass unemployment: the future of Britain.* Oxford: Blackwell, 1982.

26 Gorz, André, *Farewell to the working classes: an essay in post-industrial socialism.* London: Pluto Press, 1982.

27 Donnison, David, *A radical agenda: after the new right and the old left.* London: Rivers Oram, 1991.

28 Trainer, F.E., *Abandon affluence!.* London: Zed Books,1985, pp194-196, 10.

29 Quoted by Girardet, Herbert, 'Scarred sacred land', in *The Guardian,* 23 August 1991, p33.

30 Blackwell, Trevor and Seabrook, Jeremy, *The politics of hope.* London: Penguin, 1988.

31 Marquand, David, in *The Guardian,* 9 November 1990.

32 *The Observer,* 28 June 1992. Quoted by Paul Rogers, co-author with Malcolm Dando of *A violent peace: global security after the cold war.* London: Brasseys, 1992.

33 World Commission on the Environment and Development, as above (ref. 10), xi.

34 Gore, Al, *Earth in the balance: ecology and the human spirit.* Boston: Houghton Mifflin/London: Earthscan, 1992.

35 Robbins, John, *Diet for a new America.* Walpole: Stillpoint, 1989.

36 Details from the Institute for African Alternatives, 23 Bevenden St, London N1 6BH.

Part 2: So why has it all come to this ?

1 Cowan, Painton, *Rose windows.* London: Thames & Hudson, 1979.

2 Fromm, Erich, *To have or to be?* London: Jonathan Cape, 1978, p1.

3 Quoted in Schumacher, E.F., *Small is beautiful.* London: Abacus Sphere, 1974, p19.

4 For a critique of deconstructivism from a similar standpoint to this book, see Spretnak, Charlene, *States of grace: the recovery of meaning in the post-modern age.* San Francisco: Harper, 1991.

5 Meadows, D.H. and others, *Limits to growth.* London: Pan, 1983.

6 Schumacher, E.F., *Small is beautiful.* London: Abacus Sphere, 1974, p26.

7 King, Alexander and Schneider, Bertrand, *The first global revolution.* New York: Simon & Schuster, 1991.

8 Walsh, Roger, *Staying alive: the psychology of human survival.* Boulder: Shambhala, 1984, xvii-xviii.
9 See, for example, Suzuki, D.T., and others, *Zen Buddhism and psychoanalysis.* London: Souvenir Press, 1974.
10 Merton, Thomas, *No man is an island.* Tunbridge Wells: Burns & Oates, 1955, ix.
11 Spretnak, Charlene, as above (ref. 4).
12 Suzuki, D.T., *Essays in Zen Buddhism III.* London: Rider, 1970, p214.
13 Fromm, Erich, *Psychoanalysis and Zen Buddhism,* in Suzuki, D.T. and others, as above (ref. 9), pp87-88.
14 Eliot, T.S., 'East Coker', in *Four quartets.* London: Faber & Faber, 1944.
15 Becker, Ernest, *The denial of death.* New York: Free Press, 1974, p26.
16 Blyth, R.H., *Zen and Zen classics.* New York: Random House, 1978.
17 Vaclav Havel, at the Oslo Conference on Hate, 1990, reported in *The Guardian,* 19 September 1990.
18 Merton, Thomas, *The seven storey mountain.* London: Sheldon, 1948, p205.
19 *Fourth world review,* no54 1992. Letter from Barbara Panvey.
20 Kohr, Leopold, *The breakdown of nations.* London: Routledge & Kegan Paul, 1957.
21 Pirsig, Robert M., *Zen and the art of motorcycle maintenance.* London: Bodley Head, 1974.
22 Ferguson, Marilyn, *The aquarian conspiracy.* London: Routledge & Kegan Paul, 1981. (A classic of American new age ideology.)
23 Griffin, Susan, 'The way of all ideology' in her *Made from this Earth.* London: Women's Press, 1982.
24 Orwell, George, *The collected essays, journalism and letters* (eds. Sonia Orwell and Ian Angus). New York: Harcourt Bruce Jovanovich, 1968, v3, pp293-299.
25 Hogen Daido Hamahata, *The other shore.* ed. Kate Carne. Privately published, 1986.
26 Gospel of St.Matthew 10:34.
27 Carmichael, Alexander, *Carmina Gadelica.* Edinburgh: Oliver & Boyd, 1900-1961, v2 pp315-316.

Part 3 Environmentalism: the reactive response

1 World Commission on the Environment and Development *Our common future* [Brundtland Report]. Oxford: Oxford University Press, 1987, xii.
2 Fuller, Richard Buckminster, *Operating manual for spaceship Earth.* London: Feffer & Simons, 1969.
3 Social and Community Planning Research, *British social attitudes.* Aldershot: Dartmouth Publishing, 1992
4 Paddy Ashdown, interviewed in *Green Line* no. 69 February 1989, pp12-14.

5 Minnesota attorney general Hubert Humphrey III, quoted in Plant, Christopher and Judith, *Green business: hope or hoax*. Hartland: Green Books, 1991, p13.

6 Sale, Kirkpatrick, 'Perplexity of progress', in *Resurgence*, no. 139 March/April 1990.

7 World Commission on the Environment and Development, as above (ref. 1).

8 Quoted in Elkington, John and Burke, Tom, *The green capitalists*. London: Gollancz, 1987, p179.

9 *The Guardian*, 2 December 1990.

10 Davis, John 'Towards a wasteless society', in *New economics*, no. 9 Spring 1989.

11 Ophuls, William, *Ecology and the politics of scarcity*. San Francisco: W.H. Freeman, 1977

12 Trainer, F.E., *Abandon affluence!*. London: Zed Books, 1985, p242.

13 See, for example, Elkington, John and Cairncross, Frances, *Costing the Earth*. London: Business Books, 1991.

14 Reported in *Green line*, no. 86 April 1991.

15 Max Nicholson, quoted in Elkington, John and Burke, Tom, as above (ref. 8), p158.

16 Mackenzie, Dorothy, 'Towards minimal chic' in *Resurgence*, no. 143 November/December 1990, p20.

17 Porritt, Jonathon and Winner, David, *The coming of the Greens*. London: Fontana Collins, 1988. pp140-141.

18 Porritt, Jonathon and Winner, David, as above (ref. 17), pp134-135.

19 See, for example, Simon, Julian L and Kahn, Herman, *The resourceful Earth*. Oxford: Blackwell, 1984.

20 *The Guardian*, 22 November 1991, p32.

21 Pearce, David and others, *Blueprint for a green economy*. London: Earthscan, 1989.

22 Bowers, John, *The conservationists' response to the Pearce Report*. Telford (23 Donnerville Gardens, Admaston, Shropshire): BANC, 1990.

23 Jacobs, Michael, *The green economy*. London: Pluto Press, 1991, pp99 and 107.

24 Ekins, Paul, 'Growth without end', in *The Guardian*, 12 July 1991.

25 Pearce, David, 'Economics, equity and sustainable development', in Ekins, Paul and Max-Neef, Manfred, *Real life economics*. London: Routledge, 1992, pp69-76.

26 Schwartz, Eugene, *Overskill*. New York: Ballantyne, 1971.

27 Davis, D. and others, 'International trends in cancer mortality in France, West Germany, Italy, Japan, England & Wales and the USA', in *The Lancet*, 336(8713), 25 August 1990, pp474-481.

28 Bertell, Rosalie, *No immediate danger*. London: Women's Press, 1985.

29 Pearce, David and others, *Sustainable development: economy and environment in the Third World.* Aldershot: Gower/ Brookfield: Edward Elgar, 1990.

Part 4: The radical green alternative

1 Ophuls, William, *Ecology and the politics of scarcity.* San Francisco: W.H. Freeman, 1977, p13.

2 Bramwell, Anna, *Ecology in the twentieth century: a history.* New Haven: Yale University Press, 1989, p195. (For fuller treatment of green nazism see Bramwell, Anna, *Blood and soil: Walter Darre and Hitler's 'Green Party'.* Oxford: Kensal Press, 1985).

3 Hardin, Garrett, 'Tragedy of the commons', in *Science,* 162 (1968), pp1243-1248. (Reprinted in Daly, Herman E., *Towards a steady state economy.* San Francisco: W.H. Freeman, 1973, pp133-138).

4 Ophuls, William, 'The politics of a sustainable society', in Pirages, D. (ed.) *The sustainable society,* New York: Praeger, 1977, p16.

5 Ophuls, William, *Ecology and the politics of scarcity.* San Francisco: W.H. Freeman, 1977, pp226-227.

6 See, for example, Daly, Harman E. and Cobb, John B., *For the common good: redirecting the economy towards community, the environment and a sustainable future.* Boston: Beacon Press, 1989/London: Green Print, 1990.

7 Goldsmith, Edward, 'The ecology of war', in *The Ecologist,* v4, p125.

8 Goldsmith, Edward, *The great U-turn: deindustrialising society.* Hartland: Green Books, 1988.

9 Bookchin, Murray, *The modern crisis.* Philadelphia: New Society Publishers, 1986, p34.

10 Bookchin, Murray, as above (ref. 9), pp56,59.

11 Ellen, Roy F., 'What Black Elk left unsaid: on the illusory images of Green primitivism', in *Anthropology today,* 2(6) 1986, pp8-12.

12 I have drawn here on the papers collected in Howell, Signe and Willis, Ray, (eds.), *Societies at peace: anthropological perspectives.* London: Routledge & Kegan Paul, 1989.

13 Eibl-Eibesfeldt, I., *The biology of peace and war.* Thames & Hudson, 1979, p161.

14 Fox, Matthew, *Original blessing.* Santa Fe: Bear & Co, 1983.

15 For example, compare *Economics for the future* (Federal White Paper no4) with *Costing the earth* (Federal Green Paper no23); London: Liberal Democrats, 1991.

16 Porritt, Jonathon and Winner, David, *The coming of the Greens.* London: Fontana, 1988, pp9,11.

17 Goldsmith, Edward and others, *Blueprint for survival.* London: Penguin, 1972.

18 Pepper, David, *The roots of modern environmentalism.* Beckenham: Croom Helm, 1984, p118.

19 Porritt, Jonathon, in *Resurgence,* no136 September/October 1989, p7.

20 In *Fourth world review,* no33 1989, p28.

21 Alty, Janet, 'The Green Party and the political process', in *Green line,* no76 November/December 1989, p10.

22 Michels, Robert, *Political parties.* New York: Collier Books, 1962.

23 Williams, Raymond, *Towards 2000.* London: Chatto & Windus, 1983, p123.

24 Kelly, Petra, 'Towards a Green Europe and a Green world', in Dodds, Felix (ed.), *Into the twenty-first century.* Basingstoke: Green Print, 1988, p108.

25 Commoner, Barry, *Ecology and social action.* Berkeley: University of California Press, 1973.

26 Robertson, James, *Future wealth: a new economics for the twenty-first century.* London: Cassell, 1990.

27 Ekins, Paul and Max-Neef, Manfred, *Real life economics: understanding wealth creation.* London: Routledge, 1992.

28 Ryle, Martin, *Ecology and socialism.* London: Radius Century Hutchinson, 1988.

29 Ekins, Paul, 'The new economics', in Ekins, Paul (ed.), *The living economy: a new economics in the making.* London: Routledge & Kegan Paul, 1986, pp354-355.

30 Spangler, David, 'Revelation: birth of a New Age', in Bloom, William (ed.), *The new age: an anthology of essential writings.* London: Rider, 1991, p28.

31 Laing, Ronald, *The politics of experience.* London: Penguin, 1967.

32 See Wilber, Ken, *Eye to eye: the quest for the new paradigm.* Boston/Shaftesbury: Shambhala, 1990. (On spiritual paradox and levels of consciousness his *No boundary* (Shambhala, 1979) is recommended).

33 Rivers, Patrick, *The stolen future.* Basingstoke: Green Print, 1988, p180.

34 Dauncey, Guy, *After the crash: the emergence of the rainbow economy.* London: Green Print, 1989, p260.

35 Hillman, James, *We've had a hundred years of psychotherapy and the world is getting worse.* San Francisco: Harper, 1992.

36 Simmonds, J.L., *The emerging new age.* Santa Fe: Bear & Co, 1990, p216.

37 Berman, Morris, 'Metapolitik', in *Resurgence,* no115 March/April 1986, pp17-19.

38 Seabrook, Jeremy, *The myth of the market.* Hartland: Green Books, 1990, pp102-103.

39 For a valuable discussion on the prepersonal and transpersonal see Wilber, Ken, as above (ref. 32) p224.

40 Wood, Kate, *The destiny challenge: a record of spiritual experience and observation.* Forres: New Frequency Press, 1992.

41 Spangler, David and Thompson, William Irwin, *Reimagination of the world: a critique of the new age, science and popular culture.* Santa Fe: Bear & Co, 1991. pp31, 17.

42 Batchelor, Stephen, 'Buddhist economics reconsidered' in Badiner, William Hunt (ed.), *Dharma Gaia: a harvest of essays in Buddhism and ecology.* Berkeley: Parallax Press, 1990, p179.

43 Seed, John and others, *Thinking like a mountain: towards a council of all beings.* Philadelphia: New Society Publishers, 1988

44 From an interview in *Mother Jones*, May/June 1989.

45 Hardin, Garrett, 'The immorality of being soft hearted', in *The relevant scientist*, no1, November 1989, p18.

46 'Deep ecology vs social ecology': speech to National Gathering of US greens, Amherst, Mass. 1987.

47 Interviewed in *Green line*, no. 73, June 1989, p13.

48 Batchelor, Stephen, as above (ref. 42), p180.

49 Snyder, Gary, *Practice of the wild.* San Francisco: North Point, 1990, p68.

50 Quoted by Kirkpatrick Sale, in *Resurgence*, no143, November/December 1990.

51 Bradley, Ian, *God is Green.* London: Darton, Longman & Todd, 1990.

52 Cooper, Tim, *Green Christianity.* London: Spire Hodder & Stoughton, 1990, p68.

53 Interviewed in *Resurgence*, no144, January/February 1991, pp24-27.

54 De Waal, Esther (ed.), *The Celtic vision: selected and edited from the 'Carmina Gadelica', by Alexander Carmichael.* London: Darton, Longman & Todd, 1988, p5.

55 McDonagh, Sean *To care for the Earth: a call to a new theology.* London: Geoffrey Chapman, 1986.

56 McDonagh, Sean, as above (ref. 55), p82. (Teilhard appears only fleetingly in McDonagh's later book, *Greening of the Church* (Chapman, 1990)).

57 Leech, Kenneth, *True God: an exploration in spiritual theology.* London: Sheldon, 1985, p418.

58 Boff, Leonardo and Clodovis, *Introducing liberation theology.* New York: Burns & Oates, 1987, p13, 9.

59 Fox, Matthew, *Creation spirituality*, San Francisco: Harper, 1991.

60 Fox, Matthew, as above (ref. 14).

61 Interviewed in *Resurgence*, as above (ref. 53).

62 Rilke, Rainer Maria, *Letters to a young poet*, trans. K.W. Maurer. London: Langley, 1943, p248.

63 Merton, Thomas, 'Contemplative prayer', quoted in Castle, Tony (ed.), *Thomas Merton on prayer.* London: Marshall Pickering, 1989, p22.

64 Spretnak, Charlene, *States of grace: the recovery of meaning in the post-modern age*. San Francisco: Harper, 1991, pp142-143.

65 Heilbrunn, Carolyn, *Towards a recognition of androgeny*. New York: Knopf, 1964.

66 Feldman, Christina, *Woman awake: a celebration of women's wisdom*. London: Arkana, 1990, p134.

67 Whitmont, Edward, *Return of the Goddess*. London: Arkana, 1987, p190.

68 Reuther, Rosemary Radford, *Sexism and God talk*. Boston: Beacon, 1983, p73.

69 Reuther, Rosemary Radford, *New woman/new earth: sexist ideologies and human liberation*. New York: Seabury, 1975, p204.

70 Collins, Sheila D., *A different heaven and earth*. Valley Forge: Judson, 1974, p161.

71 Warren, Karen, 'Feminism and ecology: making connections', in *Environmental ethics*, 9(1), Spring 1987, pp3-20.

72 Touraine, Alain, 'La révolution culturelle que nous vivons', in *Nouvel observateur*, 1 August 1978.

73 Joint declaration of European green parties, 23 January 1984. Reproduced in Parkin, Sara, *Green politics: an international guide*. London: Heretic, 1989, pp327-328.

74 Mill, John Stuart, *Utilitarianism, liberty and representative government*. London: Everyman, 1910, pp363-364.

75 Tönnies, Ferdinand, *Community and association*. London: Routledge, 1974.

76 Spretnak, Charlene, *The spiritual dimension of green politics*. Santa Fe: Bear & Co, 1986, pp29-30.

77 Both quotations are from Ascherson, Neil, *Games with shadows*. London; Radius Century Hutchinson, 1988, p4.

78 For a discussion of green and nationalist perspectives in the Welsh context see Jones, Ken H., 'On the endangered species list?', in *Planet: the Welsh internationalist*, no74, April/May 1989, pp78-83.

Part 5: Shaping the future and Epilogue

1 Ophuls, William, *Ecology and the politics of scarcity*. San Francisco: W.H. Freeman, 1977, p241.

2 Porritt, Jonathon, in Inglis, Mary and Kramer, Sandra (eds.), *The new economic agenda*. Findhorn: Forres, 1985 p24.

3 Kohr, Leopold, *The breakdown of nations*. London: Routledge & Kegan Paul, 1957, pp2 and ix-x.

4 Sale, Kirkpatrick, *Human scale*. London: Secker & Warburg 1980, pp130 and 159.

5 Sale, Kirkpatrick, as above (ref. 4), pp60 and 498.

6 Sale, Kirkpatrick, as above (ref. 4), pp508-509.

7 Papworth, John, *Fourth world review*, no36, 1989.

8 Schumacher, E.F., *Small is beautiful.* London: Abacus Sphere, 1974, p29.

9 Schumacher, E.F., as above (ref. 8), p54.

10 Green Party, *Manifesto for a sustainable society.* London: Green Party, 1989. As amended at the 1992 Autumn Conference, para. PG200

11 Schumacher, E.F., as above (ref. 8), p202.

12 Green Party, as above (ref. 10), paras. DC200-203.

13 Green Party, *Manifesto for a sustainable society.* London: Green Party, 1989, p44, para. AD103. This section was replaced at the Party's 1992 Autumn Conference by one which more exclusively emphasised decentralisation.

14 Green Party, as above (ref. 13), pp44-45 para. AD105. Replaced in Autumn 1992 by a text which simply states that 'A redistribution of wealth between areas may continue to be necessary . . . There should be no economic incentive for a wealthy area within a district or region to opt out' (para DC203).

15 Trainer, F.E., *Abandon affluence!.* London: Zed Books, 1985, p249.

16 Ophuls, William, as above (ref. 1), p184.

17 Robertson, James, *Future wealth: a new economics for the twenty-first century.* London: Cassell, 1989, p81.

18 Schumacher, E.F., *Good work.* London: Abacus Sphere, 1980, pp66-67.

19 Dauncey, Guy, 'The new local economic order', in Ekins, Paul (ed.), *The living economy.* London: Routledge & Kegan Paul, 1986, p269.

20 Ryle, Martin, *Ecology and socialism.* London: Radius Century Hutchinson, 1988, pp46, 77.

21 Interviewed by Ed Vulliamy in *The Guardian,* 9-10 December 1989.

22 Nove, Alec, *The economics of feasible socialism.* London: Allen & Unwin, 1983.

23 Seabrook, Jeremy, *The myth of the market.* Hartland: Green Books, 1990, p188.

24 Porritt, Jonathon, 'Going Green with envy' in *Resurgence,* no 143, November/December 1990, pp15-19.

25 Trainer, F.E., as above (ref. 15), p263.

26 Trainer, F.E., as above (ref. 15), p205.

27 Mulgan, Geoff and Wilkinson, Helen, 'The enabling and disabling state' in Ekins, Paul and Max-Neef, Manfred, *Real life economics.* London: Routledge, 1992, pp340-352.

28 Green Party, as above (ref. 13), p42 para. DC203.

29 Ascherson, Neil in *The Independent on Sunday,* 18 November 1990, p23.

30 Sennett, Richard, *The fall of public man.* Cambridge: Cambridge University Press, 1977, p264.

31 Sennett, Richard, as above (ref. 30), p267.

32 Hofstede, Geert, *Culture's consequences: international differences in work related values.* London: Sage, 1980.

33 *The European,* no2123, June 1991.

34 See Henderson, Hazel, *The politics of the solar age.* New York: Anchor Doubleday, 1981, pp303-4.

35 Ophuls, William, as above (ref. 1), p136.

36 Pepper, David, 'Radical environmentalism and the labour movement' in Weston, Joe, *Red and green.* London: Pluto Press, 1986, pp115-139.

37 Robertson, James, as above (ref. 17).

38 Robertson, James, *The sane alternative: a choice of futures.* The Old Bakehouse, Cholsey, Wallingford, Oxon: The author, rev. edn. 1983, p93.

39 Robertson, James, as above (ref.17), p10.

40 For a study of the social composition of the green movement and how this relates to characteristic green attitudes and values, see Cotgrove, S., *Catastrophe or cornucopia: the environment, politics and the future.* Chichester: Wiley, 1982.

41 Dahrendorf, Ralf, *Class and class conflict in industrial society.* London: Routledge & Kegan Paul, 1959.

42 Robertson, James, as above (ref. 38), p108.

43 For more in this vein, see Adar, Marge and Howell, Sharon 'The subjective side of power' in Plant, Judith (ed.), *Healing the wounds: the promise of ecofeminism.* Philadelphia: New Society Publishers, 1988/London: Green Print, 1989.

44 Seabrook, Jeremy, *The idea of neighbourhood.* London: Pluto Press, 1984, p94.

45 Dauncey, Guy, as above (ref. 19), pp264-272.

46 Mulgan, Geoff and Wilkinson, Helen, as above (ref. 27).

47 *The Guardian,* 19 December 1990.

48 Carroll, Lewis, *Through the looking glass.* London: Gollancz, 1986, Chapter VI.

49 Dauncey, Guy, *After the crash: the emergence of the rainbow economy.* Basingstoke: Green Print, 1988.

50 Quoted in Ekins, Paul, *New world order: grassroots movements for social change.* London: Routledge, 1992, pp114, 202.

51 NACLA, *Report on the Americas,* xxiii(4), November/December 1989, p22. (475 Riverside Dr, Suite 454, New York, NY 10115).

52 Schneider, Bertrand, *The barefoot revolution.* London: Intermediate Technology, 1988.

53 Plaid Cymru and Green Party (Ceredigion & Pembroke North) *Towards a green Welsh future/ Tua'r dyfodol gwyrdd Cymreig.* Talybont (Dyfed): Y Lolfa, 1992. Distributed by Ceredigion Green Party, Trewylan, Ffordd Bryn-y-Mor, and Plaid Cymru, 32 Heol-y-Wig, both in Aberystwyth, Wales. Comprises a joint policy manifesto and reprints of five discussion papers.

54 See Osmond, John, *The democratic challenge.* Llandysul: Gomer, 1992.

55 Barry Maycock in *Green line,* no79, June 1990.

56 Salzman, Lorna, 'A dream ends, a nightmare begins' in *Fourth world review*, no50, 1992, p12.

57 Capra, Frijtof and Spretnak, Charlene (eds.), *Green politics.* London: Hutchinson, 1984, p156.

58 Curle, Adam, *Tools for transformation.* Stroud: Hawthorn Press, 1990, p17.

59 Capra, Frijtof and Spretnak, Charlene (eds.), as above (ref. 57), p157.

60 Snyder, Gary, *Earth house hold.* New York: New Directions, 1968, p91.

61 Schumacher, E.F., as above (ref.8), pp249-250.

62 Frankel, Boris, *The postindustrial utopians.* Cambridge: Polity, 1987, pp265-266.

63 *The Guardian,* 20 April 1990.

64 On this 'category error', see Wilber, Ken, *Eye to eye: the quest for the new paradigm.* Boston(MA)/Shaftesbury: Shambhala, 1990, pp1-37; and on the relationship of physics to mysticism, pp133-139.

65 Irvine, Sandy and Ponton, Alec. *A green manifesto.* London: Macdonald Optima, 1988, p133.

66 Schumacher, E.F., *Guide for the perplexed.* London: Abacus Sphere, 1978, p138.

67 Quoted in Gowan, J., *Trance, art and creativity.* California: Northridge, 1975.

68 Kelly, Thomas, *Testament of devotion.* London: Quaker Home Service, 1979, p62.

69 See Ives, Christopher, *Zen awakening and society.* London: Macmillan, 1992, pp70-75.

70 Hegley, John, 'Wipe your glasses' in *The Guardian,* 20 October 1990.

71 Reported in Phipps, John-Francis, *The politics of inner experience: dynamics of green spirituality.* London: Green Print, 1990, p42.

72 *Vinaya* 1, 21.

73 Sivaraksa, Sulak, *A Buddhist vision for renewing society.* Bankok: Thai Watana Panich, 1981, p162.

74 INEB: PO Box 1, Ongkharak, Nakhorn Nayok, 26120 Thailand. Network of Engaged Buddhists; (UK): Plâs Plwca, Cwmrheidol, Aberystwyth, Wales SY23 3NB; (US): Buddhist Peace Fellowship: PO Box 4650, Berkeley, CA 94704.

75 *The cloud of unknowing,* London: Penguin, 1961.

76 Schumacher, E.F., as above (ref. 66), pp80-85.

77 From a talk given at a Buddhist Peace Fellowship retreat in March 1983 at Tassajara Zen Mountain Center, USA.

78 Feldman, Christina, *Woman awake: a celebration of women's wisdom.* London: Arkana, 1989, p52.

79 Gestalt Centre, 64 Warwick Rd, St Albans, AL1 4DL (includes deep ecology workshops); Nigel Collingwood, 67 Heights Rd, Upton, Poole, Dorset, BH16 5RD.

80 Jones, Ken, *Guidelines for compiling a green community development strategy*. 9pp typescript, available from the author, Plâs Plwca, Cwmrheidol, Aberystwyth, SY23 3NB, Wales.

81 Macy, Joanna Rogers, *Despair and personal power in the nuclear age*. Philadelphia: New Society Publishers, 1983. See also her *World as lover, world as self*. Berkeley: Parallax, 1991/London: Rider, 1993.

82 Shields, Katrina, *In the tiger's mouth: an empowerment guide for social action*. Newtown,(NSW, Australia): Millenium, 1991. (Distributed in the UK by Green Print).

83 Curle, Adam, as above (ref. 58), p25.

84 Titmuss, Christopher, 'A passion for the Dharma' in *Turning wheel*, Fall 1991, p19. (Journal of the [US] Buddhist Peace Fellowship).

Index

Index